Leaving Certificate

Geography
SRPs

James Campbell
Enda Whelton

Edco

First published 2011
The Educational Company of Ireland
Ballymount Road
Walkinstown
Dublin 12
www.edco.ie

A member of the Smurfit Kappa Group plc

ISBN 978-184536464-9

Editor: Simon Coury
Design: Identikit
Layout: Outburst Design
Cover Photography: Alamy
Illustration: Design Image

Ordnance Survey maps
Based on Ordnance Survey Ireland Permit No. 8773
© Ordnance Survey Ireland/Government of Ireland

Photograph Acknowledgements
Alamy, European Photo Services, Photocall Ireland, iStockphoto, Shutterstock

Authors

James Campbell graduated from UCD with a degree in Geography and Economics and a Higher Diploma in Education. He has over twenty years' teaching experience at Junior Certificate and Leaving Certificate Honours level and is Head of the Geography Department in Blackrock College, Dublin. James also teaches Geography and Economics at the Institute of Education, Leeson Street. He has written two earlier revision guides for the Leaving Certificate Geography course before it was revised in 2004. James is co-author of *Revise Wise Geography for the Junior Certificate*. He is passionate about his subjects and instils a great love of Geography and Economics in his students.

Enda Whelton began his teaching career in Coláiste Choilm, Ballincollig, Co. Cork, before moving to Blakestown Community School in Dublin. He currently teaches Geography in Blackrock College in Dublin. Enda is co-author of *Revise Wise Geography for the Junior Certificate*.

Website

To access solutions visit:

www.edco.ie/geographysrps

Contents

« Section 1: Physical Geography »

❖ Section 2: Regional Geography ❖

❖ Section 2: Regional Geography ❖

❖ Section 3: Maps, Aerial Photographs and Graphs ❖

❖ Section 4: Human Elective ❖

❖ Section 4: Human Elective ❖

❖ Section 5: Economic Elective ❖

Explanatory notes for exam workbook and online study guide

- This workbook is designed to be used in conjunction with two other elements: the online study guide and your own copybook or A4 pad.

- In the online study guide you can find all the fully worked-out sample answers to all questions in the workbook. As you work through the online study guide you should file sample answers in a folder to build up a bank of answers.

- As well as the sample answers, the online study guide will include the following: key hints and tips on exam timing, approximate study timing, the methods by which exam questions can be asked, coherence points for each question, exam techniques, statistics, background information, definitions and question structure.

- You or your teacher will need to log in to the Edco website at www.edco.ie/geographysrps to complete the workbook answers.

- Use your copybook to write out your answers in your own words, and to practise drawing sketches and diagrams.

- You will not have room in the workbook to draw all diagrams and sketch maps so practise drawing them into your copybook as you practise answering the related questions.

- The workbook is designed to cover all areas of the course with the exception of your option unit. That means that if you study the workbook in conjunction with the online study guide you will cover the course.

- The workbook will give for a concise and appropriate revision of the course material. It is geared towards helping you break down the entire course into the necessary information required to achieve top marks in the Leaving Certificate geography paper.

- This workbook is divided up into:
  (i) short questions,
  (ii) 20-mark questions,
  (iii) 30-mark questions.

- Short questions: The beginning of each chapter in the core units (Physical Geography, Regional Geography and Maps, Aerial Photographs and Graphs) includes information you need to know for the short questions on the Leaving Certificate exam paper.

- 20-mark questions: Some questions in the workbook are 20-mark questions which are relevant to Part A of the Physical, Regional and Elective sections of the paper.

- 30-mark questions: Most of the questions in this workbook are 30-mark questions which require 15 SRPs (Note: 1 SRP = 2 marks). They are either Type A or Type B questions.

- Type A are fill-in-the-blanks questions.

Sample Type A Question (see p. 143)

Assess the development of services, transport and tourism in a core European region of your choice.

Insert the following terms into the blanks below:

quaternary services / the Paris Bourse / the services sector / La Défense

Services

- More than two-thirds of the population of the Paris Basin work in ..*the services sector*.., with a 3 per cent increase per annum. As the demand for services such as transportation, tourism, leisure and entertainment have increased, so have the income levels. **(1 SRP)**

- In a sophisticated economy such as that of the Paris Basin there is a big demand for ..*quaternary*. .*services*.. such as finance, insurance, marketing and accounting. The financial centre is located in .*La Défense*., Paris. **(1 SRP)**

- The Parisian stock exchange, .*the Paris Bourse*., is the second largest in Europe after London. Three of Europe's largest banks have their headquarters in Paris. **(1 SRP)**

How to approach answering Type A questions

1 Each Type A 30-mark question gives you at least 15 'Significant Relevant Points' (SRPs). Each SRP is worth two marks.

2 Begin by filling in the blanks with the terms in the box above each question, as in the example above.

3 If there are some blanks you have not managed to fill then download the full answer from the online study guide.

4 Then study and learn the terms from each SRP. You may find it helpful to underline or highlight each key term.

5 Then learn the key point from each SRP.

6 Using your copybook/A4 pad write out the full answer in your own words using the key terms you learnt.

7 Allow approximately 15 minutes for a 30-mark question.

- Type B questions use prompts to guide your answers.

Sample Type B Question (see p. 26)

Explain where volcanoes occur on the earth's surface.

Introduction

1 Pacific Ring of Fire ....

Divergent plate boundaries

How to approach answering Type B questions

1 Each Type B 30-mark question gives you at least 15 prompts and each prompt represents one 'Significant Relevant Point' (SRP).

2 You need to download the answer from the online study guide. You may find it helpful to print it off.

Sample Question 1: Explain where volcanoes occur on the earth's surface.

■ Most volcanoes, but not all, occur in the Pacific Ring of Fire where plates converge and diverge. Some volcanoes also occur at hot spots. **(1 SRP)**

■ Divergent plate boundaries: at divergent plate boundaries plates separate. This is the theory of sea-floor spreading proposed by Harry Hess in 1960. **(1 SRP)**

■ When two plates separate cracks form on the ocean floor. These cracks are filled by magma which forces its way upwards from the mantle. **(1 SRP)**

■ The Magma cools, forming a new ocean floor. Along the Mid-Atlantic Ridge volcanic islands have formed, e.g. Iceland. **(1 SRP)**

3 Read the online answer, underlining the key point in each SRP. Make sure you understand each SRP and how it relates to the question.

4 Then, with the aid of each prompt, write in the key point of each SRP into your workbook.

Introduction

1 Pacific Ring of Fire *where most volcanoes occur/diverging, converging, hot spots*

Divergent plate boundaries

2 sea-floor spreading *plates separate at diverging plate boundaries/ Harry Hess 1960*

3 cracks form *when plates separate magma is forced up from the mantle*

4 Mid-Atlantic Ridge *magma cools forming new ocean floor/ volcanic islands, e.g. Iceland*

5 Then learn the key point from each SRP.

6 Using your copybook, write out the full answer in your own words using the key terms you learnt.

7 Allow approximately 15 minutes for a 30-mark question.

Note: Some questions of both types will have more than 15 SRPs. The reason for this is to give you a detailed understanding of the answer to the question you are being asked. In the exam itself you will only be required to write out 15 SRPs.

Note: Some points may be awarded for the cohesion of your answer, so take care to structure your answer. Avoid using bullet points, as marks are awarded for how you present your answer.

Physical Geography section

- You need to know only one of the following for the 30-mark questions: rivers/fluvial; coasts/sea; glaciations/ice or mass movement. You do, however, need to know them all for the short questions.

- You need to know a case study of human interaction or interference in surface processes, e.g. the impact of hydroelectric dams.

- You need to know only the weather maps, graphs and charts section for the short questions.

Regional Geography section

- You need to know only one continental/sub-continental region.

- Some regional questions will not be as clear-cut as others and some may ask you to examine the 'factors affecting' the development of an economic activity, which changes the question slightly. All the information you will need is in the workbook but the structure might need to change. For example, two factors affecting the development of agriculture in an Irish region would be physical factors and economic factors. Physical factors would include relief, soils, drainage and climate, which you will find in the physical processes answer in your chosen region, and an economic factor would be the impact of the Common Agricultural Policy (CAP), which you would find in the primary economic activities answer in your chosen region.

Maps, Aerial Photographs and Graphs section

- You will need to use graph paper for making sketches from Ordnance Survey maps and aerial photographs.

- As well as the extracts from OS maps printed in the workbook, you will also need to refer to maps used in past Leaving Certificate exam papers. If you have trouble finding them, look on the website for links.

Elective sections

- You only have to cover and learn either the economic elective or the human elective.

Option questions

- This book does not cover the option unit essay questions.

Section 1

Physical Geography

Chapter 1

The Restless Earth

(a) Introduction

« Explanations »

- The Earth (4.6 billion years old) is currently broken into seven large plates and numerous smaller ones.

- The size and position of these plates change over time.

- The edges of these plates, where they move against each other, are sites of intense geological activity, such as earthquakes, volcanoes and mountain building.

« Definitions »

Plate tectonics is a combination of three ideas:

1 **Continental drift** is the movement of continents over the earth's surface and their change in position relative to each other.

2 **Subduction** is the process in which one plate is pushed beneath another plate into the underlying mantle when plates move towards each other. It results in faulting.

3 **Sea-floor spreading** is the process whereby the ocean floor is extended when two plate move apart. As the plates move apart the rocks break and form a crack between the plates. Magma rises through the cracks and seeps out into the ocean floor forming an undersea volcano.

❖ Concepts ❖

You need to know the following concepts for the short questions.

Insert the following terms into the blanks below:

Mohorovicic Discontinuity / oceanic / asthenosphere / crust / core / lithosphere / mantle / continental

The Earth is composed of **three layers**.

1 **The** ....

Consists of iron and nickel heated to between 3000°C and 5000°C. Comprises the outer and inner core.

2 The ....

A layer of red-hot rock to a depth of 2,800km.

- **The upper mantle** comprises solid rock and is rigid.

- **The** .... lies beneath the rigid mantle: rocks are at melting point and are easily deformed. The rocks are capable of flow.

- **The** .... (Moho) is the boundary marking the change from crust to mantle.

3 The ....

The outermost layer.

There are two types of crust:

1 .... **crust**: 5km to 10km thick

- Comprises ancient and dense rocks called sima

- Sima is composed of silica and magnesium

- Basalt makes up most of the world's oceanic crust.

2 .... **crust**: 30km to 60km thick

- Composed of younger and lighter rocks called sial

- Sial is composed of silica and aluminum

- Granite is the most common rock in the continental crust.

The crust and the uppermost section of the mantle are called the .... The lithosphere is broken up into different sections called **plates**.

Insert the following terms into the blanks below:

inner core / moho / crust / outer core / oceanic crust / mantle / continental crust

(b) Global Crustal Plate Movement

Sample Question 1

With the aid of labelled diagrams, discuss the process of global crustal plate movement.

Theories

1 continental drift ....

2 thermal convection ....

3 boiling water ....

4 global crustal plate movement ....

5 diagram of theory of thermal convection

Proofs

6 matching fossils ....

7 Glossopteris ....

8 continental fit...

9 diagram of Africa and South America to prove continental fit

10 matching rocks and mountain ranges ....

History of the plates

11 Pangaea and Iapetus Ocean ....

12 diagram of Pangaea showing split into Laurasia and Gondwanaland ....

13 Laurasia and Gondwanaland ....

14 2–20cm per year...

15 diagram of Mid-Atlantic Ridge

(c) Divergent Plate Boundaries

Sample Question 2

With the aid of a diagram, explain what happens at a divergent plate boundary. In your answer refer to associated landforms.

Insert the following terms into the blanks below:

Mid-Atlantic Ridge / Black Smokers / move apart / cracks / mid-oceanic ridges / mid-ocean ridges / new oceans / the Azores / Africa / continents / Red Sea / forcing the plates apart / sea-floor spreading / 1960 / mantle / rift valley / hot water / Atlantic Ocean / dissolved minerals / new rock / magma / Harry H. Hess / glacial material / oceanic crust / chimney-like vents / bacteria

Divergent plate boundaries (boundaries of construction)

- At divergent plate boundaries, plates ……………………………… . These plates are often called boundaries of construction. **(1 SRP)**

- The process which drives the plates apart is called …………………………… . **(1 SRP)**

- Over millions of years sea-floor spreading leads to the formation of ………………………… . **(1 SRP)**

- Sea-floor spreading was proposed by …………………………… in ……… . **(1 SRP)**

- As the plates, driven by convection currents in the mantle, move apart, ……………… form on the ocean floor. These cracks are filled by …………… from the …………… . **(1 SRP)**

- This lava (magma, on reaching the surface, is called lava) spreads across the ocean floor, ……………………………………… , forming ………………………… . **(1 SRP)**

- Hess noticed that the age of the sea floor is youngest where ………………… is formed along the …………………………… . **(1 SRP)**

- The plates carrying Eurasia and North America separated over 100 million years ago along the ……………………………, moving no faster than 2.5cm per year. **(1 SRP)**

- The Mid-Atlantic Ridge lies beneath the ………………………… and extends from the North Pole to the South Pole. It reaches a height of 2,500m to 3,000m above the ocean floor. **(1 SRP)**

- The Mid-Atlantic Ridge comes to the surface forming islands, e.g. Iceland and …………………… . **(1 SRP)**

- Divergence is occurring on the east side of …………… , forming the East African …………………… . Cracks on the sea floor are being filled by magma which is causing East Africa to split from the rest of the continent, forming the ……………… and the Gulf of Aden. **(1 SRP)**

- ………………… sometimes occur at mid-ocean ridges. They are ……………………… on the floor of the ocean which emit ……………………… . Often they contain …………………………… and ……………… which support marine organisms. **(1 SRP)**

Sea-floor spreading

- There are three proofs for sea-floor spreading:

    1 The existence of .... such as the Mid-Atlantic Ridge. **(1 SRP)**

    2 The age of the sea floor is youngest where new rock is formed along the mid-ocean ridges. **(1 SRP)**

    3 Deposits of .... similar in type and age are found where .... were once attached. **(1 SRP)**

- Diagram of a diverging plate boundary **(1 SRP)**

(d) Convergent Plate Boundaries

Sample Question 3

With the aid of diagrams, explain what happens at a convergent plate boundary. In your answer refer to associated landforms.

Plate convergence

1 at convergent plate boundaries ....

2 Benioff Zone ....

3 subduction ....

Three types of plate convergence

1 Oceanic to oceanic

4 subducted ....

5 long, deep, narrow trenches and islands arcs ....

6 Mariana Trench ....

7 diagram of oceanic plates converging

2 Oceanic to continental

8 subduction ....

9 deep ocean trench ....

10 Benioff Zone ....

11 volcanic mountains ....

12 faulting..

13 diagram of oceanic plate converging with a continental plate

3 Continental to continental

14 no subduction ....

15 fold mountains ....

16 Himalayas ....

17 north-west Ireland, Scotland and Scandinavia..............................

18 diagram of continental plates converging

(e) Three Types of Plate Boundary

Sample Question 4

With the aid of diagrams, examine what happens at three different types of plate boundary.

Note: In this question you have to include five to six SRPs from each of the previous two questions (i.e. divergent and convergent plate boundaries) and five SRPs from transform plate boundaries.

Insert the following terms into the blanks below:

earthquakes / Pacific / crust / north-west / fault line / slide past each other / passive / 6cm / North American / San Andreas Fault / 1cm / conservative / north-west

Transform plate boundaries

- Transform plate boundaries are sometimes called .... or .... plate boundaries. **(1 SRP)**

- At a transform plate boundary two plates .... without the destruction or creation of .... **(1 SRP)**

- The .... is the line along which the plates slide. .... sometimes occur at transform plate boundaries. **(1 SRP)**

- The most famous fault line is the .... in western America which extends for 1,300km. **(1 SRP)**

- The San Andreas Fault line lies between the .... Plate and the .... Plate. These two plates are sliding past each other in a horizontal motion. **(1 SRP)**

- The American Plate is moving .... by ...... per year while the Pacific Plate is moving .... by ...... per year. These two plates are locked together. Energy is building up and when they unlock the energy will be released as an earthquake. **(1 SRP)**

- Diagram of a transform plate boundary **(1 SRP)**

Chapter 2
Earthquakes

(a) Introduction

« Definitions and explanations »

- An **earthquake** is a movement or tremor in the earth's crust.
- Earthquakes start miles down in the earth where there is a **fault** in the earth's crust.
- They start with a slight shaking motion which stops briefly and then starts a little stronger.
- The ground can shake for a few seconds or a few minutes.
- Earthquakes are associated with **plate boundaries** and especially with **subduction zones** where one plate plunges beneath the other.
- The crust is subjected to huge stress.
- The rocks bend and snap along a **fault line**.
- The energy is released as **seismic waves**, originating from the focus, the source of the earthquake.

❖ Concepts ❖

You need to know the following concepts for the short questions.

Insert the following terms into the blanks below:

deep / epicentre / seismic waves / fault line / shallow / focus / Pacific belt / intermediate

- Eighty per cent of all earthquakes, including the world's most devastating, occur in the ………………………… .
- The place within the earth's crust where the earthquake occurs is the …………… .
- The point on the earth's surface directly above the focus is the …………………… .
- A …………………… is a line of weakness/fracture where the rocks on either side have moved relative to one another, e.g. San Andreas Fault.

Types of earthquake

1 .... **earthquakes**

■ These are earthquakes that occur nearest the surface. Their focus is less than 70km deep.

■ The subducting plate jams, pressure builds up and an earthquake occurs.

2 .... **earthquakes**

■ Their focus is between 70km and 300km deep.

■ The subducting plate melts, magma forms and an earthquake occurs.

3 .... **earthquakes**

■ Their focus is greater than 300km deep.

■ Chemical changes may occur within the rock.

■ .... are recorded in a seismology station.

Label the diagram below using the following terms:

fault / focus / epicentre / seismic waves

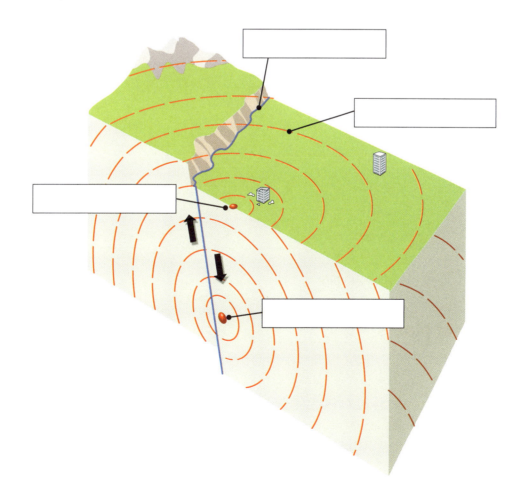

(b) Causes of Earthquakes

Sample Question 1

List and explain the causes of earthquakes.

Convergent plate boundaries

1 plates collide, subduction ....

2 Kobe earthquake ....

3 San Francisco earthquake ....

4 Peru–Chile Trench ....

5 diagram of convergent plate boundary

Divergent plate boundaries

6 plates separate ....

7 Mid-Atlantic Ridge ....

8 diagram of divergent plate boundary

Transform plate boundaries

9 plates slide past each other ....

10 56mm per year ....

11 San Andreas Fault ....

12 Los Angeles earthquake ....

13 diagram of a transform plate boundary

In the interior of plates

14 tensional forces ....

15 rift valleys ....

16 Great African Rift Valley ....

(c) Earthquake Prediction

Sample Question 2

How do geographers attempt to predict and measure earthquakes?

Insert the following terms into the blanks below:

Richter scale / animal / lasers / past earthquakes / fault line / seismic activity / increasing pressure / strainmeters / overdue / seismic gaps / the San Andreas Fault / tiltmeters / radon gas / stress / probability / severity / Haicheng / population / open-ended / seismograph / seismic waves / 33-fold increase / Chilean earthquake / earthquake damage / L'Aquila earthquake / geology / ten times / creepmeters / Charles Richter / seismic activity / 9.5 / building materials / male toads / time delay

Predicting earthquakes

- While forecasting earthquakes is difficult, the following ways are used:

1 Studying past earthquakes
- Scientists study .... to predict the possible size of earthquakes in the future. They then estimate how long it has been since the last earthquake to determine the .... that an earthquake will occur in the near future. **(1 SRP)**

2 Seismic maps
- Seismologists use seismic maps which indicate the likelihood and potential .... of future earthquakes. They locate regions where earthquakes and aftershocks have occurred in the past but are currently quiet, e.g. .... **(1 SRP)**

- These are areas along a .... that are blocked and where .... is building up. Areas which have been quiet for a long period are termed .... **(1 SRP)**

- Seismic gaps indicate areas of .... that have had little earthquake activity for a number of years. They point out areas which are long .... for an earthquake. **(1 SRP)**

3 Water and gas levels
- Water levels in wells can rise in response to .... ; .... levels also increase in the weeks and days before an earthquake. **(1 SRP)**

4 Land movement

■ ………………………… and ………………………… indicate minute land-level changes which may be due to magma rising from the mantle. ………………………… pick up strains in rock 200m below the surface. They show if the rocks are being deformed, buckled or bruised. **(1 SRP)**

■ …………… are used to measure the movement of rocks along a fault line. Any movement of rock on either side of the fault line could indicate ………………………………… . **(1 SRP)**

5 Seismographs

■ A ………………………… is an instrument that records earthquakes. Seismographs are used to measure the ………………………… which are generated by an earthquake. **(1 SRP)**

■ Increased activity on seismographs can indicate to seismologists that a large earthquake is imminent. They can also use seismographs to measure the ………………………… between earthquakes to help give a more accurate prediction of the next earthquake. **(1 SRP)**

■ The energy in these waves is measured on the ……………………………… . **(1 SRP)**

■ The Richter scale was devised by ………………………………… in 1935. **(1 SRP)**

■ It is an …………………… scale – it begins at zero but has no upper limit. Each step in the scale represents a ………………… in the energy released by an earthquake and ………………… the amount of shaking. **(1 SRP)**

■ The greatest magnitude recorded was ……… from the 1960 ………………………………… . **(1 SRP)**

■ The Mercalli scale was devised by Guiseppe Mercalli in 1902. It measures ……………………………… on a twelve-point scale – 1 indicates no damage while 12 indicates total devastation. The damage done depends on: (a) the ……………… of the area; (b) the ………………… density; and (c) the ……………… ………………………… . **(1 SRP)**

6 …………… behaviour

■ Animals are more sensitive than humans to changes in the earth. **(1 SRP)**

■ In 1975 Chinese officials evacuated the city of ……………… , a city inhabited by a million people, days before a 7.3 magnitude earthquake following observations of strange behaviour by animals. **(1 SRP)**

■ Before the ………………………………… in Italy in 2009 it was observed by scientists that even though it was their mating season, 96 per cent of …………………… departed the area five days before the earthquake struck. **(1 SRP)**

(d) Damage Caused by Earthquakes

Sample Question 3

Examine the type of damage caused by an earthquake.

Ground vibrations

1 Izmit earthquake………………………………………………………………………………………………

2 San Francisco earthquake ……………………………………………………………………………………

Liquefaction

3 soil, silt and sand . . . .

4 Mexico City . . . .

Avalanches and landslides

5 Kashmir earthquake, 2005 . . . .

Fire

6 power lines . . . .

7 Great San Francisco earthquake . . . .

8 San Andreas Fault . . . .

9 shaking . . . .

10 more damage . . . .

Tsunamis

11 destructive sea wave . . . .

12 huge amounts of water . . . .

13 65m high . . . .

14 Indian tsunami . . . .

15 Tokyo and Bangladesh . . . .

(e) Reducing Earthquake Damage

Sample Question 4

Briefly outline the factors that determine the damage an earthquake can cause and explain how earthquake damage can be reduced.

Insert the following terms into the blanks below:

Izmit / secure / fault lines / clean water / duration / time / underlying rocks / depth / lack of services / non-flammable / engineer / food / earthquake drills / wide streets / foundations / elastic buildings / unstable soil / rescue teams / fire-fighting teams / igneous / building construction / time / distance from the epicentre / disease / sedimentary / population / design / size / tents / California / Third World / energy / reinforce / shatterproof / wooden-frame / crossbeams / developed regions / homeless

Factors which influence damage done by earthquakes

- Damage caused by earthquakes depends on the following factors:
  - The .... of day and .... of year.
  - The amount of .... released by the earthquake.
  - The .... density.
  - The type of .... : the nature of the building material and the manner in which it was constructed are important. Lightweight material with flexible connections is ideal.
  - The type of .... : .... rocks (granite) will be able to withstand the tremors and vibrations better than .... rocks (limestone).
  - .... and .... of shaking of the earthquake. The greater the size on the Richter scale and the longer the ground shakes, the greater the damage.
  - .... If the epicentre is located in an urban area, the damage and loss of life will be greater. The further away from the epicentre the smaller the amount of damage.
  - .... of earthquake. Shallow earthquakes cause more damage because they occur nearer the surface. **(4 SRPs)**

Limiting earthquake damage

- The best defence is good emergency and evacuation planning. In .... such as .... the government can afford to .... and .... cities to absorb the impact of earthquakes. **(1 SRP)**
- In developing countries, i.e. '........................' countries, the results can be devastating. People are left .... , they suffer exposure to .... and suffer from a .... **(1 SRP)**

Requirements for limiting earthquake damage
- Use of .... building material. This will reduce deaths in the event of fire. **(1 SRP)**
- Improved building regulations.
  - Avoid building along .... or in areas of .... concrete structures, tie buildings down to their foundations and use .... to increase stability. **(1 SRP)**
  - Build the .... on rollers. The rollers help to absorb the shocks which in turn reduces the pressure on buildings. **(1 SRP)**
  - Construct .... and install .... windows. This ensures that energy is dissipated evenly throughout the building, allowing buildings to withstand horizontal as well as vertical pressure. **(1 SRP)**
  - .... as many household items as possible to the wall to stop them moving around and increasing the risk of injury when the earthquake strikes. **(1 SRP)**
  - Construct .... houses. These are less likely to collapse. Wood frames are flexible, enabling them to absorb stress. **(1 SRP)**
- Practise .... , so people in the affected area know what to do when an earthquake strikes. This would reduce the number of deaths. **(1 SRP)**

- ……………………………… and ………………………………………………… should be readily available to minimise loss of life. **(1 SRP)**

- ………… , ………… and …………………………… should be in place in earthquake-prone areas to help the homeless and the injured. **(1 SRP)**

■ More use of …………………………… would reduce the loss of life when buildings fall. **(1 SRP)**

  ■ The 1999 …………………… earthquake in Turkey destroyed many new apartments blocks while older ones nearby were unaffected. Investigations showed that building collapse was due to inadequate design and the use of poor building materials. **(1 SRP)**

(f) Case Study of an Earthquake: Indian Ocean Tsunami

Sample Question 5

Discuss the causes and human impact of an earthquake you have studied.

Insert the following terms into the blanks below:

the Maldives / underwater earthquakes / Somalia / magnitude 9.3 earthquake / 240km off the coast of Sumatra / Simueleu / subducted / Pacific Tsunami Warning Centre / Banda Aceh / six giant waves / more women were killed than men / 10m high / tsunami warning / 4,000 / minding children / epicentre / 50 minutes / shallow / 20m / killing tens of thousands of people / the Maldives / Sri Lanka / Andaman Sea towards Thailand / billions of dollars' worth of damage / the largest humanitarian response ever / megathrust / tilted / coral / north-west Sumatra / volcanic eruption / focus / the Pacific Ocean / upward thrust / thrust out / tsunamis / billions of tonnes of sea water / capsizing freighters / 5,000 / Kenya / 10,000 / trench / the ocean bed / eight minutes / Somalia / huge stresses / elderly parents / harbour wave / thirty minutes / geological events / throwing boats / a tsunami forms

The Indian Ocean tsunami

■ On 26 December 2004 a ………………………………………… that ripped apart the sea floor off the coast of ………………………………… was recorded. It was the second-biggest earthquake ever recorded. It was a …………………… earthquake. The ………… was 24km under …………………… . The tremors lasted …………………… . **(1 SRP)**

■ A devastating tsunami travelled thousands of kilometres across the Indian Ocean, killing people in countries as far apart as Indonesia, ……………………… , Sri Lanka and …………………… . **(1 SRP)**

■ A tsunami is defined as a series of very large waves formed when an area of water is displaced by ………………………………………… or a ………………………………… . It is a Japanese word meaning …………………………… . 'Tsu' means harbour and 'nami' means wave. ……………………… ………………… is very prone to tsunamis. **(1 SRP)**

The cause

■ .... , deep under the ocean floor, at the boundary between two tectonic plates, lies a 1200km .... called the Andaman–Sumatran subduction zone. **(1 SRP)**

■ The lower plate carrying India is being .... beneath the upper plate carrying most of south-east Asia, dragging it down, causing .... to build up. **(1 SRP)**

■ It was a .... earthquake, which occurs where one plate slips (subducts) beneath the other. These earthquakes are very powerful, damaging the ocean floor and generating .... **(1 SRP)**

■ The island of .... has been .... by the force of the earthquake, causing .... , submerged beneath the ocean for thousands of years, to be .... of the water. **(1 SRP)**

■ Deep under the Indian Ocean, at the .... of the quake, the 20m (65ft) .... of the sea floor set in motion a series of .... that devastated the lives of millions. .... , forced upward by the movement of the seabed, flowed away from the fault in a series of giant waves. **(1 SRP)**

The effect

■ Relying on seismic data alone, the scientists at the .... in Hawaii had no idea the earthquake had resulted in an ocean-wide tsunami. It was .... before a .... was issued. **(1 SRP)**

■ .... after the shaking had subsided the first wave, travelling eastwards, crashed into Sumatra. **(1 SRP)**

■ On the shores facing the epicentre the waves reached heights of .... , stripping vegetation from mountain sides 800m inland, ... and .... into the trees. **(1 SRP)**

■ The city of .... , a few kilometres around the coast, was almost completely destroyed, ... in 15 minutes. **(1 SRP)**

■ The waves continued across the .... On the shores the sea disappeared off the beaches, attracting many tourists to rescue fish left flapping on the sand. Minutes later the first waves hit. **(1 SRP)**

■ A thousand tonnes of water crashed down on each metre of beach. Waves were .... , caused .... and killed .... people. **(1 SRP)**

■ .... hit .... Over .... people died in the city of Galle. .... were killed in India. Eighty people were killed in .... , one of the lowest-lying countries on earth. The waves then hit .... – 300 people were killed. In .... only one person died. **(1 SRP)**

■ Official reports indicate that overall .... When the tsunami hit most of the men were at sea fishing. The tsunami passed under their fishing boats. The women were at home .... and .... and looking after their small .... **(1 SRP)**

■ The plight of the many affected people and countries prompted .... with donations of over seven billion dollars. **(1 SRP)**

Chapter 3
Volcanoes

(a) Introduction

Insert the following terms into the blanks below:

dormant / Mauna Loa / Vulcan / permanent / Slemish Mountain / magma (molten rock) / extinct / earth's interior / resting or sleeping / Mount Pinatubo / active / historic times / 400 million people

« Definitions and explanations »

- **Volcanoes** are openings on the surface of the earth. Volcanoes offer a window into the ………………………………… . The word 'volcano' derives from ……………… , the Roman god of fire.

- **Volcanic activity** is the process by which ………………………………………… forms inside the earth. Gases, rock fragments and dust rise through the earth's crust onto the surface.

- It is estimated that over ………………………………………… live and work in the environs of active volcanoes.

❖ Concepts ❖

You need to know the following concepts for the short questions.

The life cycle of volcanoes

- Like rivers, volcanoes have a life cycle. They start life as …………… volcanoes, and then they become …………… and finally …………… .

- **Active volcanoes** are in a state of ………………… eruption, e.g. Stromboli in the Lipari Islands, north of Sicily, also called the Lighthouse of the Mediterranean. ………………… , on the island of Hawaii, is the world's largest active volcano.

- **Dormant volcanoes** are ………………………………… after a period of volcanic activity. In 1991, ………………………… in the Philippines erupted violently, having been dormant for 600 years.

- **Extinct volcanoes** have not erupted in ……………………… , e.g. ………………………… in Co. Antrim and the Puys in the Massif Central.

Label the diagram below using the following terms:

vent / crater / magma chamber / caldera / secondary vent / pyroclastic cloud

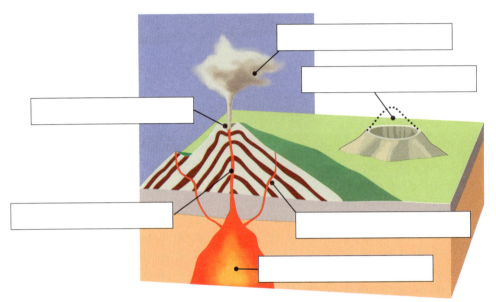

(b) Where Volcanoes Occur

Sample Question 1

Explain where volcanoes occur on the earth's surface.

Introduction

1   Pacific Ring of Fire ....

Divergent plate boundaries

2   sea-floor spreading ....

3   cracks form ....

4   Mid-Atlantic Ridge ....

5   less explosive ....

6   diagram of a divergent plate boundary

Convergent plate boundaries

7   heats up ....

8   volcano ....

9   Mount St Helens ....

10 diagram of a convergent plate boundary

Hot spots

11 warm areas ....

12 Hawaiian island chain ....

13 Mauna Loa ....

14 Pacific Plate ....

15 Yellowstone National Park ....

16 diagram of a hot spot

(c) Types of Volcanic Material

Sample Question 2

List and explain the types of volcanic material that are emitted from a volcano.

Insert the following terms into the blanks below:

sulphur dioxide / glacier bursts / Mount Pinatubo / lava / travel chaos / magma / white / destructive / Mauna Loa / Mount Eyjafjallajökull / Mount St Helens / low / explosive / less viscous / hydrogen / vents / ash, cinders and rock fragments / very destructive / glowing clouds / Mount Pinatubo / rock fragments / carbon monoxide / magma / blackened / viscous / side of a mountain / under an ice cap / glacier / much silica / high / gases / not explosive / lahar / Mount St Helens / pyroclastic material / do not travel far / constructive / Nevado del Ruiz / little silica / Colombia / silicon / acid / oxygen / basic / lava / mudflows / 18km / Iceland / flash floods

1 Lava

■ When .... reaches the surface it is called .... Some lava contains .... and is termed .... , while lava containing .... is termed .... **(1 SRP)**

■ Silica is a .... or colourless substance composed of .... and .... **(1 SRP)**

■ Acid lava flows are associated with .... plate boundaries. Silica content is .... , the flows are .... , moving slowly up the vent. Consequently, ... cannot easily escape and so acid lava flows are very .... Acid lavas .... has a high silica content. **(1 SRP)**

■ Basic lava flows are associated with .... plate boundaries. Silica content is .... ; the flows are .... , moving easily up the vent and across the surface. Basic lava flows are .... in Hawaii has low silica content. **(1 SRP)**

2 Volcanic gases

- Carbon dioxide, ... , steam, sulphur dioxide and .... are emitted during an eruption. **(1 SRP)**

- These gases form .... , allowing the .... to reach the surface. **(1 SRP)**

3 Pyroclastic material

- .... emitted by a volcano are called pyroclastic material. **(1 SRP)**

- Sometimes the pyroclastic material may mix with water to form a .... or mudflow. **(1 SRP)**

- These flows are .... The eruption of .... in .... in 1985 caused a lahar which killed over 23,000 in the valley below. The magma reacted with the .... on the mountain, resulting in .... **(1 SRP)**

- The eruption of .... in the Philippines in 1991 sent a cloud of .... 40km into the atmosphere. .... rushed down the mountain, extending .... from the eruption. **(1 SRP)**

4 Tephra

- Tephra refers to large .... and .... emitted by a volcano. **(1 SRP)**

- The eruption of .... in 1991 ejected tephra 3km into the atmosphere. The resulting ash .... the sky for days. **(1 SRP)**

5 Nuée Ardentes

- Nuée Ardentes are .... containing ash and other pyroclastic material. **(1 SRP)**

- They often move down the .... very rapidly, with devastating consequences. **(1 SRP)**

- Following the eruption of .... in 1980, a cloud of ash, steam and poisonous gas raced down the side of the mountain at 320km per hour, destroying forests, lakes and camping sites 32km away. Nine hundred were killed, 42,000 homes were destroyed and 100,000 acres of cropland were devastated. **(1 SRP)**

6 Jokulhlaups

- Jokulhlaups or .... occur when volcanoes are sited .... **(1 SRP)**

- In .... on 15 April 2010 .... erupted under an ice sheet. The resulting .... damaged nearby infrastructure and caused problems for Icelandic farmers in the area. The plume of smoke and ash led to the worst .... that Europe has ever witnessed. **(1 SRP)**

(d) Extrusive Landforms

Sample Question 3

Write an account of volcanic extrusive landforms.

Shield volcanoes

1   basic lava flows . . . .

2   broad base . . . .

3   broad, low-angled slope . . . .

4   warrior's shield . . . .

5   Mauna Loa . . . .

Lava plateaux

6   basic lava flows . . . .

7   two plates separate . . . .

8   the Antrim plateau . . . .

9   formation began 65 million years ago . . . .

Dome volcanoes

10   acidic lava flows . . . .

11   high with steep sides . . . .

12   Mt St Helens . . . .

Composite volcanoes

13   acid lava flows . . . .

14   alternating layers . . . .

15   convergent plate boundaries . . . .

16   tallest volcanoes . . . .

(e) Intrusive Landforms

Sample Question 4

Examine volcanic extrusive and intrusive landforms.

Note: In this question you have to write seven to eight SRPs from the previous question on extrusive landforms and seven to eight SRPs on volcanic intrusive landforms (see below).

Introduction

1 volcanic intrusive landforms ....
2 plutons ....
3 weathering and erosion ....

Batholiths

4 dome-shaped mass ....
5 Leinster batholith ....

Dykes

6 vertical sheets ....

Sills

7 horizontal sheets ....
8 laccolith ....
9 lopolith ....

❖ *Concepts* ❖

You need to know the following concepts for the short questions.

Insert the following terms into the blanks below:

hot springs / crater-like / geysers / Old Faithful / groundwater / black smokers / magma

Other volcanic landforms

1 Hydrothermal areas

- **Hydrothermal areas** occur when .... comes into contact with .... and hot rock. This heated water rises towards the surface, forming ....

- These are springs where the water is warmer than the temperature of the human body.

- They often contain dissolved minerals, which may have medicinal properties.

- The curative and restorative properties of Japan's hot springs have been appreciated for hundreds of years.

- .... are hot springs that eject jets of hot water and steam into the air, often rising to 30–60m.

- .... in Yellowstone National Park, USA, ejects hot water 50m into the air every 45 to 100 minutes. The steam is used to produce electricity, as in Iceland.

- .... are tall, chimney-like vents on the ocean floor, on or near mid-ocean ridges.

- They emit large amounts of mineral-rich seawater which often supports a diverse community of life.

2 Calderas

- **Calderas** are large, ... circular depressions formed when the top of a volcanic mountain is destroyed due to a very violent eruption.

(f) Advantages and Disadvantages of Volcanoes

Sample Question 5

List and explain the advantages and disadvantages of volcanoes.

Advantages of volcanoes

1 Fertile soils

1 minerals, dust, ash and cinders ....

2 Java ....

2 Formation of precious stones and minerals

3 gold, silver, lead ....

4 sulphur ....

3 Geothermal energy

5 production of electricity ....

6 hot springs ....

7 northern California ....

4 Tourism

   8 Mt Vesuvius and Mt Etna ....

   9 Piton de la Fournaise ....

Disadvantages of volcanoes

1 Loss of life

   10 Krakatoa ....

   11 El Chichon ....

2 Damage to property

   12 AD79 Vesuvius ....

   13 Mt St Helens ....

3 Environmental damage

   14 Mt Pinatubo ....

   15 blotting out sunlight ....

4 Economic effects

   16 Mt Eyjafjallajökull ....

(g) One Volcanic Landform in Ireland: The Giant's Causeway

Sample Question 6

Explain, with the aid of a diagram, the formation of one volcanic landform found in ireland.

Insert the following terms into the blanks below:

crumbled / early Tertiary period / moving northwards / 40,000 stone columns / water / surface / 35 million years / thawing / the Antrim plateau / lava plateau / equatorial / cracked skin of mud / columnar jointing / shifted / glaciation / plates / lava outflows / intensive volcanic activity / igneous activity / deep / a layer of black chocolate / freeze–thaw action / molten rock / premier geological attraction / cracks / freezing / chalk bed / fissures / hexagons / glaciated

The Giant's Causeway

- The Giant's Causeway is located at the base of basalt cliffs on the sea coast on the edge of .... in Northern Ireland. **(1 SRP)**

- It was formed during the .... 62–65 million years ago in an era of .... **(1 SRP)**

- Antrim was undergoing .... Very fluid .... was ejected through fissures in the overlying .... , forming an extensive .... The molten rock covered the chalk like .... **(1 SRP)**

- Three .... occurred, known as the Lower, Middle and Upper Basaltic. **(1 SRP)**

- At this time the Giant's Causeway would have been located in an .... region. It has been slowly .... due to the actions of the earth's .... The plates move slowly over millions of years but over that time they can travel thousands of miles. **(1 SRP)**

- The Causeway comprises .... , with the tallest reaching 12m. Most, but not all, form .... **(1 SRP)**

- The polygonal columns were formed due to a geological process called .... **(1 SRP)**

- As the molten lava which erupted from the volcanoes cooled, it would have resembled the .... left by a dried-out pond or lake. **(1 SRP)**

- The lava deposits were very .... , and as the areas below the surface began to cool and harden, the .... from the .... began to move downwards, creating deep .... **(1 SRP)**

- .... after the volcanic eruptions the area was .... and covered in water.
  (1 SRP)

- The ice and water entered the cracks between the columns, ... and .... and widening the cracks between the rocks. **(1 SRP)**

- Some rocks .... , while others were .... by the .... of the ice. **(1 SRP)**

- The combined influence of .... and .... helped to form the present shape of the Giant's Causeway. **(1 SRP)**

- Today, it is Ireland's .... , attracting thousands of tourists every year. **(1 SRP)**

- Sketch map of Ireland showing the area of the Giant's Causeway **(1 SRP)**

Chapter 4
Folding and Faulting

(a) Introduction

Folding

In the process of **folding**, a structure that once was flat may be bent or buckled into a series of wave-like folds and hollows. Folding occurs along **destructive plate boundaries** where converging plates collide and buckle.

Example:

The Himalayas were formed when the Eurasian Plate converged with the Indo-Australian Plate. Sea-floor sediments were compressed and uplifted into **fold mountains**. Fold mountains are worn down and re-shaped by weathering and erosion.

Point to note:

The process of folding is similar to pushing inwards on opposite ends of a piece of paper or pushing it up from below.

- The result of folding can be compared to a sheet of corrugated iron on a roof top.
- Folding is evident in Loughshinny, north Co. Dublin, and the Rock of Cashel, Co. Tipperary.

 **❖ Concepts ❖**

You need to know the following concepts for the short questions.

Insert the following terms into the blanks below:

symmetrical / syncline / asymmetrical / limbs / overfolds / anticline / overthrusts

Different types of fold

- .... refers to the upfold or arch.

- .... refers to the downfold or trough.

- The two arms of a fold are called ....

- Folds whose limbs and dips are uniform are described as ....

- Folds whose limbs are unequal are described as ....

- .... occur when one limb lies over the other limb.

- .... occur when one limb is pushed forward over the other limb.

Label the diagrams below using the following terms:

asymmetrical fold / syncline / overfold / simple fold / overthrust fold / anticline

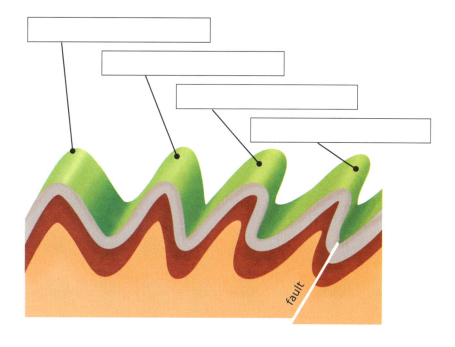

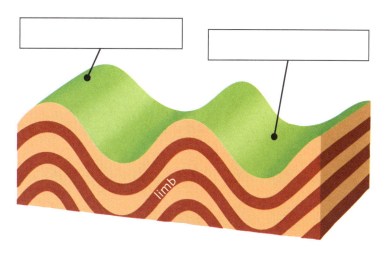

Faulting

« *Definitions and explanations* »

- **Faulting** occurs when rocks are displaced relative to each other, forming a fault line.

- A **fault line** is a fracture along which one section of the earth's crust has been displaced relative to another.

- This displacement may be **vertical or horizontal** or a combination of both. It results from compression and tension associated with continental drift.

- Fault terminology:

    1 **Scarp**: a cliff formed due to vertical displacement.

    2 **Throw**: the degree of vertical displacement.

    3 **Heave**: the degree of horizontal displacement.

(b) Three Types of Fold Mountain

Sample Question 1

Explain the formation of the three types of fold mountain.

Introduction

1 global distribution/convergent plate boundaries. . . . .

2 continental plates . . . .

Caledonian foldings

3 450 million years ago . . . .

4 Caledonia . . . .

5 weathering and erosion . . . .

6 mountainous backbone . . . .

Armorican foldings

7 270 million years ago . . . .

8 Vosges Mountains . . . .

9 Munster ridge and valley province ....

10 anticlines and synclines ....

11 plantation surface ....

12 the Burren ....

Alpine foldings

13 30 million years ago ....

14 African plate ....

15 high and more rugged ....

16 Ireland ....

17 diagram of Caledonian, Armorican and Alpine foldings

(c) Case Study: Munster Ridge and Valley

Sample Question 2

With the aid of a diagram, explain how the Munster ridge and valley were formed.

Insert the following terms into the blanks below:

Burren / east–west / old red sandstone / uplifted / valleys / rias / carboniferous limestone / equator / west Waterford / weaker / Bandon / submerged upland coasts / European plate / anticlines / Comeraghs / folded / Macgillycuddy's Reeks / V-shaped valleys / Galtees / Lee / synclines / eroded faster / equator / mountains / Cork and Kerry / African plate / Armorican / ridges

Munster ridge and valley

- The Munster ridge and valley province extends from .... into .... **(1 SRP)**
- The .... of the ridge and valley province run in an .... direction. **(1 SRP)**
- They were formed during the .... mountain-building period 270 million years ago. **(1 SRP)**
- The region comprises .... and .... **(1 SRP)**
- The limestone was deposited when Ireland lay close to the .... **(1 SRP)**
- Limestone is a .... rock than sandstone and so was .... than the sandstone. **(1 SRP)**

- The limestone was eroded to form .... or .... , while the harder sandstone formed .... or .... **(1 SRP)**

- The major rivers of south Ireland flow through the limestone valleys – the .... , Blackwater and .... **(1 SRP)**

- The .... collided with the .... 270 million years ago. **(1 SRP)**

- The limestone and sandstone rocks were .... and .... into valleys (synclines) and ridges (anticlines). **(1 SRP)**

- This folding formed the .... , ... , the .... and the Silvermines. The .... in Co. Clare was also uplifted around this time. **(1 SRP)**

- Parts of the anticlines along the south-west Cork and Kerry coastlines were flooded, forming .... **(1 SRP)**

- Rias are drowned .... , becoming wider and deeper as they approach the sea. They are features of .... **(1 SRP)**

- Diagram of anticline and syncline **(1 SRP)**

(d) Three Types of Fault

Sample Question 3

With the aid of diagrams, explain the three types of fault.

Normal faults

1 apart ....

2 rift valley and graben ....

3 vertical movement...

4 rift valleys ....

5 diagram of rift valley

6 Glenmore...

7 block mountains..

8 diagram of block mountain

9 Ox Mountains, Co. Sligo ....

Tear faults

10 plates move horizontally ....

Reverse and thrust faults

Chapter 5
Rocks

« *Definition* »

- There are **three types** of rock:

    1 **Igneous** rocks

    2 **Sedimentary** rocks

    3 **Metamorphic** rocks

Label the diagram below using the following terms:

granite / basalt / limestone / sandstone / shales / quartzite / marble and slate

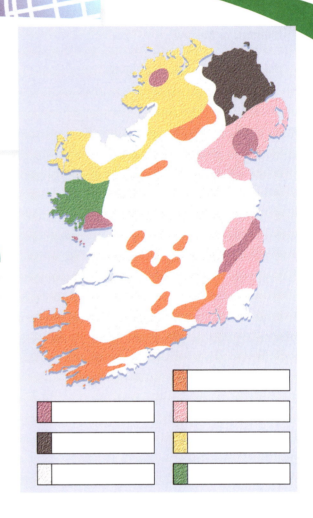

(a) Igneous Rocks

Sample Question 1

Explain how igneous rocks are formed. In your answer refer to two types of igneous rock.

Igneous rock formation

1 ignis...

2 volcanic/extrusive ....

3 plutonic/intrusive . . . .

Extrusive

4 basalt . . . .

5 quartz . . . .

6 hydrochloric acid . . . .

7 Giant's Causeway . . . .

Antrim plateau

8 65 million years ago . . . .

9 fissure . . . .

Intrusive

10 granite . . . .

11 chemical composition . . . .

12 grey . . . .

13 buildings . . . .

14 Donegal and Wicklow . . . .

Leinster batholith

15 Caledonian folding . . . .

16 molten magma . . . .

17 weathering and erosion . . . .

(b) Sedimentary Rocks

Sample Question 2

With the aid of examples, outline the different types of sedimentary rocks and explain how they are formed.

Insert the following terms into the blanks below:

sediments / lithification / organically / permeable / calcium carbonate / layers / road stones / red / Comeragh Mountains / bedding planes / chemically formed / most / compress / inorganic / cement / most common rock type / weathering / broken down / cement / strata / lakes / erosion / transported / seas / 350 million / lithification / compressed sea creatures / soluble / corals / deposited / fossils / equator / grey-white / thirty degrees south / grains / brown / Macgillycuddy's Reeks / evaporated / plaster boards / rock salts / gypsum / layers / grit roads / Carrickfergus, Co. Antrim / over one-third / hot desert climate / lake / paving stone / well solidified / bedding planes / seas / fertiliser / sand / deposited / 400 million / building material / desert climate / Kingscourt, Co. Cavan / sea / compressed

Sedimentary rocks

- Sedimentary rocks are formed due to the processes of .... and .... .When rocks are subjected to weathering and erosion the rock is .... , ... and .... as sediments. **(1 SRP)**

- These .... are laid down in .... or .... on the beds of .... and .... The strata are separated by .... .Over time, the layers are .... into sedimentary rocks through the process of ....**(1 SRP)**

There are three types of sedimentary rock:

1 Organic

2 Inorganic (mechanically formed)

3 Chemically formed (evaporates)   **(1 SRP)**

Organic
Limestone

- Limestone is an .... formed sedimentary rock comprised of .... It formed .... years ago when Ireland was near the .... and surrounded by ....**(1 SRP)**

- It was formed from the remains of .... which were laid down in .... .Consequently, it may contain ....**(1 SRP)**

- Limestone is .... and .... in water containing carbon dioxide. **(1 SRP)**

- It is the ………………………………… in Ireland, found in the Burren, Co. Clare, and the Aran Islands. It is …………………… in colour due to impurities in the rock. **(1 SRP)**

- It is used as a ……………………………… , e.g. St Patrick's Cathedral, Dublin. It is also used to make …………… and also as a ………………… when converted into lime. It can also be used as ……………………… . **(1 SRP)**

Inorganic

Sandstone

- Sandstone is an ………………… sedimentary rock formed ………………… years ago. Ireland at this time was ……………………………… of the equator and had a ……………………… . **(1 SRP)**

- It comprises ………… of …………… eroded from older rocks and ……………… on river and sea beds. **(1 SRP)**

- The top layers of sand …………… the lower layers so it is …………………………… and the different strata or layers are separated by ……………………………… . **(1 SRP)**

- The transformation from sand to sandstone is similar to the way sugar hardens after becoming damp and this transformation is called ……………………… . **(1 SRP)**

« Definitions »

Lithification is the process whereby newly deposited sediments are converted into solid rock by compression and cementation.

- Sandstone can be ………… or ………… in colour and it is used as a ……………. It is found in ……………………………… and the ……………………………………… . **(1 SRP)**

Chemically formed

Gypsum and rock salt

- Gypsum and rock salts are …………………………… sedimentary rocks. These rocks formed when water ………………… from a ………… or ……… when Ireland had a ……………………………… . **(1 SRP)**

- When ………… of the water evaporated ……………… were formed. …………… forms when ……………………………… of the water evaporated. **(1 SRP)**

- Rock salts are found in ……………………………………… and gypsum is found in ………………… ………………… . **(1 SRP)**

- Rock salt is used to ………………… and gypsum is used in the manufacture of ……………… and ……………………… . **(1 SRP)**

(c) Metamorphic Rocks

Sample Question 3

Explain the formation of metamorphic rocks. In your answer, refer to the formation of one type of metamorphic rock.

Metamorphic rocks

1   metamorphic rocks ....

2   examples of metamorphism...

3   the three types of metamorphism ....

4   thermal metamorphism..

5   regional metamorphism ....

6   dynamic metamorphism...

Thermal metamorphism

7   thermal metamorphism of limestone ....

8   subducted...

9   different colours ....

10   highly valued rock ....

Regional metamorphism

11   gneiss ....

12   great pressure ....

13   feldspar, quartz and mica...

Dynamic metamorphism

14   slate...

15   converging plate boundaries..

16   waterproof and splits easily ....

(d) The Rock Cycle

Sample Question 4

With the aid of a diagram, explain the rock cycle.

Insert the following terms into the blanks below:

weathering and erosion / sandstone / lithification / basalt / James Hutton / inorganic sedimentary rock / intrusive / pressure / thermal metamorphism / on the surface / destroyed / three stages / transported and deposited / compress / limestone / dynamic metamorphism / stress / metamorphic rocks / recycling machine / mantle / organic sedimentary rock / solidifies / below the crust / marble / magma / extrusive / slate / granite / formed / igneous / rocks

The rock cycle

- Rocks are constantly being …………… and ………………… as part of the rock cycle. **(1 SRP)**
- The rock cycle summarises the major factors affecting rocks both ………………………………………… and ……………………………………… . **(1 SRP)**
- It was proposed by ……………………………… in the eighteenth century that the upper part of the earth was a ……………………………………………… . **(1 SRP)**
- The cycle comprises ……………………………, i.e. creation, modification and destruction. **(1 SRP)**

Igneous

- …………… from the …………… cools and …………………… to form ……………………………………… . **(1 SRP)**
- ……………… is an …………………… igneous rock formed when lava cools quickly on the earth's surface, e.g. at the Giant's Causeway in Antrim. **(1 SRP)**
- ……………… is an …………………… igneous rock formed when magma cooled slowly within the earth's crust, i.e. when it intruded into the upfolds underneath mountains, as in the Wicklow Mountains. **(1 SRP)**

Sedimentary

- Igneous rocks are subjected to …………………………………… .
- The resulting fragments and sediments are ………………………………………………………… on lake and sea beds, forming sedimentary rocks. **(1 SRP)**
- The top layers ………………… the bottom layers into ………………… – the process of ……………………………… . **(1 SRP)**
- …………………, the most common rock type in Ireland, is an ……………………………………… . It was formed 350 million years ago from the compressed remains of sea creatures when Ireland was covered by a warm tropical sea. **(1 SRP)**

- ...., found on the ridges of Munster, is an ...., which was formed 400 million years ago when Ireland was located below the equator and had a desert climate. **(1 SRP)**

Metamorphic

- When the sedimentary rocks are put under .... due to heat (the movement of plates) and .... (folding) they form .... **(1 SRP)**

- .... is formed at convergent plate boundaries due to the .... (heat) of limestone. **(1 SRP)**

- .... is also formed at convergent plate boundaries due to the .... (pressure) of shale. **(1 SRP)**

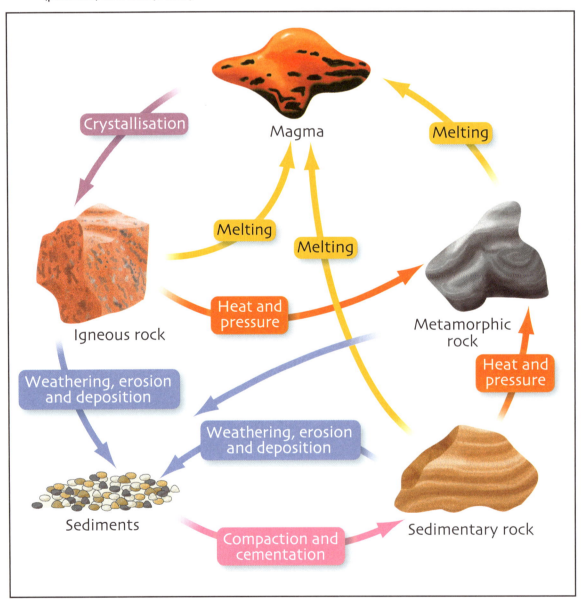

The Rock Cycle

(2 SRPs)

(e) Human Interaction with the Rock Cycle

Sample Question 5

With the aid of a case study, explain one way in which humans interact with the rock cycle.

Case study: natural gas in Ireland

1 25 per cent of total primary energy demand in Ireland . . . .

Kinsale Head

2 50km off the coast/100m of water . . . .

Seven Heads

3 30km away . . . .

The Corrib gas field

4 250 million years old . . . .

5 an anticline trap . . . .

6 a fault trap . . . .

7 70km off the coast of Mayo . . . .

8 wells . . . .

9 an anti-corrosion agent . . . .

10 terminal to process the gas . . . .

11 Shell . . . .

Advantages of the Corrib gas project

12 boost Ireland's GDP . . . .

13 60 per cent of Ireland's natural gas needs . . . .

Other sources

14 two interconnector sub-sea pipelines . . . .

15 residential, commercial and industrial functions . . . .

Chapter 6
Weathering

« Definitions »

Weathering is the breaking down or wearing away of landforms on the spot (in situ). It does not involve the removal of the material that results.

There are three types of weathering:

(a) **Mechanical** or physical

(b) **Chemical**

(c) **Biological**.

Erosion is the breaking down or wearing away of landforms and the transportation of the broken down material and its deposition elsewhere.

The main agents of erosion are rivers, seas, wind, ice and gravity.

(a) Mechanical Weathering

Sample Question 1

Define the term 'mechanical weathering', and with the aid of diagrams explain two types of mechanical weathering.

Mechanical weathering

1 physical disintegration of rocks . . . .

2 little or no vegetation cover . . . .

3 exfoliation and freeze–thaw . . . .

Exfoliation/onion weathering

4 deserts . . . .

5 expansion and contraction . . . .

7 outer layer will expand . . . .

8 exfoliation . . . .

9 moisture. . . . .

10 diagram of exfoliation/onion weathering

Freeze-thaw action

11 mountainous areas . . . .

12 rain enters cracks . . . .

13 rain falls again . . . .

14 gravity. . . . .

15 talus. . . . .

16 Croagh Patrick, Co. Mayo . . . .

17 diagram of freeze–thaw action

(b) Chemical Weathering

Sample Question 2

List and explain the four types of chemical weathering.

Insert the following terms into the blanks below:

minerals that do not contain water / carbon dioxide / calcium carbonate / the Burren / hydrogen / rounded by hydrolysis / oxygen / bauxite / rock / crumble / reacts / oxidation / feldspar / hydrolysis / iron / water / Wicklow and Mourne mountains / disintegration / mineral constitutents / carbonation / atmosphere / calcium bicarbonate / limestone and chalk / high clay content / shale / Three Rock Mountain / lose their strength / humid climates / destruction / chemical changes / kaolin / brown, yellow or red / china clay / old red sandstone / minerals / granite / tors / dissolved by rainwater / carbonic acid / chemical changes / rocks / hydration / solution

Introduction to chemical weathering

■ Chemical weathering refers to the . . . . of rocks as a result of . . . . in the . . . . of rock. **(1 SRP)**

■ . . . . is an essential requirement for chemical weathering and so chemical weathering is very active in . . . .**(1 SRP)**

- The chief processes are:
    - ....
    - ....
    - ....
    - .... **(1 SRP)**

Carbonation

- When rainwater absorbs .... as it falls through the .... it forms .... Carbonic acid weathers .... **(1 SRP)**
- The carbonic acid reacts with .... in limestone, converting it to soluble ...., which is carried away in .... **(1 SRP)**
-

$$H_2O + CO_2 \quad \rightarrow \quad H_2CO_3$$
$$\text{water} + \text{carbon dioxide} \quad \rightarrow \quad \text{carbonic acid}$$

$$H_2CO_3 + CaCO_3 \quad \rightarrow \quad Ca(HCO_3)_2$$
$$\text{carbonic acid} \quad \rightarrow \quad \text{calcium bicarbonate}$$
$$+ \text{calcium carbonate}$$

(1 SRP)
- Carbonation is very active in .... , Co. Clare. **(1 SRP)**

Hydration

- Hydration refers to the process whereby water is absorbed by .... **(1 SRP)**
- .... with a .... expand as they absorb water. **(1 SRP)**
- When these rocks absorb water they expand and .... , leading to the .... of the rock. .... is weathered by hydration. **(1 SRP)**

Oxidation

- Oxidation refers to the process whereby .... that has been .... is added to rocks containing .... The addition of oxygen causes these rocks to .... easily. **(1 SRP)**
- Oxidated rocks will have .... surfaces, e.g. .... and .... **(1 SRP)**

Hydrolysis

■ Hydrolysis refers to the process whereby .... which is present in water .... with .... in the .... to cause a series of .... **(1 SRP)**

■ .... in granite absorbs water, converting it into .... or .... **(1 SRP)**

■ Blocks of .... which have been .... often rise several metres above the surrounding land . These are .... They can be seen on .... , Co. Dublin. **(1 SRP)**

■ Hydrolysis has helped to shape the .... **(1 SRP)**

(c) Three Types of Weathering

Sample Question 3

Name and explain three different types of weathering.

Note: In this question, you have to include five to six SRPs from each of the previous two questions (i.e. physical and chemical weathering) and five to six SRPs from biological weathering below.

Biological weathering

1 the disintegration of rocks ....

Plants

2 roots ....

3 lichens and mosses ....

4 water..

Animals

5 rodents and earthworms..

6 regolith...

Humans

7 deforestation ....

8 open the soil to other processes...

(d) Factors that Control the Weathering Process

Sample Question 4

List and explain the factors that control the weathering process.

Insert the following terms into the blanks below:

freeze–thaw / mechanical / plants / weathering / biological / rapid temperature change / loosening soil / range / pore spaces / desert regions / water / exposing rocks / mountainous / steep topography / temperate climates / environmental damage / restricted / time / caves / humidity / 50m below / cooler / permeable rock / bedding planes / metre

Climate

- Chemical weathering requires .... and high temperatures. **(1 SRP)**
- Chemical weathering is prevalent in equatorial regions, but is also common in .... like Ireland, where carbon dioxide is dissolved in rainwater. **(1 SRP)**
- .... weathering dominates in regions that are arid and sub-arctic. **(1 SRP)**
- Exfoliation requires .... and a large temperature .... Exfoliation is prevalent in .... such as the Sahara Desert. **(1 SRP)**
- .... requires temperatures to fluctuate around freezing point, a plentiful supply of .... and rock with cracks and .... Freeze–thaw is prevalent in .... areas. **(1 SRP)**
- Biological weathering requires rapid growth of .... plus .... by humans, e.g. deforestation, overgrazing, overcropping. **(1 SRP)**
- It is prevalent in hot environments but also .... climates like Ireland's. **(1 SRP)**

Depth and soil cover

- Mechanical weathering is .... to the top .... of bedrock and regolith. **(1 SRP)**
- Chemical weathering can operate up to .... the surface, e.g. the .... in the Burren. **(1 SRP)**
- .... weathering is active in all soil environments. **(1 SRP)**

Rock type

- .... allows water to seep through it, accelerating the weathering process. **(1 SRP)**
- Rocks which split along .... , such as limestone, break up more easily, helping the weathering process. **(1 SRP)**

Time

- The longer the rock is exposed to the .... processes, the more .... for the weathering processes to operate. **(1 SRP)**

Plants and animals

- The actions of plants and animals influence weathering processes by .... and .... to the weathering process. **(1 SRP)**

Relief

- .... exposes more rock to weathering than horizontal surfaces. **(1 SRP)**

Chapter 7
Karst

(a) Introduction

« Definitions and examples »

Karst means **barren**. The name derives from a region in Slovenia.

Karst landscapes:

- **The Burren** in Co. Clare, Ireland (Burren = rocky/stony place)
- The Peak District in Derbyshire, Great Britain

Tower karst landscapes:

- Guilin, China
- Halong Bay, Vietnam

The weathering process in limestone areas

Rainwater, falling through the atmosphere, absorbs CO_2, forming **carbonic acid** (H_2CO_3) which reacts with **calcium carbonate** ($CaCo_3$), the cementing agent in limestone, to produce a soluble **calcium bicarbonate** ($Ca(HCo_3)_2$), which is carried away in solution.

$$H_2O + CO_2 \rightarrow H_2CO_3 \mid H_2CO_3 + CaCO_3 \rightarrow Ca(HCO_3)_2$$

This process is called **carbonation.**

Label the diagram below using the following terms:

limestone pavement / joints / underground river / dry valley / clints / grikes / gorge / bedding planes / swallow hole /

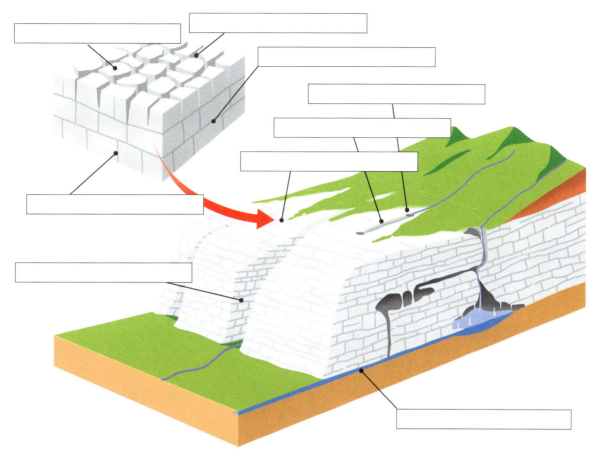

Label the diagram below using the following terms:

cavern / stalactite / stalagmite / pillar

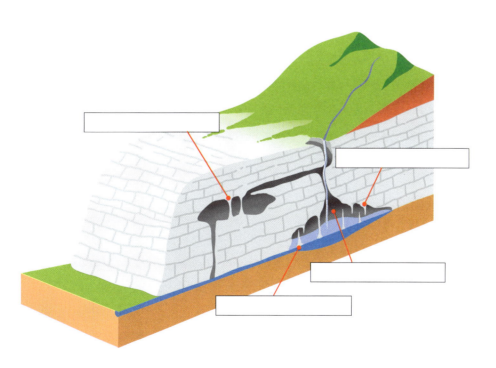

❖ Concepts ❖

You need to know the following concepts for the short questions.

Insert the following terms into the blanks below:

columns/pillars / stalagmites / curtains / limestone pavements / grikes / swallow-holes or sinkholes / dry valley / dolines / poljes / caves / clints / stalactites / karren / turloughs / fossil / swallow holes / uvalas

Surface karst features

1 ....

■ These consist of slabs or blocks of rock called .... and are separated by joints called ....

■ Small rounded hollows or depressions called .... may occur on the clint surface.

2 ....

■ These are large, funnel-shaped downward openings on the limestone/karst surface, which are carved out by a river that disappears underground.

■ A swallow-hole that is no longer used by a river becomes a .... swallow-hole.

■ A .... is one that was carved out by the force of running water but no longer has a river flowing through it.

3 ....

■ These are shallow seasonal lakes located in low-lying areas, created as increased precipitation in the winter leads to a rise in the water table.

4 Hollows

■ ....are bowl-shaped depressions where overlying soil subsides into a depression.

■ .... are formed when a series of dolines join together (100–200m in diameter).

■ .... are very large depressions formed when a series of uvalas join together. The polje at Carron in the Burren is over 60m deep and 3km in diameter.

Underground karst features

1 ....

■ An underground passage which has been enlarged to form a cave or cavern by the processes of abrasion and carbonation.

2 ....

■ These are formed by water which percolates down through limestone, evaporates when it reaches the warmer air in the cave and deposits calcite on the cave roof.

3 ....

■ These are formed on the floor of a cave by water which evaporates, leaving the calcite to build upwards.

4 ....

■ Columns/pillars are formed when stalactites and stalagmites meet.

5 ....

■ These are formed when calcite is deposited along a crack or fissure in a cave roof.

(b) How the Burren Was Formed

Sample Question 1

Explain how the Burren was formed.

The Burren

1 distinctive landscape. ....

2 lacks vegetation and surface water ....

3 over 360 sq km ....

4 unique surface features ....

5 Carboniferous geological period ....

6 skeletons ....

7 compressed ....

8 well-stratified rock ....

9 calcium carbonate ....

10 Armorican mountain-building period. ....

11 limestone is permeable ....

12 Slieve Elva ....

13 granite erratics. ....

14 forest. ....

15 Mullaghmore ....

(c) Surface Feature: Limestone Pavements

Sample Question 2

With the aid of a diagram, explain the formation of any one surface feature found on a Karst landscape.

Insert the following terms into the blanks below:

joints and cracks / grikes / carbonation / carbonic acid / Burren / uneroded rock surface / exposed flat rock / calcium carbonate / bicarbonate / clints / solution / $Ca(HCO_3)_2$ / two metres deep / plant life / resistant slabs / paving slabs / karren / limestone pavement / edges / flurting / Yorkshire Dales

Limestone pavements

- One surface feature found in the Burren is the .... Limestone pavements are a legacy of the last ice age that ended 15,000 years ago in Ireland. The ice eroded the top layers of material to reveal a massive .... when the ice disappeared. **(1 SRP)**

- Limestone pavements are formed by the process of .... **(1 SRP)**

- This is the process by which rainwater falling through the atmosphere absorbs CO_2, forming .... (H_2CO_3) which reacts with .... to produce a soluble calcium .... which is carried away in .... **(1 SRP)**

- The chemical formula for carbonation is: $H_2CO_3 + CaCO_3 \rightarrow$ .... **(1 SRP)**

- A limestone pavement is an extensive area of ...., comprising clints, grikes and karren. **(1 SRP)**

- Rainwater falling on limestone travels underground via .... in the limestone. **(1 SRP)**

- The joints are widened and deepened to form .... by the process of carbonation. **(1 SRP)**

- They may be thirty centimetres wide and up to .... **(1 SRP)**

- Soil deposits in the grikes provide a home for .... – hazel, ash, shrubs and exotic plants. **(1 SRP)**

- The more .... surrounding the grikes are not affected . These are called .... Each clint is up to a few square metres in extent. **(1 SRP)**

- Limestone pavements resemble .... **(1 SRP)**

- Carbonation also takes place on the surface of the clint, forming .... These are narrow hollows on the clint surfaces. **(1 SRP)**

- Small hollows may form on the .... of the clints due to solution. This process is termed .... **(1 SRP)**

- Limestone pavements can be seen in the .... , Co. Clare, the ...., England, and the Causses in France. **(1 SRP)**

- Diagram of limestone pavement **(1 SRP)**

(d) Underground Features: Stalactites and Stalagmites

Sample Question 3

With the aid of diagrams, explain the formation of two underground features found in limestone regions.

Insert the following terms into the blanks below:

dripstone formations / evaporation and deposition / curtains / swallow holes / percolated / evaporation / percolation / calcium carbonate / slanting ceilings / stalactites / carbonation / floor / grow upwards / the ceiling / straw stalactites / columns / deposition / warmer air temperatures / icicles / evaporated / Poll an lonain / carbonation / abrasion / underground streams / tunnels / growing downwards / bedding planes and joints / caves / stalactites / curtains / Marble Arch, Co. Fermanagh / channels / a maze of caves / water / abrasion / carrot-shaped stalactites / pillars /carbonates / stalactites and stalagmites meet / calcium carbonate / cave roof / stalagmites / formula / through cracks / Ailwee Cave, Co. Clare / water

Underground limestone features

- Rivers make their way underground via .... , following lines of weakness in the underlying rock, forming .... , caves, ... , stalagmites, ... and curtains. **(1 SRP)**

- As the river makes its way underground it .... and enlarges the .... , forming .... in the limestone rock. **(1 SRP)**

- The processes of .... (river erosion) and .... widen the channels, forming .... **(1 SRP)**

- .... is the scouring action of the load. **(1 SRP)**

- .... is the process whereby rainwater falling through the atmosphere combines with CO_2 to form a weak carbonic acid, which reacts with calcium carbonate to form a soluble calcium bicarbonate, which is carried away in solution. **(1 SRP)**

- The .... for carbonation is $H_2CO_3 + CaCO_3 \rightarrow Ca(HCO_3)_2$. **(1 SRP)**

- Over time, ... form, such as Mitchelstown Cave, Co. Tipperary, and Ailwee Cave, the Burren. **(1 SRP)**

- If the river is flowing more slowly it won't have the power to erode as easily and so it will form .... , as in Dunmore Cave, Co. Kilkenny. **(1 SRP)**

Stalactites

- Stalactites are formed by the processes of .... , evaporation and .... **(1 SRP)**

- They are formed when .... which has .... through the limestone above the cave trickles down .... in the .... **(1 SRP)**

- …………………….. takes place due to the ………………………………………… in the cave , leaving behind deposits of ………………………………. . **(1 SRP)**

- …………….. form on the cave ceiling, ………………………………. , forming …………………………….. . **(1 SRP)**

- If the straw stalactite is blocked by grit the water then flows down the outside of the tube, forming …………………………………………………………. . **(1 SRP)**

- ……………………………contains the largest free-standing stalactite in the world. **(1 SRP)**

Stalagmites

- Stalagmites are formed by the processes of ………………… and ……………………………… . **(1 SRP)**

- They are formed on the ………………… of a cave by ……………… which has not completely ……………………… on …………………… . **(1 SRP)**

- The water evaporates on the floor, leaving behind ………………………… , forming …………………… which …………………………………… . **(1 SRP)**

- Columns or ……………… are formed when ……………………………………………… meet. **(1 SRP)**

- ……………… form in the same way as …………………… , except that curtains form on ……………………………. rather than on a horizontal ceiling. **(1 SRP)**

- These features are called ……………………………………………… , as they owe their formation to water dripping through the ceiling of a cave. **(1 SRP)**

- All of the above can be found in the following caves:

  - ……………………………………………………………

  - Crag Cave, Castleisland, Co. Kerry

  - Dunmore Cave, Co. Kilkenny

  - ……………………………………………………………

  - Mitchelstown Cave, Co. Tipperary. **(1 SRP)**

- Diagram of cave/cavern **(1 SRP)**

(e) Cycle of Erosion in a Karst Area

Sample Question 4

With the aid of diagrams, explain the cycle of erosion in a karst area.

Introduction

1 a cycle of erosion ....

2 river erosion ....

Youthful stage

3 rivers flow normally ....

4 carbonation ....

5 diagrams of the youthful stage

Mature stage

6 swallow-holes ....

7 caves ....

8 dolines, uvalas and poljes ....

9 diagrams of the mature stage

Old-age stage

10 limestone has now been eroded...

11 hums...

12 underlying impermeable rocks ....

13 diagrams of the old-age stage

14 tower karst and hums ....

15 heavy monsoon rains ....

16 Burren in Co. Clare ....

(f) Human Interaction with the Burren

Sample Question 5

List and explain four ways in which humans interact with the Burren.

Insert the following terms into the blanks below:

calcium / fulachta fiadh / North Atlantic / part-time / farming / Rural Environmental Protection Scheme / burial / protection / interpretive centre / cool temperate oceanic / enclosures / endangered species / grikes / soil erosion / heat absorbing capacity / tourism / transhumance / Neolithic / encroachment / early human settlement / second jobs / agri-tourism / water systems / urban life / over 70 per cent / castles / tertiary / decline / uplands / lime-rich / grants / conserve / balance / caves / pollute / widened / waste

Flora and fauna

- The Burren is a botanist's delight. It is home to .... of Ireland's native flora. **(1 SRP)**

- The .... climate and the influence of the .... Drift provide ideal growing conditions. **(1 SRP)**

- Plants from the Arctic, Alps and Mediterranean regions are common. The plants grow in .... , which contain .... soils. The grikes also offer .... from the elements. **(1 SRP)**

- Many .... , such as pine martens, foxes, goats and hares, exist in large numbers. **(1 SRP)**

The human landscape

- There is evidence of .... in the Burren. The Burren contains eighty .... sites, indicating a higher population density in the past. **(1 SRP)**

- Poulnabrone, which is 5,800 years old, is an ancient .... chamber. There are ancient cooking sites or .... which are over 5,000 years old. **(1 SRP)**

- The Burren contains over 500 stone-built .... , indicating the presence of early farmers. There are many .... , such as Dun Aengus on the Aran Islands, as well as many abbeys. **(1 SRP)**

- As the population grew, forests were removed, leading to .... , exposing the limestone. **(1 SRP)**

- Today the human landscape is under threat from .... , as people arrive in great numbers to see this unique region. **(1 SRP)**

Agriculture

- There is evidence of .... dating back 6,000 years to the Neolithic period. Today the emphasis is on pastoral farming and .... is practised. Cattle are moved to the limestone .... in the winter, which are ideal grazing grounds due to a lack of frost and the .... of the limestone rock. **(1 SRP)**

- There is good vegetation, which is rich in .... due to the limestone base. However, farming is in decline, which has allowed hazel-scrub .... Farming is becoming a .... occupation, with many farmers having .... in Ennis, Shannon and Galway. **(1 SRP)**

- To encourage farming, ... are available to aid scrub clearance, removal of large boulders and limestone walls. Grants are also available to encourage increased silage production. However, a .... must be maintained between the needs of farmers and the protection of the unique landscape of the Burren. **(1 SRP)**

- Agricultural .... must be disposed of properly. All local water supplies in the Burren come from underground sources. Corofin obtains its water from Lough Inchiquin. The lough receives its water from underground sources. Agricultural waste could pollute underground .... **(1 SRP)**

- The number of farmers is declining due to increased mechanisation, consolidation of holdings and the attraction of .... In order to support farming, the .... (REPS) was introduced in 1995 to encourage farmers to .... the landscape. **(1 SRP)**

Tourism

- As agriculture falls into .... tourism is regarded as an option. The numbers employed in this .... economic activity are increasing. **(1 SRP)**

- The attractions for tourism include the unique surface features such as the Ailwee .... and the many festivals. .... is also developing. **(1 SRP)**

- However, while tourism might increase employment and income in the area, huge numbers of tourists could .... the delicate environment. **(1 SRP)**

- Roads would have to be .... to cater for coaches and increased volumes of traffic. On a positive note, plans for an .... at Mullaghmore have been abandoned. **(1 SRP)**

Chapter 8

Rivers

NB: Students have to be able to identify and name all features/landforms and processes of the following five sections for the short questions. However, only one section on rivers has to be learnt in depth for the long 30-mark questions.

(a) Introduction

Label the diagram below using the following terms:

mouth / basin / tributary / estuary /
source / confluence / watershed

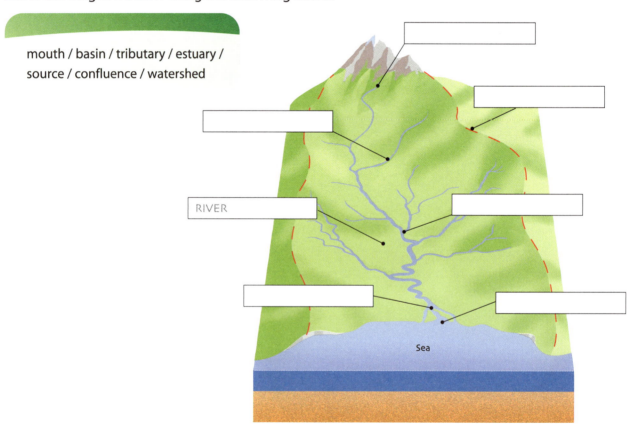

RIVER

Sea

❖ *Concepts* ❖

You need to learn the following river processes and landforms for the short questions.

Insert the following terms into the blanks below:

speed / alluvial fans / solution / traction / attrition / flood plains / suspension / solution / gorges / volume / saltation / potholes / abrasion / waterfalls / load / hydraulic action / bluffs

River Processes

Erosion

1 .... : the **weight** and **speed** and **force** of the river opens cracks and loosens rocks from the sides and bed of the valley.

2 .... : the wearing away of the bed and sides by the **scouring action** of the load (material carried by the river).

3 .... : **friction within** the load itself and **friction between** the load and the river bed.

4 .... : **dissolving** of minerals within the rock, e.g. limestone.

Transportation

1 .... : the **rolling** of rocks along the river bed.

2 .... : the **hopping** of stones along the bed.

3 .... : the **carrying** of fine particles above the bed.

4 .... : the **dissolving** of materials which are then carried elsewhere, e.g. limestone, chalk.

Label the diagram below using the following terms:

suspension / traction / solution / saltation

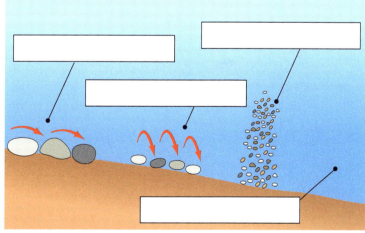

River transportation

Deposition

A river will deposit when one or more of the following occur:

1 A reduction in .... due to either

(a) flowing into a lake or sea, or

(b) flowing from steep onto gently sloping land;

2 A reduction in .... due to

(a) a period of low rainfall,

(b) flowing over permeable rocks, or

(c) high evaporation;

3 A change in the nature of the ....

It is more difficult for a river to transport boulders than soluble or suspended material so boulders will be deposited first.

River Landforms

Upper course

1 .... are circular depressions on the beds of rivers caused by the swirling action of pebbles. The swirling action deepens pre-existing hollows, similar to the potholes on roads.

2 .... occur when the bed of a river becomes suddenly steepened. When a layer of hard rock lies across a river's course the soft rocks on the downstream side are more quickly eroded than is the hard rock. The bed is steepened, forming a waterfall.

3 .... are formed when waterfalls retreat upstream. They are narrow, steep valleys. The Niagara Gorge is seven miles long and is retreating by as much as six feet per annum.

Lower course

1 .... occur when a river flows from a mountainous area with steep gradients onto a gently sloping plain, the drop in gradient and velocity resulting in deposition at the break of the slope. The dumped material builds outwards, forming a fan.

2 .... are steep slopes on the sides of rivers formed when spurs have been cut back by lateral erosion. They mark the edge of the flood plain.

3 .... are wide, open, flat areas in mature river valleys. After heavy rainfall the river's volume increases, causing it to overflow its banks and deposit mud and silt on the adjacent land. The flooded area is the flood plain and the deposited material is alluvium. Flood plains are very productive. They are bounded by the bluff line.

Label the diagram below using the following terms:

lower course / middle course / source / mouth / lake interrupts profile / upper course /
band of resistant rock / graded profile

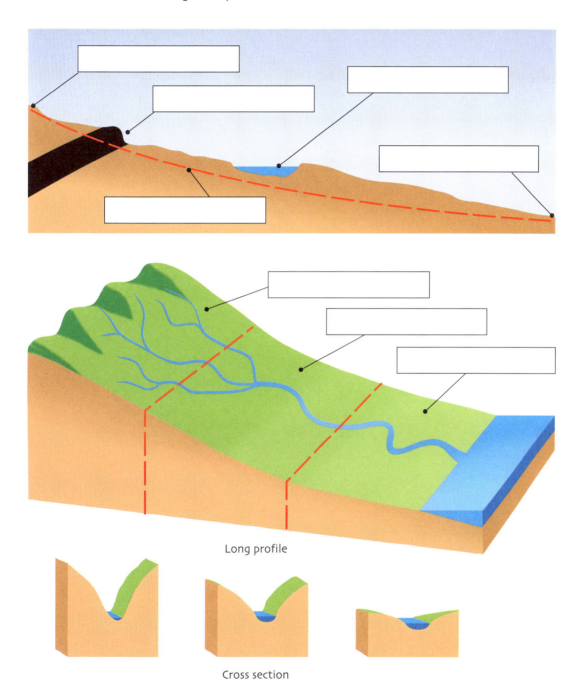

Long profile

Cross section

(b) Upper-Course Landform: V-Shaped Valley

Sample Question 1

With the aid of a diagram, discuss the formation of any feature found in the youthful stage of a river.

V-shaped valley

1. important erosive agent
2. narrow valley
3. valley floor narrow
4. the major processes
5. little water
6. erosion is vertical
7. beds and sides
8. hydraulic action
9. attrition
10. abrasion
11. weathering and erosion
12. River Liffey
13. Grand Canyon
14. lack power
15. diagram of V-shaped valley with interlocking spurs
16. River Shannon

(c) Lower-Course Landforms: Meanders and Ox-bow Lakes

Sample Question 2

With the aid of a diagram or diagrams, explain the formation of any feature found in the mature stage of a river.

Insert the following terms into the blanks below:

outside / outer bank / mort lake / abrasion / ox-bow lakes / lateral erosion / river cliffs / Inchavore River / greater / Limerick city / evaporation / meander scar / flood / hydraulic action / abrasion / ox-bow lake / River Boyne / hydraulic action / short / inner bank / River Liffey / lateral erosion / meanders / join up / evaporation / curves / volume / tributaries / meandering / deposited

Meanders and ox-bow lakes

- .... and .... are features of the mature stage. **(1 SRP)**
- The major processes involved in their formation are .... , hydraulic action, abrasion, deposition and .... **(1 SRP)**
- The river has increased in size and the .... of water is .... , because .... have joined the river. **(1 SRP)**
- .... is dominant, widening the banks, and .... becomes much more pronounced. **(1 SRP)**
- Meanders are .... in the mature stage of a river. **(1 SRP)**
- Lateral erosion in the form of .... (the weight and speed of the river) and .... (the scouring action of the load) occurs on the .... of the bend due to the greater speed of the water striking the bank there, often forming .... **(1 SRP)**
- Material eroded on the outer bank is .... on the inner bank. **(1 SRP)**
- Meanders are formed by erosion on the .... and deposition on the .... **(1 SRP)**
- Meanders are found on the River Shannon as it enters .... , on the .... near Slane, Co. Meath and the .... near Straffan, Co. Kildare. **(1 SRP)**
- As the river continues to erode laterally, the meanders grow in size and may .... **(1 SRP)**
- In times of .... the river will cut across the narrow neck (dividing land), due to .... and .... , leaving the meander cut off, forming an .... **(1 SRP)**
- The life of an ox-bow lake is .... It loses its water through .... until reeds take over, forming a .... or .... **(1 SRP)**
- Ox-bow lakes and mort lakes are found on the .... , Co. Wicklow. **(1 SRP)**
- Diagram of meanders and ox-bow lakes **(1 SRP)**

Chapter 9
Coastal Processes

(a) Introduction

You need to know the following coastal landforms for the short questions.

Insert the following terms into the blanks below:

differential erosion / fetch / peninsula / stack / swash / stump / wave-built terrace / backwash / destructive / cliffs / wave-cut platform / storm beach / cave / longshore drift / blowhole / geo / arches / waves / bay / discordant coastline / notch / beach / speed / headland / inlet / constructive / sand dune

Waves

…………… are formed as a result of the friction between the wind and the surface of the sea. Two factors determine the size of waves:

1 The …………… , which is the distance of sea over which a wave moves. The greater the fetch the more powerful the waves. Coastal erosion is therefore more evident on the western coastline of Ireland than on the eastern coastline.

2 The …………… and duration of the wind.
   Waves that move up the beach are called the …………… while the waves that move back down the beach are called the ………………… .

There are two types of wave:

1 ………………… waves are associated with deposition. They are gentle, low, flat waves.

2 ………………… waves are associated with erosion. They are steep, high waves.

Label the diagram below using the following terms:

wavelength / trough / strong swash / destructive waves / crest / strong backwash / constructive waves

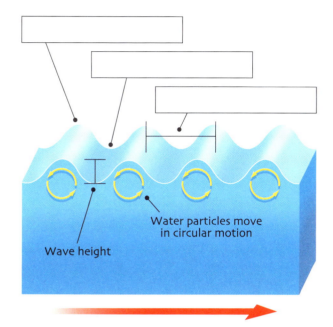

Water particles move in circular motion

Wave height

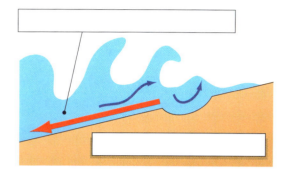

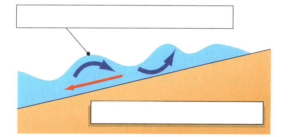

Features of coastal erosion

1 …………

- At high tide the sea finds a line of weakness along the coast.
- This line of weakness or ………… is eroded into the land by the sea.
- The land above the notch is weakened and over time will collapse into the sea, forming a cliff.
- As the cliff is eroded further inland, a …………………………………… develops, which may be seen at low tide.
- The eroded material will be carried out to sea, forming a ………………………………………… .

Examples

Cliffs: The Cliffs of Moher, Co. Clare

Wave-cut platform: Loughshinny, Co. Dublin

2 Caves

- The sea will attack a crack or a line of weakness at the base of a cliff, forming a …………… .
- If this crack extends on to the roof of the cave, the roof will be eroded, forming a ………………… .
- Over time, the blowhole will be enlarged, causing the roof to collapse forming an …………… .
- This inlet is sometimes called a …………… .

Examples

Caves and blowholes: Helvic Head, Co. Waterford

Inlets: Kinsale Harbour, Co. Cork

3 Arches

- ……………. are formed when two caves meet.
- A ……………. is formed when the arch collapses.
- A ……………. is formed when the stack is eroded to sea level.

Examples

Arch: Old Head of Kinsale, Co. Cork

Stacks: Seven Sisters at Ballybunion, Co. Kerry

Stumps: Helvic Head, Co. Waterford

4 Bays and headlands

- A ………………. is an area of water surrounded by land on three sides.
- A ………………. is an area of land surrounded by sea on three sides. A large headland is termed a ……………. .
- Bays and headlands are features of a …………………………………. where different types of rock of varying resistance approach the sea at right angles.
- Coastlines comprise hard and soft rocks so erosion is not uniform. This is termed …………………………. .

Label the diagram below using the following terms:

wave-built terrace / wave-cut platform / cliff retreats / original land surface / high-water mark / present position of cliff / overhang / low-water mark / notch

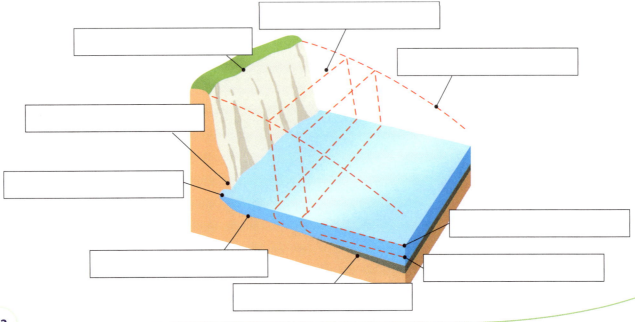

Features of coastal deposition

1 Beaches

- A …………… is formed when waves deposit material along a gently sloping coast.

- Waves which deposit material are called constructive waves.

- During stormy weather the power of the wave is increased and the wave deposits rocks and pebbles beyond the normal level of the beach, forming a ………………………………… .

Examples

Beach: Brittas Bay, Co. Wicklow

Storm beach: Killiney, Co. Dublin

2 Sand-dunes

- The wind sometimes blows sand inland, away from the sea. The sand builds up and if caught in vegetation may form a ……………………… . The inland movement of these dunes can be halted by planting marram grass and coniferous trees.

Example

Brittas Bay, Co. Wicklow

3 Sand spit

- A sand spit is a long narrow ridge of sand joined at one end to the land with the other end terminating in the sea.

- The major processes involved in their formation are ………………………………… and constructive waves.

Example

Bull Island, Co. Dublin

Label the diagram below using the following terms:

sea stump / sea cave / wave-cut platform /sea arch / geo / blowhole / fault in rock / sea stack / wave-built terrace

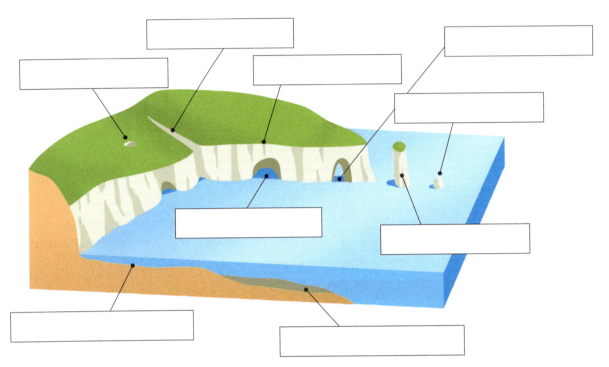

(b) Feature/Landform of Erosion: Bays and Headlands

Sample Question 1

With the aid of a diagram, explain the formation of any one feature caused by marine erosion.

Insert the following terms into the spaces below:

solution / peninsulas / bays / refraction / joints / differential erosion / sand blaster / granite / bays / hydraulic action / refraction / sheer force / deposition / corrosion (abrasion) / sedimentary / erosion / cavitation / discordant / headlands

Bays and headlands

- The major processes involved in their formation are hydraulic action, compressed air, ... and solution. **(1 SRP)**

- Bays and headlands are more likely to be found in areas where bands of hard and soft rocks are found next to each other, resulting in .... **(1 SRP)**

- More resistant bands of hard rock that stand out from the surrounding land are called .... Large versions of these are termed .... **(1 SRP)**

- The less resistant bands of rock are subject to higher levels of erosion and retreat inland, forming .... **(1 SRP)**

- As bays are cut back further, the headlands receive high-energy waves and become more susceptible to .... , while the bays receive less energy and become more susceptible to .... This process is termed wave .... Bays and headlands are features of a .... coastline. **(1 SRP)**

- Harder rocks like .... form headlands, e.g. Bray Head and Mizen Head, while softer rocks form .... , e.g. Dublin Bay and Galway Bay.

- .... is the dominant process. **(1 SRP)**

- Hydraulic action occurs when the .... of the wave exerts huge pressure on the coast. It is very effective in stormy weather. **(1 SRP)**

- The process is very effective where the coastline comprises .... rocks. **(1 SRP)**

- These rocks contain .... , faults and bedding planes. **(1 SRP)**

- The wave traps air in the cracks, which is then compressed into the cracks by the pressure of the water, forcing them apart. This is the process of .... **(1 SRP)**

- The wave then acts as a .... , throwing sand and rock fragments against the coast. This is the process of corrasive (abrasive) action. **(1 SRP)**

- The process of .... is very active along limestone coasts. **(1 SRP)**

- Headlands are subjected to wave .... The shallower water surrounding the headland results in the sea converging on the headland, leading to increased coastal erosion. As a result, caves, arches and sea stacks occur on headlands. **(1 SRP)**

- Diagram of bays and headlands **(1SRP)**

(c) Feature/Landform of Deposition: Sand Spit

Sample Question 2

With the aid of a diagram, explain the formation of one feature caused by marine deposition.

Sand spit

1 marine deposition ....

2 constructive waves. ....

3   definition of spit . . . .

4   human interaction . . . .

5   longshore drift. . . . .

6   curved or hooked . . . .

7   beaches . . . .

8   example . . . .

9   sand bar . . . .

10   lagoon . . . .

11   Wexford coast . . . .

12   deposition stops . . . .

13   increase in erosion . . . .

14   tombolo . . . .

15   diagram of spit

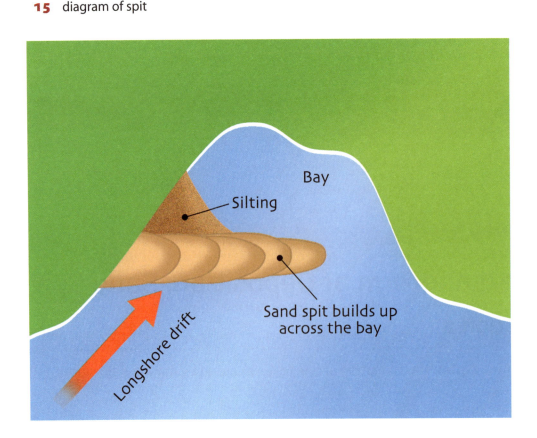

Chapter 10
Glacial Processes

(a) Introduction

Glaciation is defined as the **permanent covering of the landscape by snow and ice**, occurring in areas where summers are not warm enough to remove completely the previous winter's deposit of snow. It differs from the other agents of erosion because the resulting landforms can only be seen after the ice has melted.

❖ *Concepts* ❖

You need to know the following glacial processes and features for the short questions.

Insert the following terms into the blanks below:

truncated spurs / abrasion / hanging valleys / moraines / paternoster lakes / fjords / plucking / cirques or corries / drumlins / U-shaped valleys / 'basket of eggs' topography / ribbon lakes / drowned drumlins / erratics / eskers

Processes of glacial erosion

1 ....

- When a glacier stops due to an obstruction its ice begins to melt, forming meltwater which flows into the joints and cracks of the walls and floor of the valley through which it moves.

- This meltwater freezes and the rock in the valley now becomes part of the glacier.

- When the glacier moves downhill this country rock is plucked from the floor of the valley, forming large depressions which may become filled with water, forming ribbon lakes.

2 ....

- The plucked country rock has an abrasive sandpaper effect on rocks over which it travels. Consequently, the country rock and the glacier's load are worn down.

- The load is reduced to rock-flour while striae (scratches), showing the direction of the flow of the ice, are formed in the country rock.

- Striae can be seen on the rocks in Howth, Co. Dublin.

Features of glacial erosion

1 ....

- Glaciers travel downhill via pre-existing V-shaped valleys.

- Plucking and abrasion steepen and widen the bed and floor of the V-shaped valley.

- Unlike rivers, which swing around obstacles, forming interlocking spurs, glaciers, due to their size and power, are able to remove obstacles in their way, forming ....

- Glaciers change the valley from a V-shaped valley to a U-shaped valley.

- An example of a U-shaped valley with truncated spurs is Glendalough, Co. Wicklow.

2 ....

- These are valleys on the sides of U-shaped valleys.

- Before glaciation they entered the V-shaped valley via a gentle gradient, but overdeepening of the main valley by glaciation left these valleys hanging on the sides of the U-shaped valley.

- They now enter the main valley by means of spectacular waterfalls.

- Examples of hanging valleys are Glenmacnass Waterfall, Co. Wicklow and Powerscourt Waterfall, Co. Wicklow.

3 ....

- These are lakes on the floor of the U-shaped valley. They are formed by the plucking action of the ice.

- When two are more ribbon lakes occur side by side they form ....

- There are examples of these lakes at Glendalough, Co. Wicklow.

4 ....

- These are drowned U-shaped valleys.

- When the ice age was coming to an end, the ice melted and meltwater entered the sea, causing the sea level to rise and flooding the surrounding land.

- An example of a fjord is Killary Harbour, Co. Mayo.

5 ....

■ These are features of erosion, and are the birthplace of a glacier, occupying the head of a glaciated valley.

■ They are armchair-shaped depressions surrounded on three sides by high rock walls with an opening at the front (the lip) through which the glacier moved.

Label the diagram below using the following terms:

interlocking spurs / truncated spur / glacier / paternoster lakes / arête / V-shaped valley / hanging valley

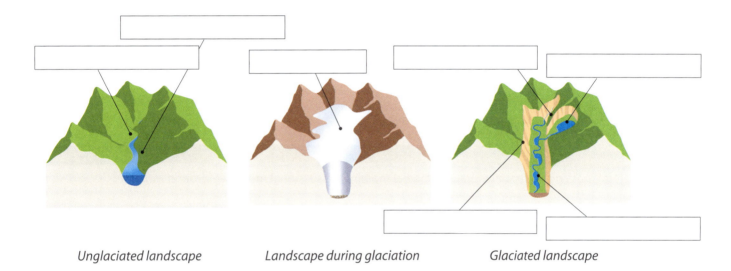

Unglaciated landscape   *Landscape during glaciation*   *Glaciated landscape*

Features of glacial deposition

1 ....

■ These are rocks which are out of place.

■ They are rocks which were transported by the ice from their source area and deposited in areas where their rock type would not normally be found.

■ Examples are the pieces of Mourne granite found in the Burren region, Co. Clare.

2 ....

■ These are small rounded hills, up to 60m in height.

■ They were formed when boulder clay, found in moraines, was compressed into small hills.

■ In appearance they resemble half an egg, and when they appear in groups they form a ....

■ Sometimes they may have been drowned by the rising sea level after the ice has melted, forming ....

■ These can be seen in Clew Bay, Co. Mayo.

3 ……………………

- Eskers are long, winding ridges comprising layers of sand and gravel.

- They are formed due to friction between the bottom layer of ice and the ground over which the ice moves.

- This friction produces meltwater, a river underneath the ice. When the ice disappears the river dries up too, as the river owes its life to the ice.

- Examples include the Eiscir Riada along the Dublin–Galway Road.

4 ……………………

- When ablation is greater than accumulation the ice deposits material. Material deposited by the ice is called drift.

- Different types of moraine are 'terminal' (front), 'lateral' (sides) and 'medial' (centre).

- The major processes involved in their formation are melting and deposition.

Label the diagram below using the following terms:

lateral moraine / terminal moraine / medial moraine / recessional moraine / ground moraine

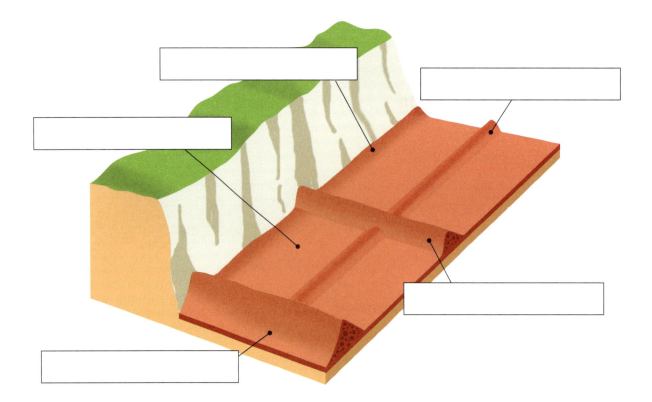

(b) Feature/Landform of Erosion: Cirques

Sample Question 1

With the aid of a diagram, discuss the formation of a feature caused by glacial erosion.

Insert the following terms into the blanks below:

contours / plucking / birthplace / arête / armchair-shaped depressions / widens and deepens / the Devil's Punchbowl / rotational slip / erosion / extrusion flow / bergschrund / tarn / freeze–thaw action / firn / corries / nivation / pyramidal peak

Cirques

- Cirques or .... are features of .... **(1 SRP)**

- The major processes involved in their formation are .... , abrasion, freeze–thaw action, gravity and extrusion flow. **(1 SRP)**

- Cirques are the .... of a glacier, occupying the head of a glaciated valley. **(1 SRP)**

- They are .... surrounded on three sides by high rock walls with an opening at the front (the lip), through which the glacier moves. **(1 SRP)**

- They are formed by .... Snow accumulates in a sheltered hollow, normally on the north or north-east sides of a mountain, and is transformed into .... and over time into ice. **(1 SRP)**

- The ice .... the hollow by freeze–thaw action. **(1 SRP)**

- The hollow is further widened by the circular scouring called .... and the plucking action of the ice as it moves downhill under the influence of .... and gravity. **(1 SRP)**

- The ice moves away from the back wall, forming a crevasse called a .... **(1 SRP)**

- All of the loosened rocks are worn down by abrasion. This combined action of plucking and abrasion is called .... **(1 SRP)**

- Corries are recognised on Ordnance Survey maps by the closeness of the .... on three sides. **(1 SRP)**

- If the corrie contains a lake it is called a .... , e.g. Upper and Lower Lough Bray in the Wicklow Mountains. **(1 SRP)**

- When two corries form back to back, a jagged knife-edge ridge forms. This ridge is called an .... , e.g. the Conor Pass, Co. Kerry. **(1 SRP)**

- A .... is formed when three or more cirques form back to back, e.g. Carrauntoohil, Co. Kerry and the Matterhorn in the Alps. **(1 SRP)**

- Lough Doon and Lough Duff in the Dingle Peninsula and .... in Mangerton Mountain, Co. Kerry are corries. **(1 SRP)**

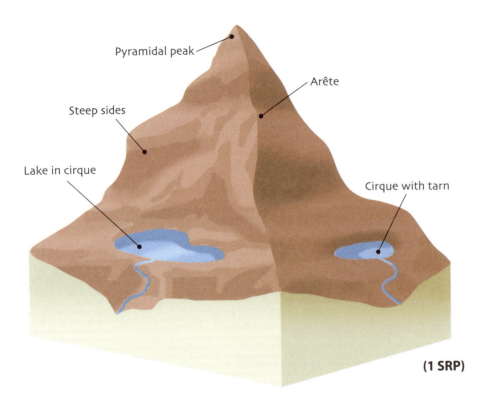

Pyramidal peak

Arête

Steep sides

Lake in cirque

Cirque with tarn

(1 SRP)

(c) Feature/Landform of Deposition: Moraines

Sample Question 2

With the aid of a diagram, discuss the formation of one glacial landform caused by glacial deposition.

Moraines

1 drift ....

2 glacial deposition ....

3 processes..

4 no sorting ....

5 seen after the ice retreats ....

6 lateral moraine ....

7 medial moraine..

8 terminal moraine ....

9 recessional moraine..

10 ground moraine ....

11 apron-like deposition ....

12 glacial till ....

13 may block valleys ....

14 Glendalough is a dammed lake..

15 example of moraine..

Chapter 11
Processes of Mass Movement

(a) Introduction

Mass movement: The processes of weathering produce **regolith** – a layer of loose material which moves downhill either through the actions of agents such as ice, rivers and wind or under the influence of gravity. The process of movement brought about by gravity is termed **mass movement**.

❖ Concepts ❖

You need to know the following features of mass movement for the short questions.

Insert the following terms into the blanks below:

blanket bogs / soil creep / lahars / loose boulders / solifluction / earthflows / rotational slumping / rockslides and rockfalls / subsidence / mudflows / bogbursts

Features of rapid mass movement

1 ....
- They are very similar to earthflows except that they have a greater proportion of water.
- The speed of flow depends on the gradient.
- They are common after volcanic eruptions, where rainfall may turn volcanic ash into mud that moves downslope, damaging towns and villages.
- These are termed ....

2 ....
- These are very common in the .... of Ireland.
- Following heavy rain, the bog becomes saturated and moves downslope.
- A bogburst occurred at Derrybrien in the Slieve Aughty Mountains in 2003.

3 ....

- The downslope movement of water-saturated soil in areas where the saturated water is unable to penetrate the underlying rock.

- They occur in humid regions where there is an abundant supply of moisture and where the rocks are weathered.

4 ....

- This occurs when the base of a slope is undercut by weathering and erosion or by human activities.

- The upper part of the slope falls down or slumps.

- It is very common along fault lines or bedding planes.

- It occurs along the north Antrim coast.

5 ....

- The former involve the collapse of large quantities of bedrock, while rockfalls involve the collapse of ....

- They occur in mountainous areas which have been subjected to glaciation and river action and along cliffs subject to coastal action.

- Human activity can also cause rockslides and rockfalls.

6 ....

- This is vertical downward movement of the earth's surface brought about by the removal of material from under the surface of the ground by mechanical or chemical weathering.

- Subsidence occurs in the Burren.

Features of slow mass movement

1 ....

- Its effects can be seen in the form of leaning trees, electricity poles and walls.

2 ....

- This occurs in periglacial environments.

- In periglacial environments the ground remains frozen all year round, except for a melting of the surface layers in summer.

- When the surface layer melts it becomes waterlogged and begins to move downslope over the frozen subsoil.

Label the diagram below using the following terms:

slumping or rotational slide / mudflow / earthflows / rockfall / soil creep / rockslide

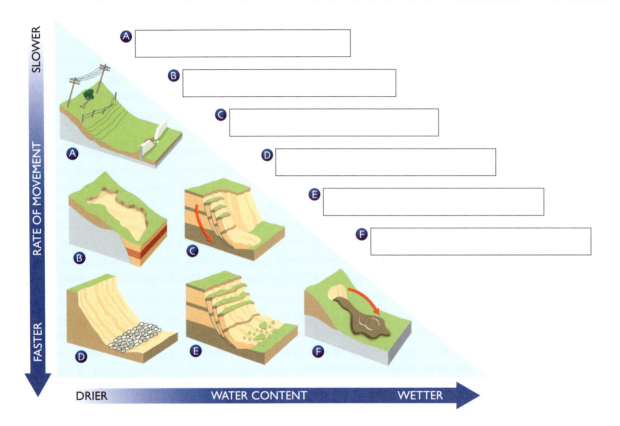

(b) Slow and Rapid Mass Movement

Sample Question 1

Explain, with the aid of labelled diagrams, examples of slow and fast mass movement.

Insert the following terms into the blanks below:

top few / frozen / waterlogged /expansion and contraction / earthflows / gradient / periglacial / volcanic eruptions / lahars / Nevado Del Ruiz / gravity / blanket / saturated / solifluction / leaning trees / mountains / soil creep / bogbursts

Slow mass movement

(a) ....

- It goes almost unnoticed. **(1 SRP)**

- Its effects can be seen in the form of .... , electricity poles and leaning walls. **(1 SRP)**

- It takes place in the .... metres of the soil. **(1 SRP)**
- It is accomplished through the .... of soil caused by freeze–thaw action, heating and cooling or the actions of humans and animals. **(1 SRP)**
- The loosened material moves downslope under the influence of .... and builds up on the upslope side of hedges and walls. **(1 SRP)**

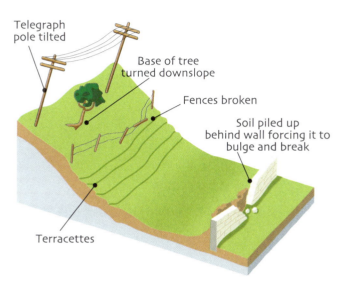

Telegraph pole tilted

Base of tree turned downslope

Fences broken

Soil piled up behind wall forcing it to bulge and break

Terracettes

(b) ....

- This occurs in .... environments. **(1 SRP)**
- In these environments the ground remains .... all year round except for a melting of the surface layers in summer. **(1 SRP)**
- When the surface layer melts it becomes .... and begins to move downslope over the frozen subsoil. **(1 SRP)**

Rapid mass movement

(a) Mudflows

- Mudflows are very similar to .... except that mudflows have a greater proportion of water. **(1 SRP)**
- The speed of flow depends on the .... **(1 SRP)**
- Mudflows are common after .... where rainfall may turn volcanic ash into mud which moves downslope, damaging towns and villages. **(1 SRP)**
- These mudflows are termed .... **(1 SRP)**
- Following the eruption of .... in Colombia in 1985 a lahar formed due to melting ice and snow. It moved down the mountain rapidly, killing 21,000 people. **(1 SRP)**

■ Diagram of mudflow

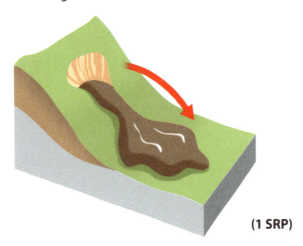

(1 SRP)

(b) ....

- They are very common in the .... bogs of Ireland. **(1 SRP)**
- Following heavy rain the bog becomes .... , moving downslope. **(1 SRP)**
- This occurred at Derrybrien in the Slieve Aughty .... in 2003. **(1 SRP)**

(c) Types of Rapid Mass Movement

Sample Question 2

With the aid of diagrams, discuss various types of rapid mass movement.

Earthflows

1 saturation ....

2 humid regions ....

3 curved scar ....

4 deposited material ....

5 diagram of earthflow

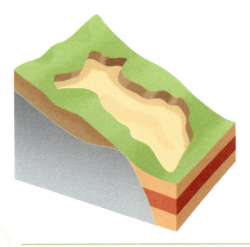

Rotational slumping

6 undercutting base of slope . . . .

7 slope falls . . . .

8 common along fault lines . . . .

9 diagram of rotational slumping

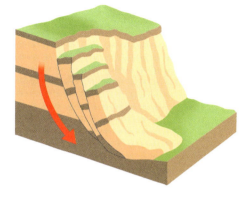

Rockslides and rockfalls

10 collapse of material . . . .

11 mountainous areas . . . .

12 human activity . . . .

13 block rivers . . . .

14 Co. Wicklow . . . .

15 diagrams of rockslide and rockfall

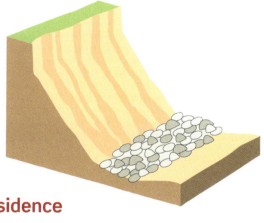
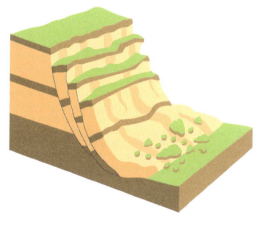

Subsidence

16 vertical movement . . . .

17 mining . . . .

18 caves . . . .

Chapter 12

Isostacy and Fluvial Adjustment

(a) River Rejuvenation

Label the diagram below using the following terms:

bluff / new flood plain / incised meander / paired terraces / old flood plain / bluff

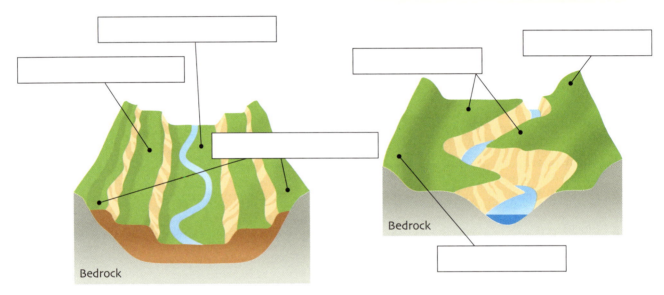

Bedrock

Bedrock

Sample Question

Explain the term 'river rejuvenation'. In your answer refer to any two landforms formed by river rejuvenation.

Insert the following terms into the spaces below:

asymmetrical / steps / drop in sea level / renewed vertical erosion / knickpoint / erode further into the alluvium / graded profile / overgrown with vegetation / glaciation / a fall in the level of the sea / plate convergence / high evaporation / profile of equilibrium / entrenched / steepen the gradient / base level / narrower / extra energy / downcutting / vertical and lateral erosion / rejuvenated / new waterfall / vertical erosion / river terraces / meandering / symmetrical / ingrown / drought / paired / drop in sea level / isostatic change / glaciation / a rise in the level of the land / the river entered the sea / vertical downcutting / vertical erosion / River Dodder at Terenure / hydraulic action / steep-sided valleys / winding gorge / incise

1 Isostacy

■ Rivers seek a .... or .... This profile is achieved when rivers arrive at their mouth – the sea or lake. This is called their .... , i.e. the lowest point to which a river can flow. **(1 SRP)**

■ The base level can change due to .... or .... relative to the level of the sea.

(a) A fall in sea level

■ Sea level may fall following a .... , during a period of .... or during a period of .... **(1 SRP)**

■ All of these reduce the amount of water entering the world's rivers, which in turn reduces the volume of water entering the world's oceans, which over a period of time may lead to a .... **(1 SRP)**

(b) A rise in land level

■ A rise in land level relative to sea level is termed .... **(1 SRP)**

■ Land level may rise due to .... or the uplift of land after a period of .... **(1 SRP)**

■ Both of these movements .... and the river is encouraged to renew its process of .... again. The river now has renewed capacity to erode – it has been .... **(1 SRP)**

■ Diagram of river achieving its ideal profile **(1 SRP)**

Note: Discuss two of the following three landforms, i.e. knickpoints, paired terraces or incised meanders, as features of river rejuvenation.

2 Landforms

(a) Knickpoints

■ A knickpoint occurs as a result of a .... If the sea level falls, the river loses it graded profile and the lower sections of the river are left perched above the sea. **(1 SRP)**

■ The river therefore has .... , which it uses to renew .... on its bed. This process of incision works its way back upstream, until a .... is formed. **(1 SRP)**

■ A knickpoint, often indicated by the presence of a .... , shows the place where .... before it was rejuvenated, e.g. the River Shannon, south of Lough Derg. **(1 SRP)**

■ Diagram of knickpoint **(1 SRP)**

(b) Paired terraces/river terraces

■ A rejuvenated river has the ability to .... which it already has deposited on its bed. **(1 SRP)**

- The processes of .... and .... recommence. Hydraulic action is the process whereby the weight and speed of the river opens cracks and loosens rocks from the sides and bed of the valley. **(1 SRP)**

- This results in a new but .... bed at a lower level within the old channel, giving rise to a series of .... which can be .... with steps on the opposite side of the valley. These are called .... **(1 SRP)**

- Sometimes, the terraces are difficult to see as they are often .... Paired terraces can be seen on the .... , and the Liffey Valley, Strawberry Beds, Co. Dublin. **(1 SRP)**

- Diagram of paired terraces **(1 SRP)**

(1 SRP)

(c) Incised meanders

- If a river had been .... before rejuvenation the .... will .... or cut back the meanders even more, forming a .... **(1 SRP)**

- Two types of incised meander are .... meanders and .... meanders. **(1 SRP)**

- **Entrenched meanders** are incised meanders with .... and a .... profile. .... is the dominant process. **(1 SRP)**

- **Ingrown meanders** are incised meanders with one side of the valley being steep and the other side being gentle, i.e. an .... profile. The dominant processes are .... **(1 SRP)**

- Diagram of incised meander **(1 SRP)**

Chapter 13
Human Interaction with Surface Processes

(a) Human Interaction with Rivers

Three Gorges Dam

Sample Question 1

Referring to a case study of your choice, discuss how humans interact with rivers.

Case study: the Three Gorges Dam

1 hydroelectric dam ....

2 end flooding..

3 mass transportation of rock and load ....

Advantages of the project

Flood control

4 prone to overflowing ....

5 1954: 33,000 drowned ....

Improved air quality

6 consumption of coal ....

Improved navigation along the river

7 number of ships ....

Afforestation

8 increased planting of trees ....

Waste management

9 70 per cent of the waste water is treated..

Disadvantages of the project

Displacement of millions of people

10 1.5 million will have been displaced ....

Water quality has declined

11 the submergence of mines..

Wildlife is being affected

11 Siberian crane ....

River bank erosion

12 erosion of the reservoir ....

13 landslides ....

14 seismic fault ....

Sedimentation

15 area devoted to afforestation reduced ....

(b) Human Interaction with the Coast

Sample Question 2

Referring to a case study of your choice, discuss how humans interact with coastal processes.

Case study: Bull Island, Co. Dublin.

1   human interaction ....
2   200 years old ....
3   great south wall ....
4   north wall ....
5   2.81km long ....
6   spit created...
7   wave refraction ....
8   sand dunes ....
9   recreational amenity ....
10 bird sanctuary ....
11 interpretive centre ....
12 UNESCO biosphere ....
13 kite surfers and walkers ....
14 planted marram grasses...
15 map of bay

Bull Island

Chapter 14

Weather and Weather Maps

(a) Short Question Answers

❖ Concepts ❖

You need to know the following concepts only for the short questions.

Insert the following terms into the blanks below:

six major wind systems / latitude / cold / synoptic or weather chart / Beaufort scale / atmospheric pressure / occluded / millibars / seven / high / winds / south-westerlies / falls / left / isobars / anemometer / ocean currents / warm / hectopascals / Campbell Stokes / relief / wind vane / convectional / cyclonic / low pressure and high pressure / depressions / anticyclones / weather station / Stevenson screen / weather / fronts / cold / temperature / degrees Celsius / isotherms / rain gauge / right / Ferrel's law / isohyets / knots / rain shadow / aneroid barometer / prevailing wind / rises / cloudy days / wet-and-dry-bulb thermometer / percentage / millimetres / isohels / warm / precipitation

« Definition »

………………… is the result of changes in temperature, rainfall, wind, atmospheric pressure, humidity and sunshine at a particular place at a particular time.

1 ……………………………

- The sun provides heat for planet earth.
- However, the sun's heat is not evenly spread over the earth's surface due to latitude and the spherical shape of the earth.

« Definition »

………………… refers to angular distance north or south of the equator. The further away a place is from the equator, the colder it is.

2 ....

- The atmosphere surrounding the planet is made up of a number of gases.

- Their weight acting upon the earth is called pressure.

- Pressure is measured in ....

- There are two types of pressure: low pressure and high pressure.

- Air that is heated expands and .... into the atmosphere, resulting in low pressure.

- Air that is cooled becomes heavier and ...., forming an area of high pressure.

- There are .... zones of pressure on the earth, three zones of low pressure and four zones of high pressure.

- Pressure is low at the equator due to the great heat from the sun's rays.

- The warm air rises and drifts towards 30°N and 30°S.

- At this latitude the air is colder and .... pressure exists.

3 ....

- They always blow from areas of high pressure to areas of low pressure.

- This movement from high pressure to low pressure is responsible for the earth's ...., three of which occur in the northern hemisphere and three in the southern hemisphere.

- The three winds of the northern hemisphere are:
  (a) the north-east polar winds
  (b) the ....
  (c) the north-east trade winds.

- The three winds of the southern hemisphere are:
  (a) the south-east trade winds
  (b) the north-westerlies
  (c) the polar winds.

- Winds in the northern hemisphere are deflected to the .... while winds in the southern hemisphere are deflected to the .... This deflection occurs according to ....

- The .... is the name given to the most frequent wind that blows in an area. In Ireland the prevailing wind comes from the south-west.

4 ....

- They occur due to the unequal heating of the sea.

- They are movements of water from hot areas to cold areas.

- The North Atlantic Drift influences Ireland. It is a .... current which passes the west coast of Ireland. It ensures that Irish ports are kept ice-free during the winter.

- The Labrador Current is a .... current which affects Greenland and Canada. This cold current causes temperatures to drop, causing harbours and ports to freeze up during the winter.

5 ....

- There are three types of rainfall.

.... rainfall

- This occurs when moisture-laden air coming in from the sea is forced to rise over mountains.
- When this air rises it cools and condensation takes place .
- Rain then falls on the windward side of the mountain.
- The leeward or sheltered side of the mountain receives little or no rain.
- It is a .... area.
- Relief rain occurs along the west coast of Ireland.

.... rainfall

- This occurs in equatorial climates and on hot sunny days in Ireland.
- The sun's rays heat the ground. The warmed air rises.
- As it rises, it cools. Condensation occurs. Clouds are formed and rain falls.

.... (frontal) rainfall

- This occurs when warm air meets cold air.
- When warm air meets cold air the warm air is forced to rise. As it rises, it cools, condensation occurs, and clouds form. Heavy showers can result.

6 .... (ascending and descending air)

- Ascending or rising air and descending or falling air create different weather patterns.

Low pressure

- When air is warmed it rises, creating low pressure.
- As it rises, it cools and condensation occurs, forming clouds which bring rain.
- .... or cyclones are associated with low-pressure areas.
- They bring strong winds, heavy rainfall and ....

High pressure

- Cold air falls, forming high pressure.
- As the cold air falls, it gets warmer.
- There is no condensation and clouds do not form, so rainfall is unlikely to occur.
- These areas of high pressure are called ....
- During the summer they bring clear blue skies and sunny weather.

7 ....

- These are the boundries between cold and warm masses of air, e.g. tropical and polar air.
- There are three types of front:

.... fronts

- These occur when a mass of cold air meets a mass of warm air.
- The cold air mass cuts under the warm air mass.
- They result in a rise of atmospheric pressure, a fall in temperature, heavy showers and a veer of wind.
- They are shown on a synoptic chart by a blue line with triangles. The triangles indicate the direction the warm air is travelling.

.... fronts

- These occur when a mass of warm air meets a mass of cold air and rises over the cold air.
- They are associated with a rise in temperature, cloud formations and heavy rain, followed by showers and a change in wind direction.
- They are shown on a synoptic chart by a red line with semicircles. The semicircles indicate the direction the warm air is travelling.

.... fronts

- These occur when warm and cold air meet in a depression and the warm air is lifted over the colder air.
- They are associated with a fall in temperature and rain.
- They are shown on a synoptic chart by a purple line with circles and triangles which indicate the direction the air is travelling.

Measuring Weather

- All of the elements that make up weather are measured in a ....
- The measurements from the weather station are shown on a ....
- They show local, national or global maps, fronts, isobars, cyclones and anticyclones.
- These synoptic charts are so called because they represent a synopsis of the weather at a particular time.

1 Measuring temperature

- A maximum and minimum thermometer measures temperature.
- The maximum thermometer measures the highest temperature of the day.
- The minimum thermometer measures the lowest temperature of the day.
- Temperature is measured in ....
- .... are lines on a map joining places of equal temperature.

2 Measuring precipitation (rainfall)

- Rainfall is measured by a ………………………… .
- Rainfall is measured in ………………………… .
- ………………… are lines on a map joining places of equal rainfall.

3 Measuring wind

- Weather forecasters are interested in wind direction and wind speed.
- Wind direction is recorded and wind speed is measured.
- A ……………………… shows wind direction. The arrow on it points in the direction from which the wind blows.
- Wind speed is measured by the rotating cup ……………………………… .
- Wind speed is expressed in …………… or kilometres per hour.
- Wind speed is also measured by the ……………………………… .
- It is a series of numbers ranging from 0 to 12 to describe different wind speeds and their effect on the environment.

4 Measuring atmospheric pressure

- Atmospheric pressure is measured by an ……………………………………… .
- It consists of a hollow metallic box with a vacuum.
- As atmospheric pressure rises or falls the box either moves inward or outwards.
- A needle, which is attached to the box, indicates the pressure of the air in the box.
- Pressure is measured in millibars or ………………………… .
- ………………… are lines on a map joining places of equal pressure.

5 Measuring humidity

- Humidity is a measure of the amount of water vapour in the atmosphere.
- A …………………………………………………………… (hygrometer) is used to measure humidity.
- The dry-bulb thermometer is an ordinary thermometer.
- The wet-bulb thermometer is kept wet.
- Evaporation from the wet-bulb thermometer results in its temperature being lower than that of the dry-bulb thermometer.
- The difference between the two indicates the relative humidity of the air.
- Relative humidity is expressed as a ……………………… .

6 Measuring sunshine

- Sunshine is measured with a …………………………………… sunshine recorder.

- This is a small glass sphere which focuses the sun's rays onto a graduated card.

- When the sun shines the rays burn a mark onto the card and the length of the mark indicates the number of hours of sunshine for that day.

- ………………… are lines on a map joining places of equal sunshine.

7 …………………………………………

- The thermometers and barometers are housed in this.

- It is a white box with louvered sides which allows the air to pass freely through.

Section 2

Regional Geography

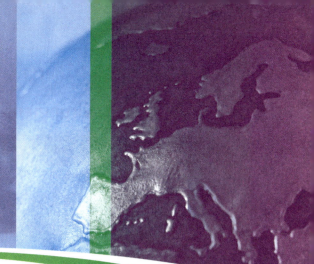

Chapter 15
Regional Introduction

Insert the following terms into the blanks below:

local autonomy / language / karst / small tertiary (services) sector / tectonic folding / hinterland / well developed manufacturing sector / large services sector / religion / infertile agricultural land / precipitation / small, underdeveloped manufacturing sector / temperature / de-industrialisation / fertile agricultural land / folding

The Physical Environment

Region Type	Examples and Comments
Climatic Region	cool temperate oceanic/maritime (western Europe) ■ A climatic region is one where .... and .... are similar.
Mountainous Region	the Alps (Europe) ■ .... due to plate tectonics creates mountain ranges that are different from the surrounding area.
Geomorphological Region	the Burren (Ireland) the Munster ridge and valley (Ireland) ■ Geological processes created the .... landscape of limestone pavements and caves whose characteristics are different from those of the surrounding area. ■ .... created the Munster ridge and valley province in south Munster.

The Economic Environment

Region Type	Examples and Comments
Core Region (well developed)	Paris Basin region (France)
	Scania region (Sweden)
	South and East region (Ireland)
	■ Core regions have .... conducive to capital-intensive agriculture, a .... due to favourable geographical location and a diversified urban economy with a .... , e.g. high-value financial (quaternary) services.
Peripheral Region (underdeveloped)	Mezzogiorno region (Italy)
	Border, Midlands and West region (Ireland)
	■ Peripheral regions have .... conducive to subsistence farming, a .... due to marginal geographical location and a .... due mainly to a small urban population.
Region of Industrial Decline	Nord-Pas-de-Calais region (France)
	Sambre Meuse region (Belgium)
	■ These regions were once thriving industrialised regions but declined due to local resources such as coal being exhausted. This is called ....

Note: Economic regions may be core, richer, developed regions (high per-capita income) or peripheral, poorer, underdeveloped regions (low per-capita income). They are therefore intrinsically linked to the human environment and have become known as **socio-economic regions**, i.e. social and economic.

The Human Environment

Region Type	Examples and Comments
Cultural Region	Wallonia region (Belgium)
	Basque region (Spain)
	■ These are regions which are defined by .... or ....
Urban/Nodal Region	Dublin (Ireland)
	Paris (France)
	Malmo (Sweden)
	■ This is composed of two areas: the city itself and its surrounding ....

Political/ Administrative Region	Four different types:

1 Supranational (e.g. EU)

2 National (e.g. Ireland)

3 Devolved (e.g. Scotland)

4 Local (e.g. Cork county council)

- These are regions created to govern and control. They exist at different levels and control different aspects of people's lives, e.g. National = finance and foreign affairs, Local = road maintenance, refuse collection.

- Devolved government is like Home Rule, i.e. it gives …………………… …………………………… or decision-making powers to a region, e.g. concerning cultural affairs, education, economic development.

Remember, there are **five** regions to be studied in detail for this question: two Irish, two European and one non-European.

	Name of sample region	Type of region
Irish	Border, Midlands and West (BMW)	Peripheral
	South and East (Dublin focused)	Core
European	the Mezzogiorno (Italy)	Peripheral
	the Paris Basin (France)	Core
Non-European	south-west USA or India	Continental/subcontinental

Points to note

The five key regions have to be studied under the following headings:

- physical processes
- primary economic activities
- secondary economic activities
- tertiary economic activities
- human processes

Chapter 16

Region 1: Peripheral Irish Region

The Border, Midlands and West (BMW)

Sample part A 20-mark question

Draw an outline map of Ireland and name the following:

- the BMW region
- two urban centres, i.e. cities or large towns
- two mountain ranges
- two drainage features, e.g. rivers
- two major routeways, e.g. key roadways
- one geomorphological feature

« Background Information »

- The BMW is made up of thirteen counties and has a population of 1.1 million.
- The BMW is a peripheral Irish region.

(a) Physical Processes

Sample Question 1

Outline the physical processes associated with a peripheral Irish region you have studied.

Insert the following terms into the blanks below:

mild / podzol soils / 1,000mm / fjords / poorly drained river flood plains / peat soils / frontal or cyclonic / rugged mountains / gley soils / maritime / shallow brown earth soils / gently undulating lowland area / upland blanket bogs / relief / cool temperate oceanic / lakes / warm / regulates the temperature range / 3,000mm / south-westerly winds / rias

Relief

- The western part of the region along the Atlantic seaboard is composed of ……………………
  ……………………… . These mountains were formed during the Caledonian folding, and stretch from
  the Bluestack Mountains in Donegal in the north of the region to the Mweelrea Mountains in Mayo in
  the south of the region. The east of the region consists of a ……………………………………
  ………………………………… . This forms the western part of the central plain. **(1 SRP)**

- The original coastline has been submerged as rising sea levels at the end of the last ice age flooded the
  river valleys, forming ………… , e.g. Clew bay, and the glaciated valleys forming …………… , e.g. Killary
  Harbour. **(1 SRP)**

Drainage

- Drainage is impeded in most areas of the region due to the ………………………………………… along
  the western seaboard and the glacial deposited boulder clay in the midlands and the border area with
  Northern Ireland. **(1 SRP)**

- This gives rise to many ………… , e.g. Lough Erne and Lough Mask, and ………………………………
  ………………………………… , e.g. along the River Shannon. **(1 SRP)**

Soils

- The region consists of infertile, poorly drained soils which are prone to waterlogging and leaching, due
  to high levels of precipitation.

  - ………………… soils are to be found on upland areas along the western seaboard where
    precipitation levels are highest. These soils have a poor mineral content, are shallow due to glacial
    erosion and of little value for any type of farming.

  - ………………… soils, which are to be found in the border areas of the region, are derived from
    glacial deposits of boulder clay and therefore are prone to waterlogging, limiting their use for farming
    and as a result are more suited to forestry.

- .... soils, which are found scattered throughout the region, suffer from leaching and contain a hardpan which inhibits drainage and thus limits their use for agriculture.

- .... soils are found in the east of the region on the central lowlands and these are conducive to pastoral farming. **(2 SRPs)**

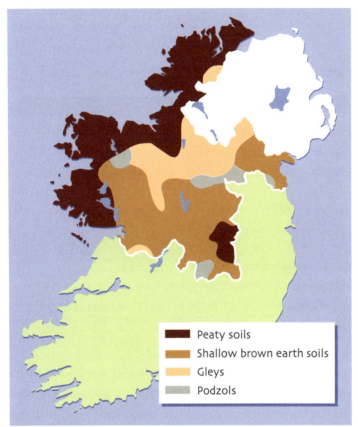

Soils of Ireland

Legend:
- Peaty soils
- Shallow brown earth soils
- Gleys
- Podzols

Climate

- The region has a .... or .... climate characteristic of western Europe. **(1 SRP)**

- Factors which influence this type of climate are:
  - The prevailing ....
  - Altitude
  - Distance from the Atlantic Ocean
  - The North Atlantic Drift current
  - Latitude. **(2 SRPs)**

Temperature

- Temperatures are .... in summer, averaging 15–17°C, and winter temperatures are colder but yet .... , averaging 4–5°C. **(1 SRP)**

- The warm North Atlantic current .... in the region, i.e. the difference between the average highest temperature and the average lowest temperature annually is small, at only 11°C. **(1 SRP)**

Precipitation

- Precipitation is predominantly in the form of rain that falls throughout the year, with a winter maximum. Total rain ranges from ……………… per annum on the western seaboard to ………… per annum in the east of the region. **(1 SRP)**

- ……………………………………… rainfall occurs in the region due to belts of low pressure created out in the Atlantic and brought onshore by the south-westerly winds. **(1 SRP)**

- …………………… rainfall occurs on the mountains of the west coast, resulting in high levels of precipitation, while the central lowlands are in the rain shadow and receive much lower rainfall levels. **(1 SRP)**

(b) Primary Economic Activities

« Background Information »

Types of farming

Arable farming

- Tillage crops, e.g. sugar beet and potatoes.
- Cereal crops, e.g. wheat and barley.

Pastoral farming (grassland):

- Dairying, i.e. milk production from cows.
- Dry stock farming, i.e. beef from bullocks.
- Sheep and goats, e.g. lamb, wool and milk.

Market gardening (horticulture)

- Fruit crops, e.g. citrus fruits such as oranges.
- Tree crops, e.g. grapes and pears.
- Salad crops, e.g. lettuce and tomatoes.

Sample Question 2(a)

Outline the development of agriculture in a peripheral Irish region you have studied.

Problems with agriculture

1 capital intensive . . . .

Physical problems

2 difficult topography. . . . .

3 peripheral geographical location . . . .

Socio-economic problems

4 age profile of farmers ....

Consequences of these problems

5 off-farm jobs..

6 out-migration and rural depopulation ....

Agricultural activities in the region

7 cattle sold as stores ....

8 unsuitable for market gardening ....

9 sheep farming popular...

10 low income from farming ....

Impact of the EU

11 Common Agricultural Policy...

12 Guarantee Fund ....

13 Guidance Fund ....

14 quota system ....

15 2003 CAP reforms/REPS ....

Sample Question 2(b)

Outline the development of fishing and fish farming (aquaculture) in a peripheral Irish region of your choice.

Insert the following terms into the blanks below:

reduced / total allowable catch (TAC) / Common Fisheries Policy in 2003 / linear / inshore fishing / continental shelf / pelagic / overfishing / depletion / Irish Conservation Box / doubled / natural sheltered harbours / super-trawler / mackerel millionaires / giant winches / undervalued / fish processing / fish support facilities

Fishing

- The west coast of the BMW region has a number of natural or physical advantages to aid the development of the fishing industry:

    - Close proximity to the rich fishing grounds of the North Atlantic.

    - The deeply indented coastline provides .... , e.g. fjords such as Killary Harbour.

    - The warm waters of the North Atlantic Drift ocean current attract many fish species to the area.

    - The shallow, gently undulating .... provides a rich supply of fish food, called plankton. **(2 SRPs)**

Fishing activities in the region

- Until the 1960s fishing was underdeveloped. It was small-scale and widely dispersed among many small fishing villages dotted in a .... pattern along the western seaboard. **(1 SRP)**

- Fishing boats were small wooden vessels suitable only for .... , and most jobs in the sector were part-time. **(1 SRP)**

- From the 1960s onwards, investment in and development of the fishing sector in the region led to the following:

    - Development of .... in the region was concentrated in the ports of Rossaveal (Ros an mHil) in Co. Galway and Killybegs in Co. Donegal.

    - Killybegs is Ireland's largest fishing port and is now the base for an open-ocean or .... fleet of large super-trawlers which can fish hundreds of miles out to sea.

    - This development of technologically advanced super-trawlers with .... , echo and sonar equipment reduced the overall numbers employed directly in fishing, but the effects of this were offset by the creation of over 1,500 jobs in onshore fish-processing. **(1 SRP)**

- Joining the EU in 1973 led to dramatic changes in the region's fishing industry as we opened up our international waters to other European countries, e.g. Spain. This resulted in .... and a dramatic .... of fish stocks, which in turn led to the implementation of the Common Fisheries Policy (CFP) in 1983. The main aim of the CFP is to create a free market in fish and conserve fish stocks. **(1 SRP)**

Impact of the Common Fisheries Policy

- Other EU countries such as Spain gained free access to Irish territorial waters, exposing our underdeveloped fishing industry to increased competition from technologically advanced fleets, but we did succeed in restricting their access to the .... **(1 SRP)**

« Definition »

The **Irish Conservation Box** is an area around the west and south coasts of Ireland where only Irish fishermen can fish.

- To reduce overfishing, the EU fixes a .... to each species of fish within its territorial waters, and each country is allocated a percentage or quota of this TAC. **(1 SRP)**

- Ireland's quota is very small, at 11 per cent of the TAC, despite the fact that we possess 16 per cent of EU territorial waters. In retrospect, Ireland .... the importance of ensuring development of its fish resources in return for ensuring benefits from the Common Agricultural Policy. **(1 SRP)**

- A significant number of small, wooden inshore fishing boats have been scrapped and the Irish fishing fleet is now dominated by a small number of large, technologically advanced fishing trawlers. The advent of the .... has exacerbated the problems of overfishing. **(1 SRP)**

- Despite quota restrictions, the value of fish landings has increased significantly in the BMW region and the owners of these large fishing trawlers operating out of Killybegs became known as the .... **(1 SRP)**

- A revised .... further reduced the TAC and it also restricted boats fishing in the Atlantic to nine days per month. **(1 SRP)**

- The future of the fishing industry in the region looks grim, as the TAC will probably be .... in the future. **(1 SRP)**

Fish farming (aquaculture)

- The indented coastal inlets and sheltered bays of the region have created many natural advantages for the development of fish farming and downstream .... The industry now accounts for a significant proportion of the fish being processed. **(1 SRP)**

- The industry has .... its output from 30,000 tonnes in 2000 to 60,000 in 2008, and created over 2,500 jobs in different farms dotted along the western seaboard. **(1 SRP)**

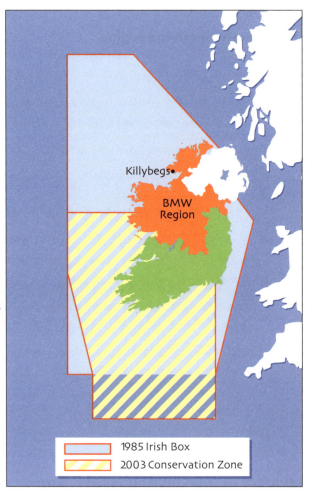

Killybegs•

BMW Region

	1985 Irish Box
	2003 Conservation Zone

(c) Secondary Economic Activities

Sample Question 3

Assess the development of manufacturing industry in a peripheral Irish region you have studied.

Insert the following terms into the blanks below:

poor transport infrastructure / the industrial development authority (IDA) / over-reliance / Údarás Na Gaeltachta / geographic isolation / European Regional Development Fund / European structural funds / taxes or tariffs / free trade / low corporation tax / nodal centre / brain drain / an international recession / craft industries / low-cost producers / Objective 1 status / foreign direct investment (FDI) / out-migration / population / information technology (IT) / M6/M4 motorways / large urban centres / high-tech, knowledge-based industry

Problems with manufacturing

- A number of problems have served to stunt industrial development in the BMW region since the 1950s.
  - A .... , i.e. a lack of motorways and limited access to mainland European markets, economically isolated the region.
  - The peripherality or .... of the region, i.e. the region's location on the fringe of Europe, has discouraged large-scale inward investment.
  - An unskilled workforce with low standards of education. Significant numbers of those who are highly educated migrated to the Dublin area due to the availability of highly skilled jobs. This created a .... , reducing the pool of skilled workers available to manufacturers in the region, and therefore discouraged the development of high-value manufacturing industry.
  - A low population density exists as a result of .... , and therefore the regional market for manufactured goods is small. **(2 SRPs)**

Government solutions

- Two Irish government agencies were set up for the task of economic development:
  - .... Its job was to promote the country, including the BMW region, as a suitable location for industrial development, by means of grants and incentives.
  - .... This organisation focused on the social, economic and cultural developments of the Gaeltacht areas, e.g. Connemara. **(1 SRP)**
- The European Union also helped the economic development of the region by granting it the then-named .... , thus enabling it to receive the maximum grant aid through the following funds:

- The .... , which assists with education and training.

- .... , which are focused on developing transport and communications in the region. **(1 SRP)**

Changing developments in manufacturing

Stage 1: 1922–60 (native manufacturing)

- Prior to 1960 all native manufacturing was protected against cheaper imports by the government. They imposed .... to increase the prices of imported goods, making the Irish products relatively cheaper on the shop shelf, thus ensuring the survival of native industry. **(1 SRP)**

- Two dominant industries emerged which were dispersed around the small towns of the region:

  - Textile (clothing) industry, e.g. woollens (Foxford).

  - Food processing industry, e.g. bacon-curing factories (Castlebar and Claremorris). **(1 SRP)**

Stage 2: 1960–80 (low-value manufacturing from foreign MNCs)

- During the 1960s and 1970s the Irish government's .... policy led to a rapid growth in manufacturing employment as branch plants of predominantly American multinational companies (MNCs) were attracted to small rural towns in the region where they mass-produced basic industrial goods. **(1 SRP)**

- Initial reasons for the influx of MNCs to the region were:

  - Government grants

  - .... (12.5 per cent)

  - Cheap land

  - Cheap labour

  - Ready-to-occupy factories

  - Support in recruiting and training workers by the IDA

  - Easy access to EU markets after 1973. **(1 SRP)**

Stage 3: 1980–90 (economic recession)

- During the 1980s .... had a profound affect on the region's economy, as many low-cost branch plants of MNCs closed or downsized. **(1 SRP)**

- The opening up of the Irish market to foreign competition from .... in Eastern Europe and South-East Asia led to the closure of many textile and food-processing industries, e.g. Fruit of the Loom in Co. Donegal. The result was that job losses were particularly significant in small towns scattered throughout the region. **(1 SRP)**

Stage 4: 1990–2008 (high-value manufacturing from foreign MNCs)

- During the Celtic Tiger era, from the 1990s till recently, the Government promoted the region as a location for high-tech industry and this led to a new wave of .... **(1 SRP)**

« *Definition* »

Foreign direct investment (FDI) is investment from multinational companies who locate subsidiaries in Ireland.

Note: A subsidiary is a factory controlled by a more powerful company, called the parent company. For example, Microsoft's parent company is in the US.

- Galway city became the dominant location for high-tech knowledge-based industry in the region due to the following factors:
  - Galway is the region's capital and it has become a ………………………………… and focus of routeways for road, rail, sea and air transport networks.
  - The city's university (NUIG) and institute of technology (GMIT) provide over 22,000 skilled graduates needed for ……………………………………………………………………………… .
  - The city has an ultra-modern telecommunications network and modern serviced industrial estates, e.g. Ballybrit. **(1 SRP)**
- The rapid economic growth of high-tech manufacturing industry in Galway city is reflected by an increase in ………………………… of over 50 per cent during the Celtic Tiger era. **(1 SRP)**

Evaluation of manufacturing activities

Positive developments

- A variety of high-tech foreign-owned MNCs have located in the region, focusing on ………………… …………………………… , e.g. Hewlett Packard, and the electrical equipment sector, which employs over 6,000 people in the Galway region. **(1 SRP)**
- Domestic industries have also developed in the region, such as …………………………………… , e.g. Galway crystal, and fish-processing factories, e.g. Killybegs. **(1 SRP)**
- Infrastructure and communications in the region have been improved significantly, with the construction of the …………………………………… to Dublin city, the development of Knock and Galway airports and Galway harbour, and the introduction of broadband internet access throughout the region. **(1 SRP)**

Negative developments

- There is an …………………………………… on foreign MNCs who might decide to pull out of Ireland if their profit margins were to decrease, and this has already occurred in the low-cost manufacturing sector, where operations have been transferred to Eastern Europe and South-East Asia. **(1 SRP)**
- High-tech industry is predominantly attracted to …………………………………… and as a result many small towns with populations of under 5,000 have failed to attract high-tech industries and only Galway city has managed successfully to attract large-scale high-value investment. **(1 SRP)**
- Overall, manufacturing is still a lot smaller in scale compared to the south and east region, and industrial productivity and wages are still lower than the national average. **(1 SRP)**

(d) Tertiary Economic Activities

Sample Question 4

Assess the development of transport, tourism and services in a peripheral Irish region you have studied.

Transport

1 fringes of a national network . . . .

2 deficit in transport infrastructure . . . .

Government strategy

3 National Development Plan 2000–06 . . . .

4 strategic road corridors . . . .

Impact of Transport 21 plan

5 National Development Plan 2007–13 . . . .

6 Atlantic Corridor and western rail corridor . . . .

Tourism

7 most valuable activity . . . .

8 scenic beauty/cultural towns/outdoor activities . . . .

Problems with tourism

9 lack of infrastructure/Shannon stopover abandoned . . . .

10 seasonal and expensive . . . .

Future strategy

11 year-round industry . . . .

12 improve infrastructure . . . .

13 upgrade marketing and advertising . . . .

Services

14 small regional market . . . .

15 improvements in communications ....

16 decentralisation ....

(e) Human Processes

Sample Question 5

Assess the development of human processes in a peripheral Irish region you have studied.

Population

1 only 27 per cent of national population...

2 rural depopulation..

3 physical factors ....

4 socio-economic factors ....

5 unemployment and emigration ....

6 brain drain..

7 increased dependency ratio...

Solutions to stimulate regional development

8 balancing regional development ....

9 grant aid from Cohesion Fund...

10 National Development Plans ....

How NDPs will develop the region

11 National Spatial Strategy: industries/services...

12 National Spatial Strategy: Gateway Innovation Fund...

Urbanisation

13 increased population of urban centres...

14 Galway city ....

15 multi-functional settlements ....

16 Western Development Commission ....

Chapter 17

Region 2: Core Irish Region

The South and East

Sample part A 20-mark question

Draw an outline map of Ireland and name the following:

- the south and east region
- two urban centres, i.e. cities or large towns
- two mountain ranges
- two drainage features, e.g. rivers
- two major routeways, e.g. key roadways

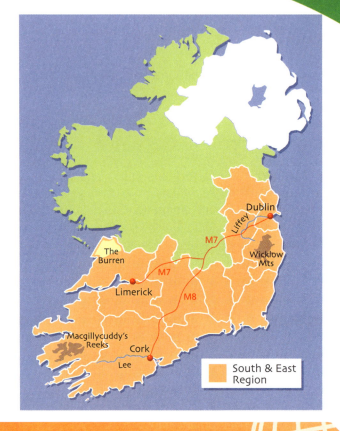

« Background Information »

- The south and east is a distinctive Irish core region made up of thirteen counties, with a population of 2.9 million.

- The region's focal point is the city of Dublin, which is the capital and the largest city in Ireland, with a population of 1.2 million. It is a primate city (six times bigger than Cork, Ireland's second biggest city).

(a) Physical Processes

Sample Question 1

Outline the physical processes associated with a core Irish region you have studied.

Relief and drainage

1 low-lying, undulating topography ....

2 south-west coast ....

3 well-drained ....

Soils

4 brown earth soils ....

5 fertile alluvial soils ....

6 peat soils ....

Climate

7 cool temperate oceanic ....

8 factors influencing climate ....

Temperature

9 warm summer/mild winter ....

10 east/south-west difference ....

11 ocean current regulates range ....

Precipitation

12 rain ....

13 frontal/cyclonic ....

14 rainfall decreases from west to east ....

15 relief ....

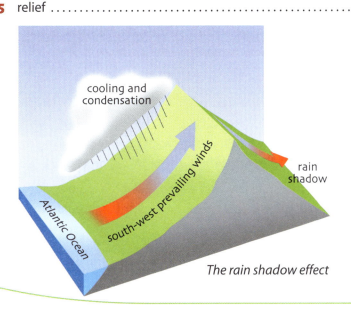

The rain shadow effect

(b) Primary Economic Activities

Sample Question 2

Outline the development of agriculture in a core Irish region you have studied.

Insert the following terms into the blanks below:

malting barley / a long grass-growing season / arable farming / well-drained / large and profitable farming units / 3,000mm per annum / low-lying, undulating / large urban market / market gardening / capital-intensive farming / new farm practices / glasshouses (greenhouses) / more prosperous forms of agriculture / intensive horticultural practices / cereal crops / high-value dairying / dry stock farming / pastoral farming / EU subsidies / light, well-drained sandy soils / wheat

The south and east region is the most fertile and productive agricultural region in Ireland due to a combination of physical and socio-economic factors.

Physical factors

- Much of the region has a .... (gently sloping) topography which facilitates the use of heavy machinery. Most of the region is covered by brown earth soils and alluvial soils on river flood plains – both of which are fertile, well-drained soils ideal for .... **(1 SRP)**

- The east of the region has a long growing season of over 280 days and rainfall is evenly spread throughout the year. This is ideal for .... , i.e. cereal and tillage crops. **(1 SRP)**

- The south of the region receives higher rainfall levels and is therefore more suited to intensive .... particularly dairying. **(1 SRP)**

Socio-economic factors

- A significant number of farmers in the region possess .... whose productivity levels are well above the national average, and therefore farmers can afford the most modern machinery to maximise their output. **(1 SRP)**

- A .... of nearly 1.8 million people exists in the GDA (Greater Dublin Area), which is conducive to capital-intensive .... , e.g. fruit and vegetables in north Co. Dublin. **(1 SRP)**

- Farmers are on average much younger, more well educated, more innovative and more willing to adopt .... than their counterparts in the BMW region. **(1 SRP)**

- Farmland is more expensive in this region and therefore farmers use the land more intensively to receive a bigger return. Farms in the region are assisted by .... through the Common Agricultural Policy (CAP). **(1 SRP)**

Three types of agricultural activity

■ Farms in the region are larger, more modern and productive, specialising in .... , e.g. market gardening, arable farming and dairy farming. **(1 SRP)**

1 Arable farming in the east

■ In the east of the region the .... low-lying topography, coupled with fertile brown earth soils and less than 700mm of rain spread evenly throughout the year, make the area conducive to capital-intensive arable farming. **(1 SRP)**

■ Arable farming in the region is focused on .... , predominantly wheat and barley, which are intensively farmed and specialised for certain markets.

  ■ .... is supplied to bakeries, e.g. Brennan's, and biscuit manufacturers such as Jacobs.

  ■ .... , i.e. barley with a high starch content, is used in the brewing (beer, e.g. Guinness) and distilling (whiskey, e.g. Jameson) industries.

  ■ Protein-rich barley is used to produce food for feeding to animals during the winter months. **(1 SRP)**

2 Pastoral farming in the south

■ The south of the region has a well-drained and gently undulating topography with fertile brown earth soils, with the exception of the mountainous areas along the western coastline. **(1 SRP)**

■ Rainfall levels are high, with up to .... on the western seaboard, which decreases with distance from the Atlantic Ocean, leading to a .... , thus favouring capital-intensive pastoral farming. **(1 SRP)**

■ Large areas of Munster consist of large farming units sited on lush pastures which focus exclusively on .... , backed by large EU quotas, e.g. the Golden Vale area in Tipperary. **(1 SRP)**

■ .... (beef farming) is also practised as stores (young cattle up to two years old) reared in the BMW region are brought to the richer pasturelands of the south for fattening and finishing. **(1 SRP)**

3 Market gardening (horticulture) in north Co. Dublin

■ The high cost of land in the Dublin region results in .... between the towns of Rush and Lusk in north Co. Dublin. The development of capital-intensive horticulture is favoured by .... , an undulating landscape, low rainfall levels, frost-free climatic conditions and a growing season of over 300 days. **(1 SRP)**

■ High-value horticulture in north Co. Dublin is based on the production of fresh fruit and vegetables, many of which are produced in .... The perishable nature of the produce is the dominant reason for such business being based in close proximity to the GDA, which provides a large market of 1.8 million people. **(1 SRP)**

(c) Secondary Economic Activities

Sample Question 3

Outline the development of manufacturing in a core Irish region you have studied.

Introduction

1 region with most urban centres ....

2 favourable geographical location...

3 main concentration of manufacturing ....

Changing developments in manufacturing

4 native manufacturing ....

5 low-value manufacturing/branch plants ....

6 government grants ....

7 cheap labour ....

8 economic recession..

9 competition from low-cost producers ....

10 high-value manufacturing ....

11 knowledge-based industry...

Advantages of Dublin

12 region's capital/port ....

13 modern communications network/national education centre ....

14 ICT in Dublin..

15 pharmaceuticals in Cork..

(d) Tertiary Economic Activities

Sample Question 4(a)

Outline the development of transport in a core Irish region you have studied.

Insert the following terms into the blanks below:

port tunnel / Terminal 2 / gateways / quality bus corridors (QBCs) / focus of routeways / National Spatial Strategy 2002 / CASP strategy / redistribution of wealth / hubs / motorway and rail / Transport 21 plan / barrier-free tolling / green route programme / interurban junctions / metro light rail system / dredging of Dublin port / Atlantic road corridor / transport infrastructure / Luas lines / integrated / deficit / strategic road corridors

Introduction

- The .... in the south and east region is well developed relative to that of the BMW region. It is focused on Dublin city, which is a nodal centre and primate city, and consequently a .... for all road and rail routes. **(1 SRP)**

- Until 2000 there was a .... in high-quality transport infrastructure, e.g. motorways, within the GDA and from Dublin city to other key urban centres designated as gateways in the region, e.g. Cork, Limerick and Waterford. **(1 SRP)**

Government strategy to develop transport

- Part of the Irish government's National Development Plan (NDP) 2000–06 was to upgrade transport systems, e.g. roads, in line with the .... **(1 SRP)**

Explanation

National Development Plans were designed to transform Ireland and create a better quality of life for all its people by:

- improving infrastructure and promoting balanced and sustainable regional development;

- promoting skills and education for high-value employment;

- .... to foster an inclusive society.

Explanation

The **National Spatial Strategy 2002** involves the large-scale development of the following:

- .... : the development of other large urban centres, e.g. Cork, to counteract the dominance of Dublin.

- .... : smaller urban centres that will help to disperse development away from gateways.

- Strategic road corridors: to provide efficient links between gateways, hubs and Dublin.

- In the south and east region the development of transport under the NDP 2000–06 focused primarily on the development of .... infrastructure. **(1 SRP)**

Impact of Transport 21 plan (2005-15)

- The government's .... envisages spending €33 billion under the National Development Plan 2007–13, which is earmarked for infrastructure development. **(1 SRP)**

Within the GDA

- Within the GDA, apart for the upgrade of the M50 motorway, including .... and free-flow .... , the emphasis for transport development is on building an .... public transport system focusing on the following projects: **(1 SRP)**

  - The construction of two new .... to Lucan and Glasnevin, the joining of the current Tallaght and Sandyford Luas lines in the city centre, and extending these lines to Citywest and the Docklands on the Tallaght line and to Cherrywood on the Sandyford line.

  - The upgrading of the Maynooth, Navan and Kildare railway lines to DART lines.

  - Building an underground .... from the city centre to the airport called Metro North and a Metro West from Tallaght to Ballymun via Clondalkin, Lucan and Blanchardstown.

  - Extending the number of .... to speed up travelling times for Dublin buses. **(2 SRPs)**

Note: Most of these public transport developments will be postponed or cut back due to the economic recession.

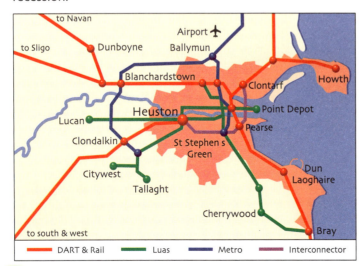

The development of public transport

- Other transport projects in the GDA are the .... to accommodate larger passenger ferries and cargo vessels, as the busy port accounts for over 50 per cent of all foreign trade. The completion of the .... removed over 9,000 trucks a day from the city centre. **(1 SRP)**

- Dublin airport is the dominant airport hub in the country, accommodating over 22 million passengers in 2007, leading to the need for the construction of .... **(1 SRP)**

Rest of the south and east

- Transport 21's impact on the rest of the south and east region is predominantly focused on the completion of .... linking other major urban centres to Dublin city:

  - M7 (Limerick city to Dublin city)

  - M8 (Cork city to Dublin city)

  - M9 (Waterford to Dublin city)

  - M11 (Rosslare harbour to Dublin city). **(1 SRP)**

- In Cork the NDP focuses on the .... to integrate public transport systems, including the .... of improved bus priority and the opening up of the Cork city to Midleton rail link. It also focuses on the construction of the Atlantic road corridor, i.e. the motorway, to Limerick and the upgrading of the N28 road from Cork city to Ringaskiddy port. **(1 SRP)**

- In Limerick the NDP focuses on construction of the N18 .... , i.e. motorway, to Galway via Shannon airport, the completion of the southern ring road, a tunnel under the Shannon and development of the western rail corridor. **(1 SRP)**

Sample Question 4(b)

Outline the development of services and tourism in a core Irish region you have studied.

Services

1 two-thirds of the national population. . . . .

2 large consumer market . . . .

3 quaternary services . . . .

4 International Financial Services Centre (IFSC) . . . .

5 factors which led to the growth of financial services. . . . .

6 spin-off services . . . .

7 European headquarters of internet services. . . . .

Tourism

8 75 per cent of national tourist revenue. . . . .

Tourism in Dublin

   9   city break destination . . . .

   10 most popular point of entry . . . .

Attractions of the region

   11 churches/architecture/museums . . . .

   12 shops/cultural quarter . . . .

   13 150,000 jobs directly . . . .

Tourism in the rest of the region

   14 scenic beauty. . . . .

   15 cultural towns . . . .

   16 outdoor activities . . . .

   17 global downturn. . . . .

(e) Human Processes

Sample Question 5(a)

Assess the development of population dymanics in a core Irish region you have studied.

Insert the following terms into the blanks below:

chronic traffic congestion / planned overspill satellite towns / over half the land area / National Spatial Strategy 2002 / coastal cities / National Development Plan 2 / lowest bridging point / commuter belt / Transport 21 plan / job opportunities / political capital and administrative centre / trading links / greater Dublin area (GDA) / Celtic Tiger era / rural to urban migratory trend / natural increase / dependency ratio / immigration / immigration offices / urban spine / urban sprawl / commuter culture / inbound / outbound / decentralisation programme / 73 per cent / strategic development zone (SDZ) / inner-city decline / urban renewal and urban redevelopment

Population

- The south and east region covers just . . . . of the country, but has . . . . of the population, and therefore its density of population is nearly three times higher than that of the BMW region. **(1 SRP)**

- Seventy-five per cent of the population of the region live in urban centres, especially in the GDA, which has a population of 1.7 million out of the 2.9 million in the region. Other relatively large centres of the region would be the . . . . of Cork, Limerick and Waterford, all of which have populations of over 50,000 people. **(1 SRP)**

- The distribution of population in the region is related to a combination of physical, historical and economic factors:

  - Physical factor: All major cities of the region are located at the .... of large Irish rivers. **(1 SRP)**

  - Historical factor: Dublin's status as the country's .... was established when it became the centre of British rule in Ireland during the colonial period. **(1 SRP)**

  - Economic factor: Most major cities of the region are located on the coast and have developed due to .... with other countries, especially those in Europe. **(1 SRP)**

- The populations of urban centres in the region have increased significantly, but nowhere is this more evident than in the ....

Focus on population growth in the GDA

- A combination of the following factors has led to the exponential growth in the population of the GDA since the beginning of the ....

- A .... : Its central geographic location to the UK and other EU markets and a highly developed communications network increased the attraction of the city for high-value manufacturing and services. This led to the provision of high-value jobs which, coupled with numerous third-level institutions and many social activities, have attracted many young people from rural areas to the city. **(1 SRP)**

- .... : Provision of jobs has led to many young people settling down, getting married and starting families in the GDA, resulting in a population increase in the region, particularly outside the Dublin city area, i.e. in the .... The region therefore has a low .... **(1 SRP)**

« Definition »

The **dependency ratio** is the ratio of the working to the non-working population. It is used to analyse the economic effect or reliance of the young and the elderly, i.e. the non-working population, on the working population.

- .... : The GDA has become a focal point for immigrants in Ireland, thus becoming a multi-ethnic society, for the following reasons:

  - Ninety per cent of foreign flights arrive in Dublin and therefore it is the first stop for many immigrants. Immigrants might have a familiarity with Dublin as they would have heard of the city before arriving and they may assume that, being the biggest city in the country, ... might be more plentiful.

  - The government .... are located in the city, so those applying for refugee status would stay until their applications have been processed.

  - Jobs are more plentiful and therefore easier to find in the GDA than in any other urban centre in the region. **(2 SRPs)**

Problems with the rapid population growth of the GDA

- .... : The M50 ring motorway, initially earmarked as an urban by-pass of Dublin city, has become an .... This spine has become a prime location for industrial parks (e.g. Sandyford) and shopping centres (e.g. Dundrum and Blanchardstown). The result is that the M50 ring-road has long since reached its capacity of 100,000 vehicles a day and this has led to traffic congestion, particularly during rush-hours.

- .... into the surrounding countryside has consumed many old villages and turned them into suburbs, e.g. Blackrock and Tallaght.

- .... took place as most young people were rehoused in the new suburbs, leaving the inner city areas with an ageing population lacking vibrancy.

- A .... was created when new suburbs outside the city developed into dormitory towns. Commuters now spend hours every day sitting in long rush-hour traffic queues going .... to the city centre in the morning and .... back to the suburbs in the evening. **(2 SRPs)**

Solutions to problems created by the rapid growth of the GDA

- The .... (2007–13) aims to address issues such as traffic congestion and urban sprawl, and to promote social inclusion and develop transport links, both within Dublin and with the rest of the country.

- The .... aims to address issues such as balancing regional development, integrating transport networks and developing the hubs, gateways and strategic road corridors.

- The .... aims to construct an underground metro system, along with extending Luas lines, DART lines and Quality Bus Corridors (QBCs).

- The government has planned a .... to relocate government departments to various towns and cities outside the GDA.

- .... were constructed outside the city to limit uncontrolled urban sprawl and reduce commuting into the city centre, e.g. Adamstown.

Focus on Adamstown

- It was designated a .... to speed up the planning of a 200-acre site in west Dublin.

- It has been designed as a self-contained sustainable town and has a planned maximum population of 25,000 people.

- It contains a mixture of housing and apartments and all modern services such as schools, shopping centres and a commuter rail station. **(1 SRP)**

- .... programmes to upgrade districts in the city which have run into disrepair. This includes the pedestrianising of city streets and conserving historical buildings to make the city a more appealing place to live in. **(3 SRPs)**

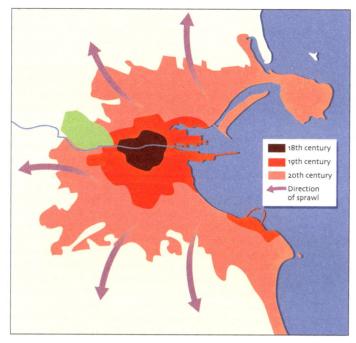

The growth of Dublin city

Sample Question 5(b)

Outline the development of human processes in a core Irish region you have studied.

Note: In this question you need to discuss seven to eight SRPs on population dynamics from the previous question and seven to eight SRPs from the urbanisation question below.

Urbanisation

1   renewal ....

2   redevelopment ....

Redevelopment

3   Dublin Docklands Development Authority...

4   global financial institutions..

5   Grand Canal Theatre ....

6   social and affordable housing ....

7   infill development ....

Renewal

8   tower blocks built in the 1960s ....

9   Ballymun Regeneration Ltd ....

10   key aspects of the scheme ....

Chapter 18

Region 3: Peripheral European Region

The Mezzogiorno (Italy)

Sample part A 20-mark question

Draw an outline map of Italy and name the following:

- a peripheral European region
- two urban centres, i.e. cities or large towns
- one mountain range
- two drainage features, e.g. rivers
- one major routeway, e.g. a roadway
- one geomorphological feature

Autostrada del Sole

Apennines

Volturno River

Olfanto River

Naples
Mt Vesuvius

The Mezzogiorno

Palermo

《 Background Information 》

The Mezzogiorno is a peripheral European region.

(a) Physical Processes

Sample Question 1

Discuss the physical processes in a peripheral European region you have studied.

Insert the following terms into the blanks below:

thin, infertile and heavily denuded / weathered lava / Atlantic low-pressure belt / Apennine / Tyrrhenian Sea / coastal lowlands / relief rainfall / permeable / rain shadow / terra rossa / alluvial / warm, temperate oceanic climate / Azores high-pressure belt / convectional / small, fast-flowing streams / alpine mountain-building movement / tectonic activity / rugged mountain terrain / frontal (cyclonic) rainfall / drained and irrigated / Adriatic

Relief

- The relief of the region is .... , consisting mainly of the .... Mountains, which stretch 1,050km down through peninsular Italy. Eighty-five per cent of the region is classified as upland or mountainous, with 45 per cent too steep for any economic activity to develop. **(1 SRP)**

- The Apennines are extremely high as they were formed during the .... around 65 million years ago, and the highest peak is Gran Sasso d'Italia (the Great Rock of Italy) at 2,914m. **(1 SRP)**

- The .... comprise only 15 per cent of the land area of the region and are discontinuous, as the Apennines run directly to the sea in some areas, inhibiting the development of communications, e.g. transportation such as motorways. **(1 SRP)**

- The region is also prone to .... such as earthquakes (2002 earthquake in Molise and Puglia) and volcanic eruptions (Vesuvius 1944 and Etna 2008). **(1 SRP)**

Drainage

- Most of the region's rivers are .... that flow in a radial pattern off the Apennines, e.g. Volturno, Pescara and Basento. Many rivers experience flooding during winter but dry up during the summer droughts as a result of the Mediterranean climate. **(1 SRP)**

- In limestone areas rainwater drains underground due to the .... nature of the rock, creating subterranean streams and cave systems. **(1 SRP)**

- Many of the coastal lowlands are made of poorly drained mudflats and marches, but many of these have now been .... , e.g. Metaponto in the Gulf of Taranto. **(1 SRP)**

Soils

- Soils in the high Apennines, which account for nearly 50 per cent of the region's land area, are .... due to weathering and erosion. **(1 SRP)**

- .... soils derived from weathered limestone, with their characteristic red colour, are found mainly in the south of the region and are subject to soil erosion, but can be used for growing vines and olives successfully if irrigated and fertilised. **(1 SRP)**

- The only fertile soils in the region are .... found on river flood plains, e.g. the Volturno River and the volcanic soils of Campania around Mt Vesuvius that are derived from .... and therefore have a high mineral content. **(1 SRP)**

Climate

- This region has a classic Mediterranean climate or .... , i.e. hot, dry summers and mild, moist winters.

Summer

- The region experiences hot, dry summers due to the .... , resulting in cloudless skies and warm sunshine.

- Summer temperatures average 28–30°C with warm, dry north-easterly winds from continental Europe.

- Summer rain is .... in brief bursts of torrential downpours and thunderstorms due to rapid heating from the sun. **(2 SRPs)**

Winter

- The region experiences mild, wet winters due to the ....
  (depression), resulting in cloud formation and rain.

- Winter temperatures average 17–18°C with moist, mild south-westerly winds from the Atlantic.

- Two types of rainfall occur in winter:

  - .... in upland areas due to the Apennines.

  - .... created by the low-pressure belt. **(2 SRPs)**

- Annual rainfall levels range from 900mm in the west along the .... to 400mm in
  the east along the Adriatic. The lower amounts fall along the .... as it is in the ....
  .... of the Apennines. **(1 SRP)**

(b) Primary Economic Activities

Sample Question 2

Outline the problems in the development of agriculture in a peripheral European region you
have studied.

Physical problems

1 difficult physical environment . . . .

Historical problems

2 latifundia . . . .

3 minifundia . . . .

4 braccianti . . . .

5 sharecropping . . . .

6 extensive farming . . . .

Solutions to agricultural problems

7 Cassa plan and ERDF . . . .

8 government subdivided land . . . .

9 reafforestation . . . .

10 irrigation . . . .

11 Autostrada Del Sole . . . .

Modern arable farming

12 Campania – high value crops . . . .

13 vines and olives . . . .

14 citrus fruits . . . .

Modern pastoral farming

15 extensive grazing of sheep and goats . . . .

16 irrigation . . . .

(c) Secondary Economic Activities

Sample Question 3

Examine the development of manufacturing industry in a peripheral European region of your choice.

Insert the following terms into the blanks below:

cathedrals in the desert / Apulian aqueduct / grants / emigration / brain drain / discouraged inward investment / low-value outputs / Cassa plan / low-value manufacturing / growth poles or centres / state-owned industry / 300,000 new, well-paid jobs were created / ERDF / Autostrada Del Sole / heavy industry / tide of migration / Apennines / Vanoni plan / low rainfall levels / over-reliance on state-owned industries / no wide-scale industrialisation / Mafia

Problems with manufacturing

- A number of problems served to stunt industrial development in the region prior to 1950.
  - It had been by-passed by the Industrial Revolution at the end of the nineteenth century and therefore . . . . had occurred.
  - Limited supply of energy or raw materials, e.g. hydroelectric power was not viable due to . . . . in summer.
  - An unskilled and uneducated workforce; those who were educated migrated to the north of Italy, creating a . . . .
  - Remoteness from the large markets of northern Italy and central Europe due to its peripheral geographical location . . . .

- A poor transport infrastructure predominantly due to the mountainous landscape of the .... that served to isolate the region even further.

- A high dependence on limited .... in the primary sector meant that there was little to process for industry. **(3 SRPs)**

Government solutions

- It was through the Italian government's .... and the .... that priority was put on promoting industrial development from 1957 onwards through the following initiatives. **(1 SRP)**

  - It created .... for investment and development, such as Naples. They also tried to develop an industrial triangle between the cities of Bari, Taranto and Brindisi to mirror the powerful industrial triangle of the north of Italy between Milan, Turin and Genoa. **(1 SRP)**

  - Under the .... infrastructure was improved, including the construction of the Autostrada Del Sole motorway, and the deep-water sea port at Taranto. **(1 SRP)**

  - The government forced .... to locate 60 per cent of all heavy industry in the region, e.g. the steel manufacturer Finsider located in Taranto. **(1 SRP)**

  - It provided .... , loans, subsidies and tax incentives to companies in order to relocate to the region. **(1 SRP)**

The impact of the CASSA plan and ERDF

Positive developments

- Over .... while over two million low-paid jobs were lost in agriculture. Nevertheless it did diversify the economy, i.e. reduce the over-reliance on agriculture. **(1 SRP)**

- The Italian government was successful in developing a world-class infrastructure, including motorways, e.g. .... , and irrigation schemes, e.g. the .... , which have allowed for the development of the very profitable food-processing industry. **(1 SRP)**

- The development of .... such as petrochemicals, car assembly, shipbuilding and steel manufacturing has been very successful. **(1 SRP)**

Negative developments

- Unemployment is still high today at over 20 per cent, especially in inland areas, and there is still a .... to the richer northern Italy and .... to the USA. **(1 SRP)**

- The capital-intensive projects to develop heavy industry became known as .... , and they failed in their bid to attract spin-off and downstream industries. **(1 SRP)**

- There is still an .... and corruption, particularly associated with the .... , prevented private inward investment. **(1 SRP)**

- Overall the sector experienced limited growth from 20 per cent of the labour force in 1950 to 25 per cent in 2008, but it did succeed in changing from .... jobs to high-value, well-paid manufacturing jobs. **(1 SRP)**

(d) Tertiary Economic Activities

Sample Question 4

Assess the development of transport and tourism in a peripheral European region of your choice.

Transport

1 Cassa plan ....

2 Autostrada Del Sole motorway ....

3 motorway on the east coast ....

Tourism

4 accessibility of the region ....

5 scenic beauty ....

6 year-round tourism ....

7 historical sites ....

8 government strategies to develop tourism..

Positive impacts

9 increased standard of living ....

10 spin-off jobs ....

11 supplements farm income ....

Negative impacts

12 tourists hike up prices..

13 pressure on the environment...

14 ruining natural beauty ....

15 advantages outweigh disadvantages ....

(e) Human Processes

Sample Question 5

Outline the development of human processes in a peripheral European region you have studied.

Insert the following terms into the blanks below:

> high population density / increasing / malaria ridden / migrated / average family size / pull / small hilltop villages / empowered / low population density / family planning / regional development policy / decreasing / plush / coastal lowlands / unemployment / higher wages / quota system / emigrated / distribution / life expectancy / urban areas / centre of administration and commerce / three million / thousands of immigrants / third largest city / economic burden / Catholic Church / eradicated / outward migration

Population

- The total population of the region is 22 million. The .... of population is related to the region's topography. The Apennine Mountains have a ...., while the coastal lowlands have a .... **(1 SRP)**

- Traditionally the birth rate and .... in the region was higher than the more affluent northern Italy, but this trend is changing as the region has developed economically. **(1 SRP)**

- The reasons why the birth rates have decreased are:
  - Women have been .... , i.e. they can decide for themselves whether or not they want to have children.
  - The influence of the .... on issues such as contraception has declined.
  - Women are educated about ....
  - Investment from the Italian government's Cassa plan and the EU's ....
    .... has developed the region economically. **(2 SRPs)**

- Economic development in the region since the 1950s has increased the ....
  due to improvements in quality of life in areas such as healthcare and nutrition. **(1 SRP)**

- Overall the proportion of young people under the age of 18 is .... , while that of the over-65s is .... **(1 SRP)**

Out-migration

- Since 1951 over five million people have left the poorer Mezzogiorno region and ....
  to the more prosperous north of Italy. **(1 SRP)**

- Up to ten million people .... in the last century, to predominantly non-European countries such as the USA and Australia before 1945, and to European countries such as Germany and France after 1945. **(1 SRP)**

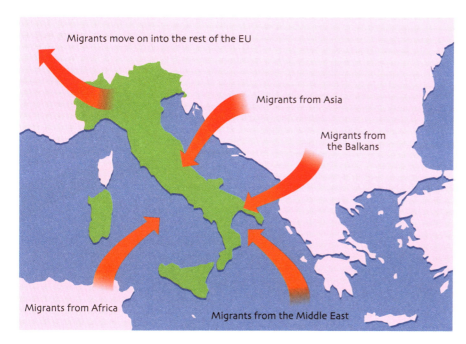

Migration into the Mezzogiorno

- Since the 1970s, however, there has been a significant decrease in .... due to the modernisation of the region. **(1 SRP)**

- .... factors to out-migration from the region were .... , overpopulation, isolation, infertile soils and poverty. **(1 SRP)**

- The .... factors of the host countries were the employment and education opportunities, a more attractive environment and .... **(1 SRP)**

In-migration

- The collapse of communist regimes in Eastern Europe in the 1990s, coupled with the civil war in the former Yugoslavia and poverty in Africa, brought .... across the Adriatic and Mediterranean seas to the region. **(1 SRP)**

- The .... placed on the Italian government has led to the introduction of a .... , which limits the number of immigrants admitted each year from each source area. Despite this, illegal immigration is still a serious problem. **(1 SRP)**

Urbanisation

- Approximately 70 per cent of people in the region live in .... , most notably the cities of Naples, Palermo and Bari. Each province in the region has developed its own .... , e.g. Naples in Campania, Bari in Apulia and Palermo in Sicily. **(1 SRP)**

- Naples, with a population of ...., is the administrative and commercial capital of the region and is Italy's .... and second largest port. **(1 SRP)**

- Prior to the 1950s most people in the region lived in .... in the Apennines away from the .... coastal lowlands. **(1 SRP)**

- Under the Cassa plan malaria was .... and industry and tourism were developed. This led to the migration of people from hilltop rural villages to the cities and towns on the .... **(1 SRP)**

Chapter 19

Region 4: Core European Region

The Paris Basin (France)

Sample part A 20-mark question

Draw an outline map of France and name the following:

- a core European region

- an urban centre

- two drainage features, e.g. rivers

- a major routeway

- a port

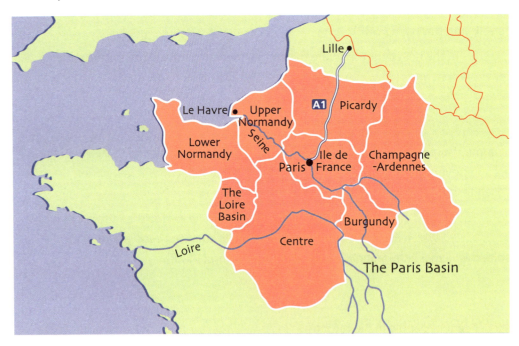

《 *Background Information* 》

- The Paris Basin is a distinctive European core region with a population of 21 million, stretching 500km east to west and 300km north to south.

- The region's focal point is the city of Paris, which is the capital and largest city in France, with a population of 12 million, and is a primate city.

(a) Physical Processes

Sample Question 1

Outline the physical processes associated with a core European region you have studied.

Relief

1 saucers of sedimentary rock..

2 Île-de-France ....

3 scarps or côtes..

4 cliff-like slope..

Drainage

5 River Seine ....

6 Le Havre..

7 well-drained ....

Soils

8 limon, clay and chalk..

9 scarp slopes are fertile ....

Climate

10 north-west: cool temperate oceanic ....

11 characteristics of cool temperate oceanic ....

12 south and east: transitional climate ....

13 influence of maritime and continental climates ....

14 characteristics of transitional climate ....

15 rainfall levels..

(b) Primary Economic Activities

Sample Question 2

Outline the development of agriculture in a core European region you have studied.

Insert the following terms into the blanks below:

> very large by European standards / geological saucers / Île-de-France / granary of France / long growing season / guaranteed prices / excellent transport network / backed by EU subsidies / large domestic market / European market / dairy production / limon / viticulture / market gardening (horticulture) / undulating (gently sloping) topography / Seine / dairy industry / pays

Agriculture

- The Paris Basin is known as the .... due to its very productive agricultural sector. **(1 SRP)**

- The reasons for this are a combination of physical and socio-economic factors.

Physical

- Most of the basin is covered by a thick layer of .... , which has weathered into an easily worked, stoneless fertile soil. **(1 SRP)**

- The region has a .... with long hours of summer sunshine and summer temperatures averaging 20°C, which is ideal for intensive cereal production, e.g. wheat, maize and barley. **(1 SRP)**

- The basin has an .... , which facilitates the use of heavy machinery. **(1 SRP)**

Socio-economic

- Farms are .... , i.e. most are over 400 hectares, and therefore farmers can afford the most modern machinery to maximise their output. **(1 SRP)**

- The basin has an .... to allow for quick and efficient delivery of all farm produce. **(1 SRP)**

- All farms in the basin are .... through the Common Agricultural Policy. **(1 SRP)**

- The basin has a .... (population of 21 million) centred on the city of Paris, which has allowed for the development of very successful dairy and market gardening industries. **(1 SRP)**

■ The basin is also centrally located and very accessible to the much larger central .... to sell its produce. **(1 SRP)**

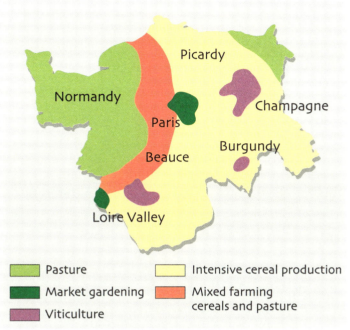

Pasture

Market gardening

Viticulture

Intensive cereal production

Mixed farming cereals and pasture

Agriculture in the Paris Basin

■ A key characteristic of the region is that different areas, known as .... , specialise in different forms of intensive farming. **(1 SRP)**

■ This is because the basin is composed of .... of sedimentary rocks laid down inside each other, which gives rise to a wide variety of agricultural production in different areas. **(1 SRP)**

■ Normandy in the north-west has a cool, temperate oceanic/maritime climate, similar to that of Ireland. Precipitation all year round is conducive to .... Much of this dairy is processed into cheese, e.g. Camembert, and other big dairy producing companies, such as Danone, are located in the region. **(1 SRP)**

■ Adjacent to the large urban centre of Paris, high-value .... is the dominant agricultural activity as there is a daily demand for fresh fruit and vegetables. **(1 SRP)**

■ Around the flood plain of the river .... alluvial soils favour intensive cereal production. **(1 SRP)**

■ The .... region consists of:

  ■ Brie, which is well known for its butter and cheese production, and which has a very modern and capital-intensive .... Prices are kept high as the intervention price from the EU guarantees high profits.

  ■ Beauce, which is known for its intensive, highly mechanised cereal production. Output per hectare rose dramatically after the foundation of the EU as a result of ....

  ■ The Champagne region, which is famous for its .... , mainly its sparkling wine. These wines are grown on the south-facing scarp of the Falaise Île-de-France and are famous throughout the world. **(1 SRP)**

(c) Secondary Economic Activities

Sample Question 3

Assess the development of manufacturing in a core European region you have studied.

Introduction

1. very large consumer market..
2. Paris: dominant hub..

Heavy industry

3. accessible to deep barge traffic..
4. Seine navigable to Le Havre..
5. transportation highly efficient..
6. car assembly..

Light industry

7. seventeen universities..
8. technopoles..
9. fashion centre..
10. printing and publishing..
11. footloose industry..
12. cosmetics and perfume..

De-industrialisation

13. low-cost industry has relocated..
14. reasons for de-industrialisation..
15. counteract through high-value manufacturing..

(d) Tertiary Economic Activities

Sample Question 4

Assess the development of services, transport and tourism in a core European region of your choice.

Insert the following terms into the blanks below:

illuminations / €4 billion per annum / quaternary services / focus of routeways / vast motorway network / the Paris Bourse / the services sector / nodal point / Reims / favourable topography / TGV / Channel Tunnel / Metro / integrated ticketing system / the world's most visited city / La Défense / primate city / Louvre museum / double-decker carriages / 250,000 people / Euro-Disney / two international airports / SNCF and RER / beaches of Normandy

Services

- More than two-thirds of the population of the Paris Basin work in .... , with a 3 per cent increase per annum. As the demand for services such as transportation, tourism, leisure and entertainment have increased, so have the income levels. **(1 SRP)**

- In a sophisticated economy such as that of the Paris Basin there is a big demand for .... such as finance, insurance, marketing and accounting. The financial centre is located in .... , Paris. **(1 SRP)**

- The Parisian stock exchange, ... , is the second largest in Europe after London. Three of Europe's largest banks have their headquarters in Paris. **(1 SRP)**

Transport

- Paris is a .... and the centre of administration and economic activities in France. This is similar to Dublin city. Paris is a .... and consequently is a .... for all road and rail routes. **(1 SRP)**

- The development of the transport network has been aided by the .... , i.e. a low-lying, gently sloping, well-drained landscape. **(1 SRP)**

- The .... (French high-speed train) can travel at over 300km per hour and is linked to over 150 destinations in France. It links Paris to Brussels (administration centre of the EU) and to London via the .... The TGV has become so popular that .... have been built to cope with the demand. **(1 SRP)**

- Within Paris itself the .... link the suburbs to the city centre, and both have park-and-ride facilities. The underground .... electrical rail system provides swift transport in and around the city of Paris. All public transport in Greater Paris has an efficient .... to speed up commuting. **(1 SRP)**

- Paris also has huge underground car parks for car commuters and a ....
.... , e.g. the Boulevard Périphérique (ring-road around Paris). Paris also has ....
.... , Charles De Gaulle and Orly. **(1 SRP)**

Tourism

Tourism in Paris

- Tourism is a thriving industry in the city of Paris, which is ....
(1 SRP)

- Attractions for tourists in Paris include:

  - Historic churches and buildings, e.g. the cathedral of Notre-Dame and the Arc de Triomphe.

  - A well designed, beautiful city with gardens such as the Luxembourg Gardens and the Gardens of the Tuileries.

  - Museums such as the famous .... and the Carnavalet Museum.

  - An extensive range of high-quality shops and restaurants with famous brands such as Chanel.

  - At night, all famous monuments and buildings (276 in total) are lit up in what has become known as the .... , capturing the atmosphere of the city. **(2 SRPs)**

- The tourist industry in the Paris Basin employs over .... directly, along with many spin-off industries, and is worth nearly .... to the region's economy. **(1 SRP)**

Tourism in the rest of the basin

- .... , located in Marne-la-Vallée 30km east of Paris, is another major tourist attraction which is linked to the city centre via the TGV. **(1 SRP)**

- The preserved battlefields of the Second World War on the .... have become a popular tourist attraction, e.g. the new visitor centre on Omaha Beach, built in 2007. **(1 SRP)**

- .... is well known for its famous cathedral and its viticulture. **(1 SRP)**

(e) Human Processes

Sample Question 5

Outline the development of human processes in a core European region you have studied.

Population

1 21 million/11 in greater Paris ....

2 rural-to-urban migratory trend ....

3 birth rate 1.9..

4 multi-racial society..

5 1.5 million immigrants ....

6 immigrants live in poor quality dwellings ....

7 racial tension ....

Urbanisation

8 urban renewal and redevelopment..

9 traffic congestion ....

Schéma Directeur

10 conservation/growth centres..

11 overspill satellite towns/urban transport...

12 young professionals ....

13 La Défense ....

14 planned overspill towns...

15 agreeable lifestyle ....

Chapter 20

Region 5(A): Continental or Subcontinental Region

The South-West (USA)

Sample part A 20-mark question

Draw an outline map of the south-west USA and name the following:

- a subcontinental region
- three urban centres
- two drainage features, e.g. rivers
- two major routeways
- a port
- a mountain range

<< *Background Information* >>

- The south-west USA is a distinctive continental/subcontinental region that stretches 3,000km from the Pacific Ocean on its western border to the Gulf of Mexico on its south-eastern border.

- The region comprises the five US states, from west to south-east, of California, Nevada, Arizona, New Mexico, Texas.

(a) Physical Processes

Sample Question 1

Discuss the relief, drainage and climate associated with a continental or subcontinental region of your choice.

Relief

1 three mountain ranges...

2 basins and plateaus...

3 Central and Sacramento Valleys ....

4 Great Basin, Death Valley, high plains ....

Drainage

5 Colorado River, Grand Canyon ....

6 five dams on Colorado (Hoover Dam)..

7 Colorado and Rio Grande ....

8 Great Basin ....

Climate

9 semi-arid or arid ....

10 annual precipitation less than 250mm ....

11 factors influencing climate ....

12 five distinctive climates ....

13 five distinctive climates ....

14 Death Valley ....

15 sunbelt...

(b) Primary Economic Activities

Sample Question 2

Outline the development of primary economic activities in a continental or subcontinental region of your choice.

Insert the following terms into the blanks below:

high plains / technologically advanced / arable farming / gold / citrus fruits / availability of water for irrigation / oil / labour is cheap / pivot irrigation / agri-companies / ranching / aerial crop-spraying / Central Valley Project / viticulture / salad crops / monocultural / cowboys / very large by European standards / truck crops / extensive farming / feedlots

Introduction

- The type of agriculture varies widely throughout the region due to key factors such as .... , topography, climate and accessibility to markets. **(1 SRP)**

- The industry is dominated by large farming units owned by large, powerful food companies called .... These companies own all the stages of production including processing, marketing and distribution, and the result is that agriculture in the region is capital-intensive, market-focused, highly industrialised and .... **(1 SRP)**

- Agriculture in the region can be divided into three key areas:

    - Intensive market gardening in California.

    - Pastoral, i.e. .... , in New Mexico and western Texas.

    - Intensive cereal production in eastern Texas.

- **Note:** Most of Nevada and Arizona are not conducive to agriculture due to the arid terrain and difficult topography. **(2 SRPs)**

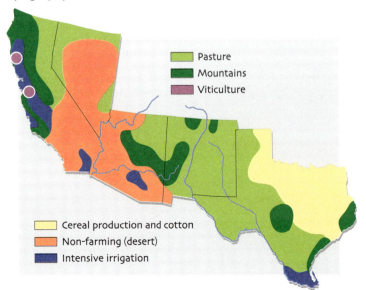

Pasture
Mountains
Viticulture

Cereal production and cotton
Non-farming (desert)
Intensive irrigation

Focus on arable farming

- …………………………………… is very intensive, focusing on the production of high-value crops such as:
  - Market gardening produce, e.g. citrus fruits and salad crops in California.
  - Cereal crops, predominantly wheat and maize, in eastern Texas. **(1 SRP)**
- Farms are ……………………………………………………………… . Most of them cover hundreds of hectares and farm …………………………………………… due to low-paid Mexican migrants. **(1 SRP)**
- Artificial irrigation, e.g. …………………………………………… , was developed in response to demands from a rapidly growing population. **(1 SRP)**

« Definition »

Pivot irrigtion is when crops are sprayed with water and fertilisers from a pipe raised on wheels which travels in a circle around the central point.

Arable farming in California

- High temperatures and rich soils make California the most influential agricultural state, producing over one-third of the fruit and salad crops and nearly 40 per cent of all ……………………………… in the USA. **(1 SRP)**

« Definition »

Truck crops are crops that are trucked across the USA on the interstate to other urban markets.

- Agriculture is technologically advanced, with …………………………………………… , pivot irrigation and mechanical harvesting. **(1 SRP)**
- The …………………………………………… , which comprises 50,000 square kilometres of irrigated land down through California, has the most intensive agricultural production in the world. **(1 SRP)**
- Examples of arable agriculture in the region:
  - ………………………………… crops, such as oranges, lemons and peaches are produced in Central Valley.
  - ……………………… or wine production is intensive in the Napa and Sonora valleys.
  - …………………………, such as tomatoes and lettuces, are grown in Sacramento Valley. **(1 SRP)**

Focus on pastoral farming: ranches and feedlots

- On the semi-arid lands of New Mexico and western Texas the agriculture is …………………………… , i.e. it is exclusively associated with ranching. Ranches are enormous farms run by small groups of workers called ………………… . **(1 SRP)**
- This type of farming is known as …………………………………………… , as low rainfall levels and sparse vegetation result in very low cattle stock per hectare. **(1 SRP)**

Extensive farming is when agricultural output is low per hectare but worker or cowboy output is high per hectare.

■ Cattle are born and reared on the .... and sold for fattening to .... owned by the agri-companies. Feedlots are where cattle are corralled and fed with concentrates and antibiotics to gain at least 1kg per day until they are big enough to be slaughtered. **(1 SRP)**

Mineral resources

■ The discovery and development of mineral resources has been a catalyst to the economic development of the region:

  ■ Texas = ... and gas.

  ■ Nevada basin = silver

  ■ California = ...

  ■ Copper, lead and zinc are also scattered throughout the region. **(1 SRP)**

(c) Secondary Economic Activities

Sample Question 3

Outline the development of manufacturing in a continental or subcontinental region of your choice.

Factors favouring industrial development

1 enterprising spirit/low population density . . . .

2 favourable geographical location/cheap labour . . . .

3 good communications network/strong military presence . . . .

Heavy industry

4 the Chemical Crescent . . . .

5 NASA . . . .

6 manufacturing military hardware . . . .

7 dual-use goods . . . .

Light industry

8 Silicon Valley/high-tech information technology . . . .

9 strong government support. . . . .

10 Stanford University . . . .

Problems with manufacturing in the valley

11 booms and recession/rapid obsolescence . . . .

Maquiladoras

12 twin cities . . . .

13 NAFTA. . . . .

14 factories both sides . . . .

15 advantages of Mexico. . . . .

16 reduced costs of production . . . .

(d) Tertiary Economic Activities

Sample Question 4

Outline the development of tourism and transport in a continental or subcontinental region of your choice.

Tourism

Areas of natural beauty

1 Bryce Canyon and Grand Canyon . . . .

2 Yosemite and Zion national parks . . . .

3 Carlsbad Caverns . . . .

Cities

4 San Francisco, Golden Gate Bridge. . . . .

5 Los Angeles, Hollywood . . . .

6 Las Vegas, gambling . . . .

Beach tourism

7 sun belt ....

8 San Diego, Santa Barbara...

Transport

9 car culture, American Dream ....

10 commuter culture ....

11 lack of public transport...

12 temperature inversion ....

Solutions to car pollution

13 tolling ....

14 car pooling ....

15 ports ....

16 airports in major cities ....

(e) Human Processes

Sample Question 5

Outline the development of population, culture and urbanisation in a continental or subcontinental region of your choice.

Insert the following terms into the blanks below:

racial discrimination / concentric circles / Latin America / ghettos / a natural increase / inward migration / diverse ethnic composition / origin is European / American Indians / commuter culture / distributed evenly throughout the region / slave trade / mired in poverty / American Dream / below the poverty line / undocumented or illegal immigrants / diseases, alcohol and a gun culture / refugees / urban sprawl / reservations / work ethic / White Anglo-Saxon Protestants / fuel costs / Los Angeles

Population

■ The region's population of 65 million is ....
due to the difficult topography, climatic variations, availability of water and other resources. **(1 SRP)**

- Population growth is higher than the national average due to:
  - Excess of births over deaths, i.e. ....
  - .... , particularly from Latin America. **(1 SRP)**

Culture

- The region has a .... , i.e. a multi-racial and multi-cultural society, with five distinct ethnic groups.

Whites/Anglos

- This group's .... They were attracted to the south-west region by the Californian gold rush and the discovery of silver in Nevada. **(1 SRP)**

- While the .... (WASPs) have been economically successful, dominating the commercial, financial and political sectors of the region, other white groups (e.g. the Irish, Italians and Poles) have had to struggle to achieve a similar level of socio-economic success. **(1 SRP)**

Native Americans

- Formerly known as .... , the majority live today in .... scattered throughout the south-west and have not as yet come to terms with the dominating white culture and lifestyle. **(1 SRP)**

- Their original way of life was destroyed by the greed of white migrants during the gold rush where they brought .... alien to the natives. **(1 SRP)**

African Americans

- They were brought to the US as part of the .... and they have experienced .... since they arrived. **(1 SRP)**

- They have been .... for generations due to discrimination experienced at the hands of the whites, and tensions led to riots in Los Angeles in 1965 and 1992. **(1 SRP)**

Hispanics

- This refers to the Spanish speakers who have emigrated from .... due to the poverty and lack of opportunity in their home country. They risk their lives crossing the heavily guarded US border in search of a better quality of life. **(1 SRP)**

- Through education, many aspire to the .... and have integrated into US society but most live .... , as opportunistic employers will exploit .... , i.e. their wages are low, with most working as agricultural labourers. **(1 SRP)**

Asians

- There are over thirty Asian cultural groups in the region and many came as .... from Korea and Vietnam. Due to prejudice in society they settled in .... as a refuge from discrimination, e.g. Chinatown in San Francisco. **(1 SRP)**

- Due to their .... and will to succeed, they have managed to integrate into US society and have been very successful in education and business. **(1 SRP)**

Urbanisation

- Around 80 per cent of the population in the south-west live in urban centres, most notably ……………………………… (population 15 million), San Francisco, San Diego, Houston and Dallas. Cities of the region are not as compact as European cities but instead they grow outwards in …………………………………………… . **(1 SRP)**

- As part of the 'American Dream' most Americans aspire to having their own car and this led to the construction of wide, grid-patterned streets resulting in …………………………………… . **(1 SRP)**

- Cheap land resulted in cities covering vast areas which have therefore become low-rise cities with a large ………………………………………… . **(1 SRP)**

- In recent years …………………………… have increased dramatically, and over time cities of the region may be forced to increase their population density, which will reduce the problem of urban sprawl. **(1 SRP)**

Chapter 21

Region 5(B): Continental or Subcontinental Region

India

Sample part A 20-mark question

Draw an outline map of India and name the following:

- a subcontinental region
- two urban centres
- two drainage features, e.g. rivers
- two major routeways
- a port
- a mountain range

« *Background Information* »

- India is located in south Asia between Burma and Pakistan. It is bordered by the Arabian Sea on the west and the Bay of Bengal on the east.

- India is the second most populous nation on earth with a population of 1.1 billion. Population increased by 21 per cent between 1991 and 2001. The present growth rate is 1.5 per cent. Seventy-two per cent live in rural areas.

- A tsunami in December 2004 caused by an earthquake under the Indian Ocean destroyed parts of the Andaman and Nicobar Islands, killing over 10,000.

(a) Physical Processes

Sample Question 1

Describe how any two of the following physical factors have influenced human activity in a continental or subcontinental region you have studied: relief, drainage, climate, soils.

Insert the following terms into the blanks below

Bay of Bengal / rain shadow / Western Ghats / leaching / prevailing winds / fold / irrigation / earthquakes / Ganges plain / densely populated / organic material / fertile alluvial soils / heavy monsoon rains / cattle and livestock rearing / Mumbai 2005 / soil erosion / hydroelectric power / western Himalayas / large-scale industrial development / Bangladesh / delta / deforestation / tourism / dry season / Indian Plate / Deccan Plateau / Thar Desert / Brahmaputra / to rise and cool / salt marshes / retreating monsoon / the Ganges / 80 per cent / Indus / heavy clay content / climatic contrasts / Hindu religion / high pressure / wet season / cotton, grains and rice / lava-covered areas

Relief

- India comprises four major physical regions:

1 The Himalayas

- The Himalayas are .... mountains formed over 50 million years ago when the .... collided with the Eurasian Plate. The Himalayas are growing by 1cm per year as a result of the ongoing collision between these plates. Consequently, ... occur in the mountains. **(1 SRP)**

Statistic

Mount Everest (8,850m), the world's highest mountain, is in the Himalayas.

■ The Indus, the Ganges and .... rivers all rise in the Himalayas. Meltwater from the glaciers in the Himalayas provides water for the rivers that flow into the .... **(1 SRP)**

■ There is very little primary economic activity due to steep gradients and altitude. However, tertiary economic activity in the form of .... is important to generate revenue, hiking in the summer and skiing in the winter. **(1 SRP)**

2 The Indus–Ganges–Brahmaputra Plain

■ These river valleys are one of the most .... parts of India as they contain .... , resulting in very rich farmland. They are also one of the most intensively farmed areas in the world. **(1 SRP)**

■ The river valleys receive .... and are home to an abundance of wildlife. **(1 SRP)**

3 The Thar Desert

■ The Thar Desert is a hot desert in western India made up of rocky soils, gravels, ... and some lakes, which gives rise to very hot summers and cold winters. **(1 SRP)**

■ There is little or no rain as the desert lies in the .... of the Bay of Bengal and the south-west monsoon. **(1 SRP)**

■ Primary economic activity is therefore limited to .... , but huge increases in population and animals have led to overgrazing and thus .... , resulting in a low standard of living. Most income now comes from tourism, e.g. desert safaris. **(1 SRP)**

4 The plateau mountains of southern India

■ The largest plateau in India is the triangular .... , comprising undulating terrain. The plateau has a dry season lasting between six and nine months and therefore vegetation is limited to scrub and deciduous broadleaved trees. **(1 SRP)**

■ On the western edge of the plateau are the .... , which fall to a narrow coastal plain that borders the Arabian Sea. On the eastern side the Eastern Ghats descend to a wider coastal plain bordered by the Bay of Bengal. **(1 SRP)**

Drainage

■ India has three major rivers: .... , the Indus and the Brahmaputra. These three rivers provide irrigation water for primary economic activity during the dry season. **(1 SRP)**

■ They are also used for transport and to generate .... for the ever-expanding manufacturing sector. Bhakra Dam on the Sutlej River is one of the highest dams in the world. **(1 SRP)**

■ The dry region of Punjab, which is shared by India and Pakistan, depends on the Indus River for vital .... water. The tributaries of the Indus are shared by India and Pakistan. **(1 SRP)**

■ The Ganges is the most important river, rising in the .... , where it gets its water from melting glaciers and snow. It flows for 2,400km to its mouth at the .... , draining almost a million square kilometres of fertile farmland so essential for the growing of rice, potatoes and wheat. **(1 SRP)**

- The river is worshipped in the ………………………………… and Hindus believe that bathing in the river washes away sins and guarantees salvation. **(1 SRP)**

- The Ganges is also good for rafting, attracting many tourists every year, but ……………………………… …………………………………………… along its banks has resulted in pollution of the river, which threatens the tourist industry. **(1 SRP)**

- The Brahmaputra rises in south-west Tibet and flows for 2,900km through the Himalayas and on into the Assam Valley before flowing into …………………… , where it joins with the Ganges to form the world's largest ………… . **(1 SRP)**

- Due to population increase and the need for more agricultural land, there is …………………………… along its banks, which has resulted in more flooding, soil erosion and siltation. However, the flooding provides alluvium so vital for agriculture in India. **(1 SRP)**

Climate

- India is a nation of ………………………………… . Climates range from deserts in the west to vast tracts of rainforests and glaciers in the snow-capped Himalayas. **(1 SRP)**

- India has four seasons: winter, which occurs in January and February, summer between March and May, the monsoon period from June to September, and the period after the monsoon from October to December. Sometimes these seasons are reduced to two, the ………………………… from mid June to September and the …………………………… from October to June. **(1 SRP)**

- The word 'monsoon' comes from the Arabic word for season. The monsoon is a seasonal change in the direction of the ………………………………… , which are determined by temperature differences between oceans and continents. Monsoons blow from the land to the sea in winter and from the sea towards the land in summer. **(1 SRP)**

- The wet monsoon extends from mid June to September. During this time the ……………………………… to the west and central India heat up, forming low pressure. Rain-bearing winds travel in from the Indian Ocean, blowing in a south-westerly direction towards the Himalayas. **(1 SRP)**

- On reaching the southernmost point of India, the wet monsoon breaks up into sections – the Arabian Sea section of the south-west monsoon and the Bay of Bengal section of the south-west monsoon. The Arabian section hits the Western Ghats, forcing the winds …………………………… resulting in heavy rainfall. **(1 SRP)**

- The Bay of Bengal section flows over the Bay of Bengal in a north-easterly direction, picking up moisture from the Bay of Bengal. Consequently, as it travels across the Indus Gangetic Plain rainfall amounts are large. **(1 SRP)**

- The dry monsoon extends from October to June. During September India starts to cool, resulting in …………………………… over India, while the Indian Ocean retains its heat. The cold winds over India blow in a north-easterly direction towards the Indian Ocean, creating the north-easterly monsoon or the ……………………………………… . **(1 SRP)**

- The monsoons account for …………………… of India's rainfall and crops such as …………………… …………… depend on the monsoons. A delay can have huge implications for the Indian economy, as witnessed during the 1990s. **(1 SRP)**

- The rains can also result in flooding, as happened in ……………………………… , with devastating consequences. Seedlings are washed away, resulting in food shortages. **(1 SRP)**

Soils

- The soils of India can be divided into four different types:

1 Alluvial soils

- Alluvial Soils are found in the valleys of the Ganges, ... and Brahmaputra. **(1 SRP)**
- These fertile soils are deposited when rivers flood their banks. They cover almost 40 per cent of India. **(1 SRP)**

2 Laterites

- Laterites are formed due to .... as a result of the heavy monsoon rains. They are mainly found in the north-east and the Western and Eastern Ghats. **(1 SRP)**
- They are red in colour but different from the red soils, as they are very acidic. **(1 SRP)**

3 Black soils

- Black soils have a .... so they retain moisture and are used for dry farming and the growing of cotton. **(1 SRP)**
- They are found in .... such as the Deccan Plateau and are underlain by the extrusive igneous rock, basalt. **(1 SRP)**

4 Red soils

- Red soils mainly occur in the eastern part of India. They are not very fertile as they do not contain sufficient .... to grow crops. **(1 SRP)**

(b) Primary Economic Activities

Sample Question 2

Examine the development of primary economic activities in a continental or subcontinental region you have studied.

Agriculture

1 worth 18 per cent of GDP ....

2 farms are small family plots ....

3 over-dependent on monsoons ....

4 half land devoted to arable..

5 rice...

6 Hindu religion ....

Government investment

7 land reform ....

8 improvements in rural infrastructure ....

9 deforrestation ....

10 20 per cent of India now forested..

Green revolution

11 double cropping...

12 high-yielding strains ....

13 rapid population increase ....

14 major producer of commercial crops ....

15 fishing..

(c) Secondary Economic Activities

Sample Question 3

Examine the development of manufacturing in a continental or subcontinental region you have studied.

Introduction

1 industry accounts for 29.4 per cent of GDP...

2 underdeveloped prior to independence ....

3 agriculture is subsistent ....

4 industry to increase GDP ....

Natural resources

5 coal to generate electric power..

6 vast reserves of iron ore for heavy industry...

7 oil wells ....

8 cirques in Himalayas used as reservoirs ....

Industry

9 four major zones..

10 food processing ....

11 textiles is the largest industry ....

12 government support for cottage industry..

13 multinational companies..

14 fast-growing high-tech centres..

15 third biggest economic power by 2035 ....

(d) Tertiary Economic Activities

Sample Question 4

Assess the development services, tourism and transport in a continental or subcontinental region you have studied.

Services

1 underdeveloped in rural areas...

2 black economy ....

3 all services state-owned..

Transport

4 Asia's largest rail network with 63,000km of tracks...................................

5 railways state-owned ....

6 road transport affected by monsoons...

7 large network of inland waterways ....

8 airline provider is Air india..

Tourism

9 spiritual significance of the Ganges..

10 7,500km of coastline ....

11 Himalayas attracts mountain climbers ....

12 wonderful beaches and tropical paradises ....

13 safaris ....

14   temples such as the Taj Mahal . . . .

15   tea plantations. . . . .

(e) Human Processes

Sample Question 5

Outline the development of human processes in a continental or subcontinental region you have studied.

Insert the following terms into the blanks below:

> Sikhism / fertile alluvial valleys / shanty towns / family planning / 800 languages / India / darker-skinned Dravidians / pushed / English / castes / symbol of life / beef / gift from the gods / missionaries / rioting / fair-skinned Aryans / rural areas into urban areas / Mumbai and Kolkata / rural migrants / pulled / services / colonial / overcrowding / specialist skills / Sunnite / Hindus / dire poverty / social institution / Pakistan

Population and culture

- Most Indians are Caucasian, belonging to two subdivisions: the . . . . in the north who make up 72 per cent of the population and the . . . . of the south who make up 25 per cent of the population. The family is a very strong . . . ., under the authority of the older male. Social life revolves around family events. **(1 SRP)**

- Most of the population lives in the . . . . of the Brahmaputra, Indus and Ganges. Agriculture is unable to feed the rapidly expanding numbers and consequently there is migration from . . . . The arrival of migrants into the poor suburbs called . . . . does not increase their standard of living as they are unable to find jobs because they lack the resources and skills required. **(1 SRP)**

- . . . . is available in rural areas. However, due to a lack of education and the need to have children to work the land, family planning has not been a success. **(1 SRP)**

- India has more than . . . . and dialects but Hindi is the national language, spoken by 41 per cent of the population. . . . . is also an official language, alongside fourteen other official languages which include Bengali and Urdu. **(1 SRP)**

- India has many religions but the majority (over 80 per cent) of the population are . . . . Hinduism is the dominant religion, which divides people into . . . . or social classes based on birth. **(1 SRP)**

- In Hinduism the cow is revered as the source of food and . . . . and consequently may never be killed. It is a protected animal in Hinduism. Most Indians do not eat . . . . Most families have at least one cow. Hindus view the cow as a . . . . to the human race. **(1 SRP)**

- The Buddhists inhabit the south of India. This religion developed in the sixth century BC. Approximately 11 per cent of the Indian population are Muslims, with most belonging to the .... branch. Islam, the Muslim faith, does not operate a caste system. **(1 SRP)**

- Between 2 and 3 per cent are Christians. Fifteen per cent of the Christians are Thomas Christians who trace their roots to a church they believe was founded in AD52 by the apostle Thomas. Most others belong to churches founded by .... and over half the Christians are Roman Catholic. **(1 SRP)**

- .... began in the sixteenth century to unite Hindus and Muslims. Less than 2 per cent of Indians belong to this faith. It is centred in Punjab in north-west India. **(1 SRP)**

- Religious tensions grew in India following independence in 1947 when two states were formed: .... , which was mainly Hindu, and .... , which was predominantly Muslim. This resulted in mass migration of millions of people. Muslims who had lived in India migrated to Pakistan and Hindu followers from Pakistan to India. There has been .... between the two rival religions. **(1 SRP)**

Urbanisation

- The rate of urbanisation in India is increasing for three reasons.
  - The .... influence: the British developed cities as centres of administration which attracted rural migrants looking for work. Such cities include .... **(1 SRP)**
  - Urban centres became the focal points for investment. Infrastructural improvements attracted more and more .... in search of work. **(1 SRP)**
  - Push and pull factors were also important. People were .... off their land due to agricultural improvements and were .... into urban centres by the prospect of a better lifestyle. **(1 SRP)**

Key urban areas

- New Delhi in the north: 12 million.
- Kolkata in the north: 13 million.
- Chennai on the south-east coast: 7 million.
- Bangalore on the south-east coast: 6 million.
- Mumbai (Bombay) on the west coast: 19 million.

(1 SRP)

- Like any major European city, Indian cities have many problems:
  - Due to .... , many people suffer from poor health.
  - Unemployment is huge, as many migrants lack the .... required for industry.
  - Many live in .... and consequently crime is widespread.
  - There is little money available to invest in .... **(2 SRPs)**

Chapter 22

The Types and Complexities of Regions

Note: The following case studies are to be covered, but only 15 SRPs are needed for each answer.

Case study 1: Ireland, north and south	Interaction of economic, political and cultural activities
Case study 2: Spain (the Basques)	(i) The importance of culture in defining a region (ii) Cultural diversity within a country
Case study 3: The European Union	(i) Impact of expansion on Ireland (ii) The future of the European Union (iii) Political and socio-economic development and expansion over time
Case study 4: Cool temperate oceanic	Focus on a climatic region
Case study 5: East/West German reunification	Impact of a changing political boundary on cultural groups
Case study 6: The Gaeltacht in Ireland	A language boundary that has changed over time
Case study 7: Dublin/Paris	(a) Urban growth and the expansion of a city boundary in Ireland (b) Urban growth and the expansion of a city boundary in Europe
Case study 8: Nord-Pas-de-Calais (France)	A region that has suffered from industrial decline

(a) Case Study 1: Ireland, North and South

Sample Question

Examine the interaction of economic, political and cultural activities in a country you have studied.

« Background Information »

- The Government of Ireland Act, 1921 divided the island of Ireland into two political regions:
  1 The Republic of Ireland, consisting of twenty-six counties, became an independent sovereign state.
  2 Northern Ireland, consisting of six counties, remained part of the UK.

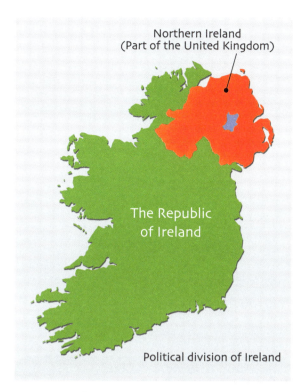

Northern Ireland
(Part of the United Kingdom)

The Republic
of Ireland

Political division of Ireland

Economic interaction

1 deteriorated during the Troubles . . . .

Focus on Republic of Ireland

2 subsistence and self-sufficiency . . . .

3 free trade and IDA . . . .

Focus on Northern Ireland

4 well developed/UK investment . . . .

5 Troubles . . . .

6 intimidating border security posts . . . .

7 improved after Good Friday Agreement . . . .

Political interaction

8 deteriorated after 1921 . . . .

9 neutrality versus involvement in Second World War . . . .

10 Troubles strained relations . . . .

11 Good Friday Agreement and referendum . . . .

12 'strands' and North–South Ministerial Council . . . .

Cultural interaction

(b) Case Study 2: Spain (i)

Sample Question 1: the Basques

Assess the importance of culture in defining a region that you have studied.

Insert the following terms into the blanks below:

Indo-European / cultural affairs / cuisine / ETA / Bilbao / 5,000 years / matadors / unique cultural identity / bombing campaigns and assassinations / rugged mountainous terrain / blood-type / peaceful co-existence / Euskera / half a million / oldest living languages / banned / ikastolas / co-official / imprisoned / Pyrenees / strategic development plan / autonomy / improved relations / parliament / Biscay / bull races / Euskadi / cattle herders / genetic differences / natural mineral resources / Basque identity / traditional heavy industry / political independence / science and technology / Romans / Pamplona

Background

■ The Basque country is a region that covers an area of over 20,000 square kilometres located next to the western end of the . . . . , along the coast of the Bay of . . . . It consists of seven districts, three of which are in France and four of which are in Spain. **(1 SRP)**

■ Three of the Spanish districts are grouped together to form one political unit called . . . . The focal point of this region is the city of . . . . (population approximately two million), which is well known for demanding . . . . **(1 SRP)**

■ The Basques have lived in the area for about . . . . and have developed their own unique cultural identity. They settled in the region long before the Celtic tribes moved to Ireland and Scotland and long before the . . . . came to Spain in 180BC . The Romans failed to conquer them due to their location in the . . . . of the Pyrenees. **(1 SRP)**

■ Their geographic isolation and therefore separation from outside influences has led to a . . . . different to that of their neighbours, i.e. the French and Spanish. The Basques have lighter complexions, than the French or Spanish, owing to . . . . , and have more genes associated with some Irish and Welsh people. Even their . . . . is different to that of other European cultural groups, as they have by far the highest percentage of blood group 'O' Rhesus-negative in Europe. **(1 SRP)**

Language

- Their language, ... , differs from all other European languages. The survival of the language has been a key factor in the survival of this distinctive cultural region. **(1 SRP)**

- The language is spoken as their first language by about .... Basques. It is one of the .... and is not related to any other language in Europe, i.e. it does not stem from the .... language base. **(1 SRP)**

- During the reign of the Spanish dictator Franco the Euskera language was .... and secret schools called .... were set up to teach the language to school-going students in defiance of his policy. Nowadays the language stands as a .... language with Spanish. **(1 SRP)**

Political conflict

- Tensions arose in the past when the Spanish government under General Franco, a fascist dictator, banned all expressions of .... , most notably the language, and .... any Basque nationalists who spoke out against the ban. **(1 SRP)**

- One group to react to the government's repression was the extreme nationalist group .... This group is responsible for the deaths of over 800 people due to its .... in its drive to gain independence. **(1 SRP)**

- In return for .... , the Spanish government granted the region a high level of .... in 1979. This had the desired effect in that it weakened support for ETA. There has been a ceasefire since March 2006. It is hoped that this will be permanent and result in .... between the Basques and the Spanish. **(1 SRP)**

- The Basques have been granted their own .... in Bilbao. It oversees local government affairs in areas such as .... , education, economic development and the environment. **(1 SRP)**

Economy

- Traditionally the Basques were .... and farmers, with a history that stretches back to the Neolithic period. Despite the Basque region consisting of only 6 per cent of the Spanish population, its .... led to the development of heavy industries such as steel and shipbuilding, which were of major economic importance to Spain. **(1 SRP)**

- In modern times there has been a decline in .... and through its .... the region now focuses on the development of numerous businesses in the areas of .... **(1 SRP)**

Conclusion

- Nowadays Basque identity is widely celebrated. Festivals have galvanised their unique culture and the city of .... has become world-famous for its .... through the streets. This involves six bulls which are allowed to chase people through the streets before being killed by .... in bullfights later that evening. **(1 SRP)**

- Even Basque .... , focused on seafood, has become more popular through Spain, and all major cities have Basque restaurants. **(1 SRP)**

(c) Case Study 2: Spain (ii)

Sample Question 2

Examine how cultural diversity can exist within a country that you have studied.

Background

1   autonomy given to Basques and Catalans...

2   local government powers ....

3   co-official languages ....

Basques

4   demanding political independence...

5   Bilbao, 2 million people ....

6   5,000 years..

7   Euskera not Indo-European ....

8   symbols of Basque identity banned..

9   ETA...

10 peaceful co-existence ....

11 ceasefire..

12 strategic regional development plan ....

Catalonia

13 very prosperous economy. . . . .

14 40 per cent of Spanish exports . . . .

15 self-sufficient . . . .

(d) Case Study 3: European Union (i)

Sample Question 1

Examine the impact of European Union expansion on Ireland.

Insert the following terms into the blanks below:

brain drain / Objective 1 status / sovereignty / foreign direct investment (FDI) / veto / depleted fish stocks / ERDF / structural change / Central and Eastern European Countries / Commission / underdeveloped / funding / export-driven economy / mass overfishing / decrease in overall influence / different political agendas / comparative advantage / new sources of raw materials / educated young workforce / expansionist policy / skilled, educated and could speak English / below their skill level / supranational / half a billion people / remittance / Western / domestic market / open free-market economy / total allowable catch / Iraq / integration / 2.2 per cent / Lisbon Treaty / centralised European defence strategy / neutrality / qualified majority voting / Eastern

Introduction

■ The future socio-economic goals of the EU's . . . . are to create an . . . . within the world's largest and most powerful trading block and to improve the lives of EU citizens through social and regional policies. This continued expansion impacts Ireland in the following ways:

Socio-economic impact

■ The expansion of the European Union (EU) in 1986 (i.e. the integration of Spain and Portugal) led to changes in the Common Fisheries Policy which resulted in a reduction in the . . . . allocated to Irish fishermen. **(1 SRP)**

■ This also led to . . . . , particularly by Spanish and Portuguese fishing fleets, in Irish territorial waters and has significantly . . . . , most notably in the Celtic Sea. **(1 SRP)**

■ The most significant socio-economic changes to Ireland as a result of EU expansion were due to the integration of the ten new member states known as the CEECs (.. ....) in 2004. This integration of the CEECs had a much greater impact on existing member states such as Ireland because their economies were much more .... **(1 SRP)**

■ A large amount of funding from the annual EU budget under the .... was originally used to improve the former peripheral .... regions such as the Border, Midlands and West region of Ireland. There has been a change of direction in income support payments and .... , which have now been transferred to the CEECs to help their underdeveloped economies. **(1 SRP)**

■ The new CEECs can provide .... , such as coal and salt from Poland. **(1 SRP)**

■ The most valuable resource to Ireland has been the immigration of an .... in our economy, as we were under-populated during the Celtic Tiger years and needed a fresh supply of young workers to fill job vacancies and to help drive our economy. At the height of the Celtic Tiger period, immigrants from Eastern European made up .... of the total working population in Ireland. **Note**: an increased labour force raises output. **(1 SRP)**

■ Most of the immigrants from Eastern Europe who arrived in Ireland since 2004 were .... , and this was a great bonus to the Irish economy. Many did, however, take jobs that were .... This led to a .... from the guest countries. **(1 SRP)**

■ The integration of new member states is important for Ireland as the now .... European Union has a market of .... This is important for Ireland as our .... is very small and other EU nations will become the market for our .... , thus increasing trade volumes. **(1 SRP)**

■ Some money earned in Ireland does leave the country through .... back to the donor country, i.e. Eastern European countries. This involves the transfer of money by a foreign worker to his or her home country. **(1 SRP)**

■ The expansion of the EU into Eastern Europe has increased Ireland's competition for attracting .... , i.e. multinational companies. The increased cost of doing business in Ireland during the Celtic Tiger boom years led to MNCs leaving Ireland for Eastern Europe, as their costs of doing business were much lower, i.e. we began to lose our .... Dell transferred a large manufacturing plant from Limerick to Lodz in Poland. **(1 SRP)**

Political impact

The future political goals of the EU involve the increased .... of all EU states and this impacts Ireland in the following ways:

■ As with all other member states, Ireland will have a continued .... within the Union as more members join, i.e. political power has to be shared out with the new member states. **(1 SRP)**

■ Only Ireland's rejection of the first Lisbon Treaty led to changes which have ensured that all member states will still have a permanent seat on the .... **(1 SRP)**

- The development of political union within the EU was to be underpinned by the 'European Constitution' and the .... Their aim is to seek .... within the Union, to exert more influence as one political unit and to allow for a more efficient running of the Union, but the result will be a loss of .... for individual countries such as Ireland. **(1 SRP)**

- A .... , i.e. a European rapid-reaction military army, would result in the loss of decision-making power of individual national governments on defence issues. Ireland, for instance, would eventually have to forgo its strategy of .... , impacting on its sovereignty. **(1 SRP)**

« Definition »

Sovereignty is the ability of a country to make decisions on issues which affect it, i.e. to rule itself on policies such as the defence of the country.

- Ireland will no longer have a .... on certain aspects of EU policy and the extension of .... will only serve to further reduce decision-making power. **(1 SRP)**

« Definition »

Qualified majority voting is a means of weighting votes where a certain number of votes above the majority are needed for a motion to be passed.

Conclusion

- Problems are created by the changes to the political structures, and there are deep divisions between member states on the issue of control of the balance of political power between large and small states:
  - There is a fear that more long-standing EU states will have less impact on the EU as it expands, and that there will be a shift of the EU centre of control from .... to .... Europe. **(1 SRP)**
  - Member states have .... , especially in relation to a centralised European defence strategy, which might compromise the neutrality of countries such as Ireland. The .... war was an example of how countries in the EU are divided on military issues. **(1 SRP)**

(e) Case Study 3: European Union (ii)

« Background Information »

- The EU has been transformed from the six-member economic community of 1957 to a 27-member political and socio-economic 'supranational union' of nearly half a billion people..

- Its future goals are to improve the economic, social and political future of the union.

  - Economic function: to create an open free-market economy and to become the world's largest and most powerful trading bloc.

  - Social function: to improve the lives of its people, particularly those in disadvantaged regions, through its social and regional policies.

  - Political function: to create a peaceful society in a continent known for its history of political conflict.

Sample Question 2

Examine the future of the European Union in relation to economic, political and sovereignty issues.

Future of economic union

1 integration of Eastern Europe ....

2 economic benefits of the EU ....

Benefits of EU expansion

3 new sources of raw materials/educated young workers ....

4 low cost of production/higher growth rates...

Economic drawbacks of EU expansion

5 financial impact..

6 economic activities underdeveloped...

7 new 'convergence' states will soak funds ....

Future of political union

8 European constitution and Lisbon Treaty ....

9 aims (three)..

10 president/qualified majority voting...

11 controlling balance of power/different political agendas ....

Future of sovereignty

12 EU given more power . . . .

13 foreign and security policy . . . .

14 compromise Ireland's neutrality . . . .

15 reforms of institutions/veto . . . .

16 qualified majority voting . . . .

(f) Case Study 3: European Union (iii)

《 *Background Information* 》

- Decisions in the EU are made by:
    1 The European Council: This consists of the first ministers of each member state, who are the final decision-makers on Union policy.
    2 The European Commission: This is the equivalent of a national civil service at European level.
    3 The European Parliament: This consists of elected MEPs from each country (736 in total).

Sample Question 3

Assess how the boundary of a political and socio-economic region you have studied has developed and expanded over time.

Background

1 one of the world's greatest success stories . . . .

Political developments

2 devastated after World War II . . . .

3 European coal and steel community . . . .

4 Treaty of Rome, 1957 . . . .

5 currently 27 members . . . .

6 1957: 6 members/1973: 9 members . . . .

7 1981: 10 members/1986: 12 members/1990: German reunification . . . .

8 1995: 15 members/2004: 25 members/2007: 27 members . . . .

9 Eastern enlargement difficult . . . .

10 treaties deepened political union. . . . .

11 Maastricht/Amsterdam/Nice . . . .

Socio-economic developments

12 initial motivation for EU was economic . . . .

13 Common Market. . . . .

14 Eurotom. . . . .

15 1962: Common Agricultural Policy . . . .

16 1974: Regional Development Fund (ERDF) . . . .

17 1987: Single European Act . . . .

18 Maastricht Treaty . . . .

19 Amsterdam Treaty/euro . . . .

(g) Case Study 4: Cool Temperate Oceanic

Sample Question

Examine, with the aid of a case study, a climatic region which you have studied.

Insert the following terms into the blanks below:

> prevailing wind / warm / North Atlantic Current / colder in winter / distance from the ocean / diurnal winter temperatures / latitude / across political boundaries / throughout the year / relief rainfall / cold / aspect / clouds / high pressure / warm in summer / maritime / frontal or cyclonic rainfall / 500mm to 3,000mm per annum / altitude / North Atlantic Current

Introduction

- A cool temperate oceanic, or . . . . , climate is to be found on the west coast of continents between 40 degrees and 60 degrees north and south of the equator, e.g. north-west Europe and the west coast of the USA. **(1 SRP)**
- The cool temperate oceanic climate of north-west Europe stretches . . . . from the north-west of Portugal to northern Norway. **(1 SRP)**

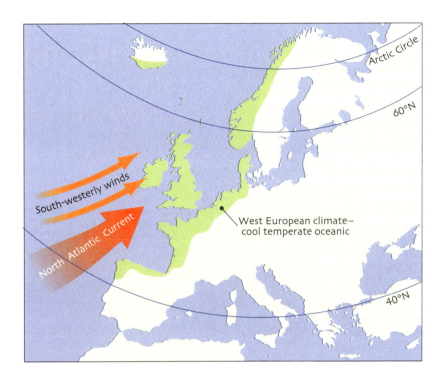

Characteristics of the climate

Temperature

- Temperatures are .... , averaging 15–17°C. Averages increase slightly from north to south and further inland from the Atlantic Ocean. **(1 SRP)**

- Daytime temperatures can reach 25°C on a sunny day with .... giving cloudless skies. **(1 SRP)**

- Temperatures are .... but still fairly mild, averaging 4–5°C in January. **(1 SRP)**

- Average .... rarely drop below freezing due to the influence of the North Atlantic Current. **(1 SRP)**

- The warm .... regulates the temperature range in north-west Europe, so that the difference between the average highest temperature and the average lowest temperature annually is small, at only 11°C. **(1 SRP)**

Precipitation

- Precipitation is predominantly in the form of rain that falls .... , with a winter maximum. **(1 SRP)**

- Total rainfall can range from .... depending on altitude, latitude and distance from the ocean. **(1 SRP)**

- Two types of rainfall occur:

  1 Relief rainfall in upland areas.

  2 Frontal (cyclonic) rainfall created by a low-pressure belt. **(1 SRP)**

- .... occurs when moisture-laden south-westerly winds from the Atlantic are forced to rise over mountains, where they cool and condense to form .... and then fall as rain. **(1 SRP)**

- .... occurs when .... air pushes .... air up, where it cools and condenses into clouds and falls as heavy rain. **(1 SRP)**

Factors influencing the climate

1 .... : This is a mild moisture-laden south-westerly wind from the Atlantic Ocean, creating low pressure, which brings rain throughout the year.

« Definition »

The **prevailing wind** is the wind that blows most often in a given area.

---

2 .... : Temperatures are much warmer at sea level as they decrease by approximately one degree for every 100m climbed above sea level.

3 .... : The warm ocean regulates the temperature range, and as a result the range increases with distance from the sea.

4 .... : This is a warm current that raises temperatures along the west coast of Europe and keeps Atlantic ports ice-free all year round.

5 .... : South-facing slopes have higher temperatures as they receive more sunlight.

6 .... : The west coast of Europe experiences temperate conditions due to its mid-latitude location, 40–60° north of the equator.

(3 SRPs)

(h) Case Study 5: East/West German Reunification

Sample Question

Examine the impact of a changing political boundary on cultural groups.

Communist East Germany GDR

Note: The city of Berlin although located in the former East Germany was itself divided between East and West

Capitalist West Germany FRG

The political division of Germany before reunification

« Background Information »

- The fall of the Berlin Wall and the Iron Curtain in 1989 led to *Deutsche Einheit* (German unity) on 3 October 1990 between the capitalist West (FRG) and communist East (GDR).

- After *die Wende* (the turning point, i.e. unification) in 1990 it was clear that forty years of separate national identities had created many differences economically, socially and culturally between the two groups.

Economic effects of reunification

1 East German state-owned companies closed. . . . .

2 large sums of money injected . . . .

3 modernising infrastructure . . . .

4 new job opportunities . . . .

5 services declined in the former West . . . .

Social effects of reunification

6 social problems/unemployment . . . .

7 mass migration to the former West/brain drain . . . .

8 pressure on housing sector/resentment of immigrants . . . .

9 fabric of society broken in the East . . . .

Cultural effects of reunification

10 West Germans distrusted . . . .

11 growth of racism . . . .

12 political dissatisfaction in the East . . . .

13 nostalgia for the East of older generations . . . .

14 West consider the East ungrateful . . . .

15 successful integration in Berlin . . . .

(i) Case Study 6: The Gaeltacht

Sample Question

Examine with the aid of a case study how the boundary of a language region can change over time.

Insert the following terms into the blanks below:

compulsory / Raidió na Gaeltachta / fluently / western seaboard / gaelscoileanna / National Development Plan / economically stagnant / English / poverty / business / extinct / national identity / daily basis / two million people / Gaeltacht area / Údarás na Gaeltachta / emigrate / TG4 / increased / Leinster / 544,000 / rural migrants / decrease / official language / small and isolated areas

Introduction

- Gaeltacht areas are places in Ireland where the Irish language is spoken on a .... (**1 SRP**)

- According to the 1851 census nearly .... were deemed to be Irish speakers. (**1 SRP**)

- Large areas of the .... and the south coast kept Irish as their spoken language. (**1 SRP**)

- From 1851 to 1926 the number of Irish speakers fell to ....(**1 SRP**)

Reasons for the decline of the language

- The west of Ireland was .... , and therefore people were forced to ...., so learning the language of the country you were emigrating to (USA or UK) made getting employment easier.

- National schools began to teach through .... after 1831.

- Irish became associated with .... and was only spoken by the poorer classes.

- English became known as the language of .... , politics and trade and this undermined the Irish language. (**2 SRPs**)

- The decline of the language was so rapid that people felt that it would be .... by the beginning of this century. (**1 SRP**)

- On gaining independence from Britain the government committed itself to supporting the Irish language as an essential part of our .... (**1 SRP**)

Government strategies for saving the language

- Irish became the .... of the state and was made .... in the school syllabus.

- An official .... was set up in 1929 and was strongly supported by the government.

- A government agency called .... was set up in 1980 to promote the economic, social and cultural development of Gaeltacht areas.

- The government invested in .... to promote education through Irish.

- The government set up .... and invested nearly £30 million in setting up the TV station .... to promote the language.

- All these measures were aimed at reducing the dominance of the English language in Ireland. (**2 SRPs**)

Successes and failures of government intervention

- At one level the measures put in place to support the Irish language were successful as the number of people who claim to be able to speak Irish has .... dramatically from just under 600,000 in 1946 to over 1.5 million in the last census. (**1 SRP**)

- The area with the most dramatic increase is .... , which would traditionally have been a predominantly English-speaking province. Perhaps this is due to the influx of .... to the greater Dublin area (west-to-east migration). **(1 SRP)**

- English is still by far the dominant language in Ireland and although many Irish people claim to be able to speak Irish, very few can speak it .... **(1 SRP)**

- There has been a dramatic .... in the boundary of the Gaeltacht and compared to 1926 the present Gaeltacht has been reduced to .... on the western seaboard. **(1 SRP)**

- Nevertheless the Irish government is committed to the survival of the Irish language and is investing around €500 million under the current .... (2007–13). **(1 SRP)**

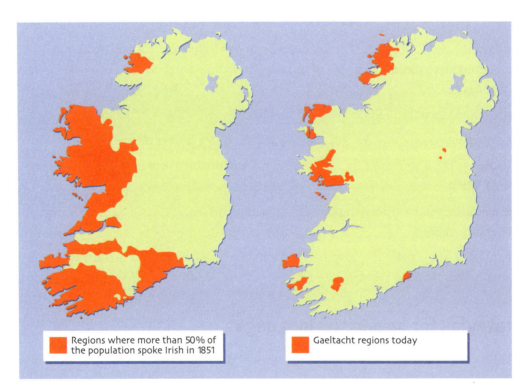

Regions where more than 50% of the population spoke Irish in 1851

Gaeltacht regions today

(j) Case Study 7(a): Dublin

Sample Question 1

Examine, with the aid of a case study, how a nodal, urban or city region may grow and expand over time.

Insert the following terms into the blanks below:

overspill towns / hubs / public transport network / greater Dublin area / high cost of land / primate city / peripheral areas / urban sprawl / centralisation of government departments / relocation / three new county councils / apartment complexes / strategic road corridors / provide essential services / expanded rapidly since the 1960s / focus of routeways / high cost of living / commuter culture / employment / reorganisation of the local authority structure / dispersal / nodal point / manageable-sized areas / gateways / Celtic Tiger era

Introduction

- Ireland's urban system is dominated by Dublin which is a .... , consisting of over one-third of the country's population. **(1 SRP)**

« *Definition* »

A **primate city** is a city which is more than twice the size of the next biggest city in that country.

- Dublin has .... , most notably in the population explosion during the Celtic Tiger era of the early 1990s to 2008. **(1 SRP)**
- The influence of the .... (GDA) has increased significantly to create an urban region that stretches over 100km from the city centre. **(1 SRP)**
- Factors which have contributed to the expansion of Dublin:

  - It is a .... and consequently a .... for all road, rail and port traffic.

  - The city became the financial, commercial, services and industrial centre of Ireland, providing much ....

  - The .... and residential property in the city forced people to look for houses or apartments outside the city centre.

  - Planning restrictions on high-rise residential developments led to ....

  - Government policy led to the .... , providing jobs in administration in the city.

  - The lack of an efficient .... led to a car commuter culture, creating urban sprawl along the main strategic road corridors out of the city. **(3 SRPs)**

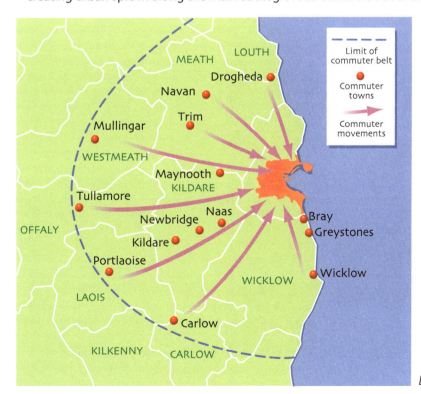

Dublin's commuter belt

Stages in the growth of Dublin city

- During the 1960s there was a significant period of growth that resulted in the .... of inner city populations to large new housing estates and .... outside the city centre, e.g. Ballymun, stretching up to 8km from the city centre. **(1 SRP)**

- Continued economic growth during the 1970s increased Dublin's population. Following this, the government decided to set up three .... (Blanchardstown, Tallaght and Clondalkin), which expanded the city to 15km beyond the city centre. **(1 SRP)**

- During the .... the competition for land and .... forced people to look for homes up to 100km from the city centre in towns such as Gorey, Portlaoise and Dundalk. This has led to a .... where many people living in the greater Dublin area have no choice but to travel long distances to and from work. **(1 SRP)**

Government solutions to rapid urban growth

1 Reform of local administration

- The exponential growth of the Dublin region has necessitated the ....
.... **(1 SRP)**

- Extreme pressure was put on the old county council structure by the rapidly increasing population of the suburbs, where the councils struggled to .... , e.g. domestic waste disposal. **(1 SRP)**

- The result was the formation of .... : Fingal, South Dublin and Dún Laoghaire–Rathdown. These more .... led to more effective administration. **(1 SRP)**

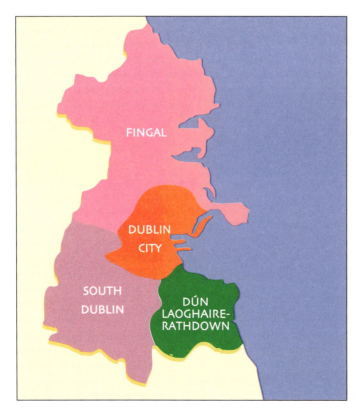

Local government in Dublin

2 Implementation of the National Spatial Strategy

■ The National Spatial Strategy was devised in 2002 to reduce Dublin's dominance and to encourage ……………… of the population away from the greater Dublin area. **(1 SRP)**

■ It included the large-scale development of the following:

  ■ Other large urban centres called ………………… , e.g. Cork, to counteract the dominance of Dublin.

  ■ Smaller urban centres called ………… that help to disperse development away from the gateways, e.g. Mallow for Cork city and Tuam for Galway city.

  ■ …………………………………………………whose function it is to provide efficient links, i.e. motorways, between gateways, hubs and Dublin. **(1 SRP)**

National Spatial Strategy 2002

3 Decentralisation

The government decentralised its departments to more …………………………………… outside the greater Dublin area. For example, the Department of Agriculture, Fisheries and Food moved to Clonakilty in west Cork. **(1 SRP)**

(k) Case Study 7(b): Paris

Sample Question 2

Examine, with the aid of a European case study, how a nodal, urban or city region may grow and expand over time.

Introduction

1 primate city and nodal point ....

Factors contributing to the expansion of Paris

2 focus of routeways/capital/high cost of land ....

3 planning restrictions/centralisation policy/commuter culture ....

Problems with the growth of Paris

4 traffic congestion ....

5 urban sprawl ....

6 population growth...

7 industry ....

8 housing ....

Solutions to problems

9 Boulevard Périphérique ....

10 new overspill towns...

11 suburban nodes ....

12 preferential axes ....

13 RER..

14 infill development ....

15 Schéma Directeur..

(l) Case Study 8: Nord-Pas-de-Calais (France)

Sample Question

Examine, with the aid of a case study, a region which has suffered from industrial (economic) decline.

Insert the following terms into the blanks below:

mass de-industrialisation / retraining / high unemployment rates / TGV high-speed rail network / competition from much cheaper coal elsewhere / Channel Tunnel / Industrial Revolution / conversion poles / industrial region in decline / natural gas / competition from Asia / renewal and redevelopment / nodal centre / technopoles, or technology parks / oil / growth phase of their lifecycles / Euralille / depletion of local coal reserves

Reasons for industrial decline

- Around the beginning of the .... , coal mining, textiles and the iron and steel industries grew rapidly in the Nord region of north-eastern France. **(1 SRP)**

- By the early 1960s the .... reduced the natural advantage of the region for heavy industry. This, coupled with competition from more modern and competitive factories elsewhere, led to rapid industrial decline. **(1 SRP)**

- Coal extraction in the Nord has ceased operation since the early 1990s due to the exhaustion of coal reserves and .... , e.g. Poland. **(1 SRP)**

- In recent times coal has been replaced by other energy sources, such as .... from the North Sea and Russian gas fields, and also by .... imported mainly from the Middle East. **(1 SRP)**

- The textile industry declined due to .... where labour costs are much cheaper, e.g. China. **(1 SRP)**

- The iron and steel industry also declined during this period of .... and thousands of jobs were lost. **(1 SRP)**

- This has had a major social impact, leading to .... and all associated social problems, e.g. an increase in crime. **(1 SRP)**

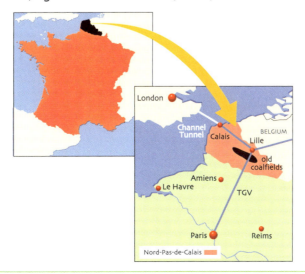

The French government's solutions

- The French government's response was to create .... , or alternative poles, for development. **(1 SRP)**

- These are used by governments to regenerate the economy of depressed regions in the following ways:

  - Building modern infrastructure, e.g. motorways.

  - Modernising cities and towns of the region through ....

  - ....workers to adapt to the needs of modern industry.

  - Attracting modern manufacturing and service industries. **(1 SRP)**

- The French government has focused on the introduction of modern economic activities that are in the .... to ensure prosperity in the future. **(1 SRP)**

Focus on the redevelopment of Lille

- The best example of economic conversion in the region is the urban redevelopment of Lille.

- Lille is now only one hour from Paris, one and a quarter hours from London and twenty minutes from Brussels since the construction of the .... **(1 SRP)**

- Lille is the most important .... in the Nord region with a population well in excess of a million people. **(1 SRP)**

- Its nodality has increased since the opening of the .... , as the Eurostar train between London and Paris travels through Lille. **(1 SRP)**

- The creation of .... for footloose high-tech industry on the city's ring motorway and the development of .... , a new international business centre, provides thousands of jobs in the secondary and tertiary sectors respectively. **(1 SRP)**

- The Nord has now transformed itself from an .... into a well-developed modern economy focusing on high-tech manufacturing and services industries. **(1 SRP)**

Section 3

Maps, Aerial Photographs and Graphs

Chapter 23

Map and Aerial Photograph Skills for Short Questions

(a) Ten Skills for Ordnance Survey Maps

Insert the following terms into the blanks below:

north / cirque lake or tarn / radial / standing stone / trellis / gentle / M 296 251 / beach / six / clustered (nucleated) / 10km² / sub-zone letter / bottom left-hand corner / representative fraction / northing / M 323 246 / contour lines / red dot / spot heights / mound / colour / triangulation pillars / glacial deposition / steep / linear / concave / convex / 6.9km / 7.8km / 12km / easting / 9km / linear scale / M 286 294 / 19km² / north-east / castle / R560 / ring forts / dendritic / M 302 253 / equal resistance / 9km² / hard and soft / 108km² / statement of scale / central area / historical settlements / north-west / deranged / 798m / dispersed

Skill 1 – Scale on maps

- Scale is the link between distance on a map and its corresponding distance on the ground.

- The scale on the Ordnance Survey Ireland map is 1:50,000, which means that 2cm on the map represents 1km on the ground.

- Scale is shown on a map in three ways:

  1 .... :
  Two divided lines, one showing distance in kilometres and one showing distance in miles. To the right of zero, distance is given in units while to the left of zero each unit is divided into tenths.

  2 .... :
  The scale is written on the map – 2cm to 1km.

  3 .... :
  The scale is expressed as a ratio between the length on the map and the actual distance on the ground – 1:50,000 – which means 1cm on the map represents 50,000cm or 500m in reality.

Skill 2 – Grid referencing

- Grid references are used to locate places on a map. The vertical lines on a map are called eastings and the horizontal lines on a map are called northings.

- A grid reference is made up of:

  1 A .... : a capital letter in blue, e.g. the letter M on the Galway OS map (see p. 199).

  2 An .... : a vertical line on a map. These digits are to be found on the top and bottom of the map.

Note

They are called 'eastings' because the digits increase as you move eastwards along the map.

3 A .... : a horizontal line on a map. These digits are to be found on the sides of the map.

Note

They are called 'northings' because the digits increase as you move northwards along the map.

- When giving a grid reference use the word **ATLAS**. First read Across the Top (AT) for the easting, and then Along the Side (AS) for the northing.

- For a four-figure grid reference always give the location at the .... of the box.

- For specific locations of places or features always give a ....-figure grid reference.

- When giving a six-figure grid reference divide each square into tenths, as shown.

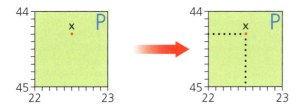

Example: Find the grid references for the following on the Galway map:

1 Tourist information centre...   ... / .... / ....

2 Megalithic tomb...   ... / .... / ....

3 Caravan and camping site...   ... / .... / ....

4 Youth hostel...   ... / .... / ....

Skill 3 – Height on maps

- Height is shown in four different ways on a map:

  1 .... : lines on a map joining places of equal height. They are drawn at 10m intervals.

  2 .... : shown by a black dot with the height beside the black dot.

  3 .... Green is used to represent lowland (land up to 200m). At 200m the colours changes to brown. The higher the land, the darker the brown becomes.

  4 .... : indicated by a black triangle with the height written beside it.

Skill 4 – Types of slope

- When the contour lines are close the slope is ....
- When the contour lines are far apart the land is ....
- When the contours are far apart at the base and close together at the top the slope is ....
- When the contours are close together at the base and far apart at the top the slope is ....

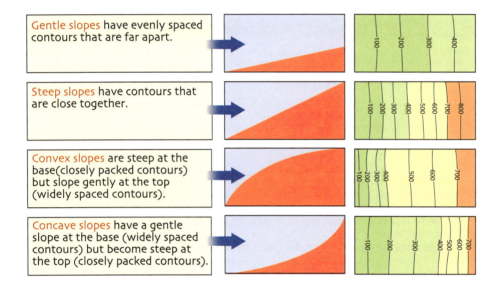

Skill 5 – Measuring distance

The straight-line method

1 Place a straight edge of a piece of paper between the two places on the map.

2 Mark each place on the piece of paper.

3 Remove the paper and place it along the linear scale at the bottom of the map to calculate the distance between the two places. State the distance in kilometres or miles.

Example: The distance from the post office in Oranmore (M 379 246) to the tourist information office in Galway city (M 302 253) is ....

Curved distance

1 Place a piece of paper along the road and on it mark the starting point of the road.

2 Each time the road changes direction, rotate the paper to follow the road.

3 While rotating the paper along the road, hold it in place with your pencil.

4 Follow this procedure until the road has been measured.

5 Mark on the piece of paper the finishing point of the area to be measured. Lift the piece of paper and place it along the linear scale.

Example: The distance between the post office in Oranmore (M 379 246) to the tourist information office in Galway (M 302 533) along the R338 and the R339 is ....

Skill 6 – Calculating area on maps

- To calculate the area of a map, multiply the length by the breadth.

   1 Count the number of grid squares along the base of the map, i.e. count the eastings.

   2 Count the number of grid squares along the vertical side of the map, i.e. count the northings.

   3 Multiply the eastings by the northings.

Remember

Each side of each square represents 1km so the answer will always be in square kilometres (km²).

Example: Galway map (p. 199): Breadth (.........) x Length (.........) = Answer (...............).

Example: Calculate the area of Lough Leane on the Killarney OS map (LC, 2006).

- Each square on the map represents 1km².

- Count up all the squares that are completely covered by water: ....

- Add the squares which are more than 50 per cent covered by water: ....

- Total squares (...............) gives you the approximate answer.

Skill 7 – Directions on maps

- North is always at the top of the map.

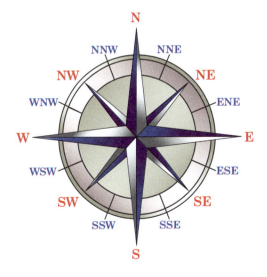

Example: Grid references on Galway map (p. 199):

1 From PO (M 379 246) to Galway Airport (M 374 284), the direction is ....

2 From Lough Atalia (M 311 257) to Ballindooly Lough (M 315 288), the direction is

....

3 From the castle (M 318 280) to the castle (M 318 302), the direction is ....

Skill 8 – Cross-sections

■ A cross-section shows how the land lies and falls along a particular line.

Examine the Ordnance Survey map extract (right) and the profile drawn along the trail that is marked in blue on the map.

Answer the questions that follow.

1 The height above sea-level at the start of the trail (A) is

....

2 The glacial landform at B is a

....

3 The road at C is the

....

4 The tourist attraction at D is a

....

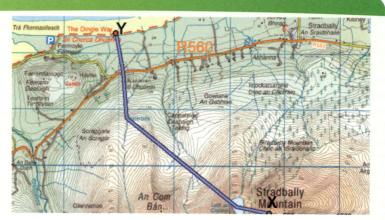

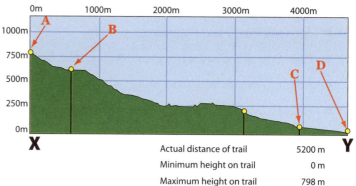

Actual distance of trail		5200 m
Minimum height on trail		0 m
Maximum height on trail		798 m

Skill 9 – Historical and rural settlement

■ Antiquities are .... which indicate a very long history of settlement in a region. Named antiquities are shown by a .... with the name beside it. Historical enclosures, which are usually ...., are shown by a small red circle.

Example: From the following grid references, name the antiquities to be found on the Drogheda OS map, (p. 200):

GR O 107 710 – ....

GR O 148 782 – ....

GR O 137 748 – ....

■ Settlements (houses) on 1:50,000 OS maps are shown by small black dots. A pattern is the shape which the settlements make when plotted on a map.

There are three main types of settlements pattern:

1 .... , where settlements patterns are built along a road, e.g. on the Galway map along the N17 at GR M 338 292 to where it exits the map at GR M 355 310.

2 .... , when a number of settlements are grouped together, e.g. on the Galway map at GR M 368 262. **Note:** These occur mainly at road junctions and especially at bridging points of rivers.

3 .... , when settlements are spaced out and evenly scattered throughout a low-lying area, e.g. in the north-west of the Galway map.

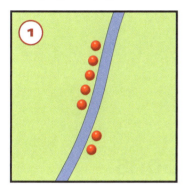 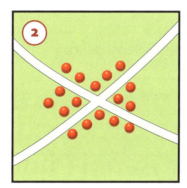 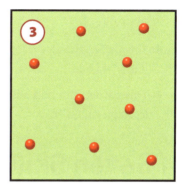

Skill 10 – Drainage patterns on maps

■ A drainage basin is the area drained by a river and its tributaries.

1 ....

  ■ This pattern resembles branches in a tree.
  ■ It develops on a level area where rocks show .... to erosion.
  ■ It is normally found in the upper and middle courses of rivers.
  ■ The River Shannon follows this pattern.

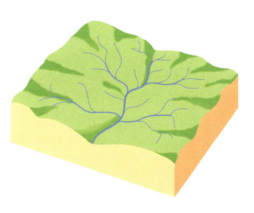

2 ....
  ■ This pattern occurs where bands of .... rocks lie parallel to each other.
  ■ Rivers flowing through the soft rocks are parallel to each other and their tributaries.
  ■ The Owenboy River, Co. Cork, follows this pattern.

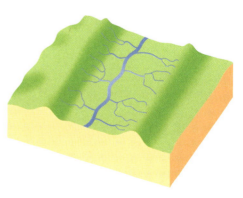

3 ....

- This pattern occurs when rivers flow from a .... , such as a mountain top.
- The pattern resembles spokes on a wheel.
- The rivers flowing off Lugnaquilla Mountain, Co. Wicklow, follow this pattern.

- ....

- This pattern occurs when rivers flow in a chaotic manner, due to wind or ice action, with small lakes forming along their courses.
- This pattern occurs in low-lying parts of Ireland which experienced ....
- This pattern can be seen in the Newport–Westport lowlands in Co. Mayo.

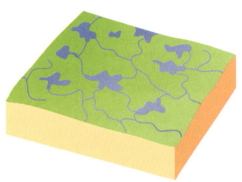

(b) Seven Skills for Aerial Photographs

Insert the following terms into the blanks below:

> leaves on trees / defensive / secondary / educational / tertiary / high oblique / no leaves on deciduous trees / north / transport / religious: church / centre foreground / right middleground / left background / traffic management yellow box: commercial / primary / oblique / industrial / agricultural / residential / tourism / compass points / recreational / low-lying / river / left foreground / port / vertical / ploughed fields / recreation or green space / bridging point / trees are multi-coloured / low oblique

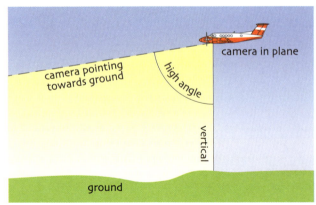

High oblique

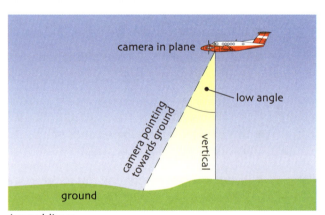

Low oblique

Skill 1 – Types of aerial photograph

- .... photographs: these are photographs where the camera is directly over the area being photographed. Scale is constant throughout. On most aerial photographs the direction arrow will be shown.

- .... photographs: these are photographs where the camera is placed at an angle when taking the photograph. Scale is not constant throughout. There are two types of these:

  - .... photographs are taken at a high angle. The camera is pointed at an angle of 60° to the ground. Part of the horizon can be seen.

  - .... photographs are taken at a low angle. The camera is pointed at an angle of 30° to the ground. The horizon is not visible.

Skill 2 – Location on aerial photographs

Vertical photographs

- Most vertical photographs contain an arrow pointing ....

- Location on vertical photographs is by means of .... in relation to another feature on the photograph, e.g. the church is found to the east of the market square.

Left Background	Centre Background	Right Background
Left Middleground	Centre	Right Middleground
Left Foreground	Centre Foreground	Right Foreground

Direction method for oblique photos

Oblique photographs

Locate the following land-use types on the Galway photograph (p. 202):

Type	Location
....	centre background
car park	....
residential	....
....	right foreground
marina	....
housing estate	....
....	centre foreground

Skill 3 – Direction on aerial photographs

- On OS maps north is always on the top. This is not necessarily the case with photographs. The photograph must be aligned in conjunction with the map, using the following approach:

  1 Draw a line joining any two major landmarks on the photograph, e.g. church and road junction.

  2 Draw a line joining the same two landmarks on the map.

  3 Compare the direction of the line drawn on the photograph with the line drawn on the OS map. This gives you the direction in which the camera was pointing.

- Practise, with the aid of your exam papers, finding the direction of each year's photograph.

Skill 4 – Functions and land-use on aerial photographs

The aerial photograph can clearly show the functions of an urban area.

- Presence of a large shopping centre: ………………………… function
- Presence of schools and universities: ………………………… function
- Presence of a large industrial estate: ………………………… function
- Presence of low-lying land: ………………………… function
- Presence of castles or towers: ………………………… function
- Presence of a large number of houses: ………………………… function
- Presence of rivers, mountains and seas: ………………………… function
- Presence of a large number of routeways: ………………………… function
- Presence of sports fields and green spaces: ………………………… function

Skill 5 – Development of settlement on aerial photographs

Certain key features on an aerial photograph will indicate factors influencing the development of a settlement.

- Flat, ……………………… land.
- A nearby ……………… .
- A bridge which would indicate that the town developed as a ……………………………… .
- A coastal location, indicating the town may have developed as a ………… .

Skill 6 – Economic activities on aerial photographs

From a photograph it is possible to determine the dominant economic activity.

- …………………… economic activities: the presence of forests, agricultural land, animals and crops in the fields; rivers and seas for fishing.
- …………………… economic activities: the presence of industrial estates and roads.
- …………………… economic activities: the presence of schools, hospitals, churches, football pitches and green space.

Skill 7 – Time of year on aerial photographs

Season	Photographic Evidence
Spring	▪ Leaves starting to appear on trees ▪ …………………………………
Summer	▪ ………………………………… ▪ Animals in fields ▪ Crops growing in fields ▪ Crowded beaches
Autumn	▪ ………………………………………… ▪ Crop arranged in bales in fields
Winter	▪ ………………………………………… ▪ No animals in fields – stall-fed ▪ Empty beaches

(c) Sketch Maps from OS Maps and Photographs

Drawing sketch maps from Ordnance Survey maps

1 Divide the map into sections.

- Find the mid-point on the top of the map and the mid-point on the bottom of the map and join them with a vertical line.
- Find the mid-point on both sides of the map and draw a horizontal line from one side to the other.
- From the top left-hand corner draw a diagonal line to the bottom right-hand corner.
- From the top right-hand corner draw a diagonal line to the bottom left-hand corner.

2 Draw a frame for the sketch map which is the same shape but not the same size as the map – usually half the length and half the breadth of the map.

3 Divide the sketch into similar sections as on the map.

4 Insert the required features on the sketch map.

5 Include a title, key and directions arrow.

6 Always use a pencil for ease of correction.

7 Always use graph paper.

Sample Question 1

Examine the Ordnance Survey map of Galway on the opposite page. Using **graph paper**, draw a sketch-map to **half scale** of the area shown. On it, show and name **each** of the following:

- The River Corrib
- An airport runway
- An area of silting/mudbank
- A sea-ferry route

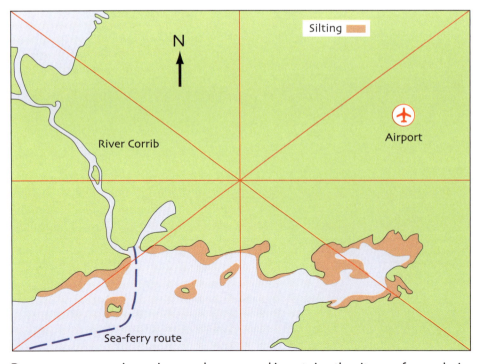

Draw your own version, using graph paper, and insert six other items of your choice on your sketch map.

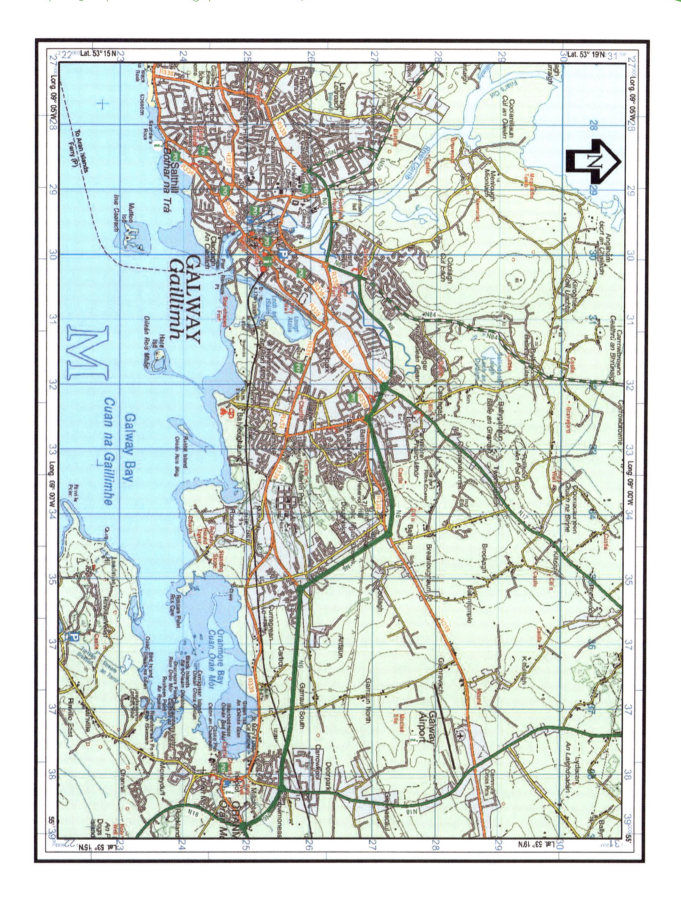

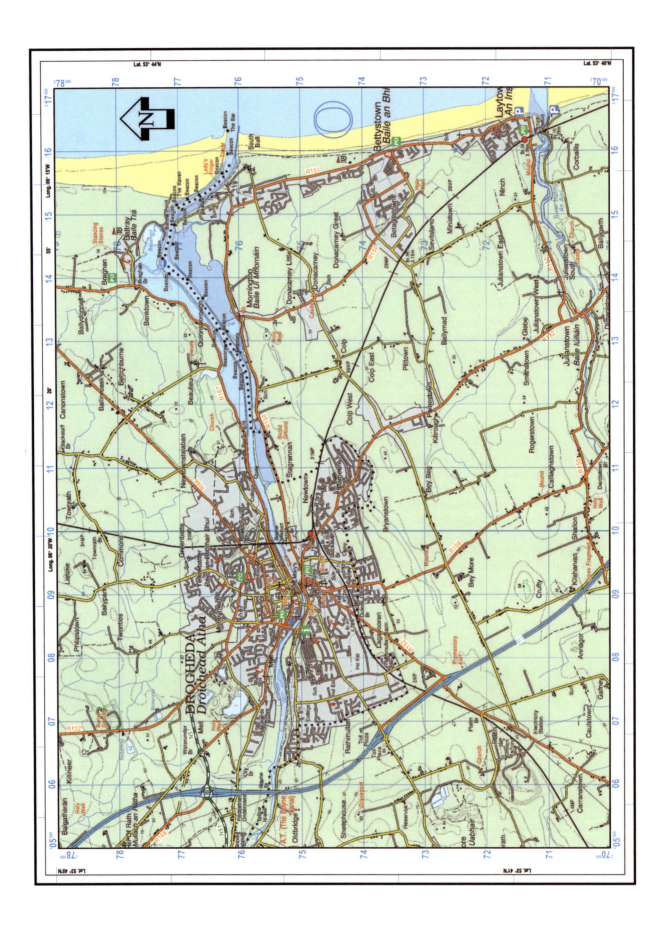

Sample Question 2

Examine the Ordnance Survey map of Drogheda on the opposite page. Using **graph paper**, draw a sketch-map **half the length and half the breadth** of the map. On it, show and name **each** of the following:

- The River Nanny
- An area of silting/mud
- A beach
- A numbered spot-height

Drawing sketch maps from aerial photographs

1 Measure the width of the photograph and divide into three. For example, if the width comes to 21cm, draw a vertical line from the top of the photograph to the bottom every 7cm.

2 Measure the length of the photograph and divide into three. For example, if the length comes to 24cm draw in a horizontal line every 8cm. The photograph is now divided into nine zones.

3 There is no rule as to what size the sketch map should be, once it is smaller than the original photograph. A good rule is to reduce each side by 4cm, e.g. if the width of the photograph is 20cm, make the sketch map 16cm wide. If the length of the photograph is 25cm make the sketch map 21cm long.

4 Divide the sketch map into nine zones. If the width of the sketch map is 15cm wide divide it by three. Therefore every 5cm drop in a vertical line. If the length of the photograph is 21cm divide it by three. Therefore every 7cm drop in a horizontal line.

5 The sketch map should now be broken up into nine different zones. Each of these zones corresponds with a zone on the original photograph. This allows for the easy transfer of information from each zone on the original photograph into its corresponding zone on the sketch map.

6 Show and name the features required.

7 Title the sketch map. Insert a key under the sketch to explain the symbols used.

Sample Question 3

Examine the aerial photograph of part of Galway below. Using **graph paper**, draw a sketch-map to **half scale** of the area shown. On it, show and name the following:

- A large church
- An area of high-rise building
- An area of water-based recreation
- An example of traffic-control street marking

Sample Question 4

Examine the aerial photograph of Drogheda below. Using **graph paper**, draw a sketch-map **half the length and half the breadth** of the area shown. On it, show and name **one** example of each of the following land uses:

- Recreation
- Religion
- Industry
- Storage

Chapter 24

Map and Aerial Photograph Skills for Longer Questions

(a) 20-mark Questions

Note: All 20-mark question require five key points, worth four marks each.

Sample Question 1: Primary activities

Using map evidence, write an account of a primary activity on the Mullingar OS map (LC, 2005).

Insert the following terms into the blanks below:

> south / burial ground / scenic beauty / parking area / 188m / carbon dioxide / early settlement / mixed woodland / Brosna / crannog / N52 / tracks / picnic site / soil erosion / coniferous / flora and fauna

There are many forested areas on the Mullingar map.

- On the south side of Lough Owel there is a large ………………… plantation at N 405 560. There is a ……………………………… at N 414 563 which people may use to gain access to the forest. However, there is no evidence of a ……………………… or caravan and camping area. The land may be subject to flooding so the only suitable land use might be forestry.

- On the eastern side of the map, between Lough Drin and Slevin's Lake, there is a large plantation of …………………………………… at N 455 564. The highest point in the forest is …………… , which contains a barrow at N 457 575, evidence of ………………………………… in the area. The forest also contains a ……………………… at N 454 575. There is a ………………… on the edge of the forest at N 448 567. Both of these features also provide evidence of early settlement. This land is probably marshy and so forestry may be the only suitable use for the land.

- There is a coniferous plantation located along third-class roads at N 415 505. The River ……………… and Lady's Canal flow to the …………… of the forest. The forest is easy to access via the third-class road coming off the national secondary road, the ……… .

- There is a coniferous plantation located along the N4 extending from N 468 531 to N 490 519, so access is easy. The forest contains two ………… – one at N 470 528, south of Marlinstown Bog, and one at N 485 525. These tracks could be used by ramblers.

- All of these forests provide ……………………………………, help to reduce ………………………………… , act as a home to ……………………………… and help to reduce the Greenhouse Effect by absorbing ……………………………… . The forests also reduce the impact of flooding as the roots absorb some of the surplus water.

Sample Question 2: Location of industry

From the Killarney map extract (LC, 2006), identify by grid reference a suitable site for the location of a major industry of your choice. Explain two reasons why you choose this site.

Exercise

Before looking at the answers below see if you can identify a location for your factory. Write down some site and situation factors relating to your chosen location.

Sample Answer

I would locate my factory at V 956 923. I choose this site for the following reasons:

Site-related factors

1 low-lying
2 readily accessible site
3 low population density
4 next to road junction

> **Point to Note**
>
> **Site** relates to the site itself.
>
> **Situation** relates to the surrounding area.

Situation-related factors

5 far from Lough Leane
6 labour from Killarney
7 accessible to railway line and N22
8 market

Exercise

Write into your copybook a brief explanation of why each of the site and situation factors was chosen.

Sample Question 3: Secondary and tertiary activities

Outline the nature of secondary and tertiary activities on the Galway map extract (p. 199).

Insert the following terms into the blanks below:

Corrib / M 302 246 / post offices / an industrial estate / M 293 253 / primary route / station / electricity transmission lines / exporting / residential / transport routes / services / industrial estates and factories / University / M 373 284

- ■ Evidence for secondary economic activity includes ....
  On the Galway map at M 325 275 there is ....

- Further evidence of secondary economic activity includes .... which allow for the movement of raw materials and the finished product. The N17 is a national .... which enters the map at M 354 310 and serves the city of Galway. It also makes Galway very accessible for workers.

- Galway is also served by a railway line. There is a railway .... at M 303 253. The railway enters the map at M 390 261. Galway Airport is located at .... Both of these would allow for the movement of exports and imports.

- In the past the River .... could have been used for importing and .... The River Corrib enters Galway Bay at ....

- Galway is also served by .... These lines enter the map at M 390 275 and enter the city at M 343 269. These would provide power for industrial, commercial and .... use.

- Galway is also served by a variety of .... vital for secondary economic activity. There are many schools, e.g. at .... , attracting families into the area. Galway .... is located at M 293 261, providing highly educated graduates for industry in the area. There are many .... , e.g. at M 290 259, which allow many of the foreign workers the opportunity to send their money home.

Sample Question 4: Ordnance Survey map versus aerial photograph

List and explain the differences between OS maps and aerial photographs.

Location

1 OS map – exact ....

2 photograph – general...

Naming features

3 OS map – named ....

4 photograph – not named ....

Communications

5 OS map – named roads ....

6 photograph – not named but include traffic patterns ....

Altitude

7 OS map – exact ....

8 photograph – general...

Land use

9 OS map – difficult to identify ....

10 photograph – great detail ....

(b) 30-mark Questions

Sample Question 1: Development of a city

With the aid of the Galway OS map (p. 199), explain three reasons why Galway city developed as a growth centre.

Insert the following terms into the blanks below:

> garda station / M 306 256 / car parks / hospitals / national primary route / M 320 310 / railway station / imports and exports / university / skills / post offices / M 390 261 / schools / industrial estate / defensive / Galway city / density of services / regional roads / tourist centre / M 328 258 / M 308 264 / star-shaped fort / national secondary roads

Galway developed as a growing economic centre for the following three reasons:

1 Focus of transport routes

- All the major roads on the map converge in .... .The ....
.... , the N17, enters the map at M 354 310 and at the roundabout on the northern outskirts of Galway (M 321 272) becomes the N6 and the R336. **(1 SRP)**

- Galway is served by two .... , the N84 which enters the map at .... and the N59 which enters the map at M 270 280. **(1 SRP)**

- Galway is also served by many ...., for example the R339 which enters the map at M 390 287. **(1 SRP)**

- There is a .... at M 303 253. The railway line enters the map at .... and runs east to west. **(1 SRP)**

- All of these forms of transport allow for the ease of movement of ...., explaining why Galway has developed as a growing economic centre. **(1 SRP)**

2 Service centre

Galway has many services.

- There is a .... at M 288 258 and a regional technical college at .... , which would educate graduates with the required .... to attract industry into the city. **(1 SRP)**

- There are .... at M 291 255 and at M 340 256 to cater for the health of the workforce and public in general. There are seven .... in Galway, e.g. at M 313 258, which allow for sending mail locally, nationally and internationally. **(1 SRP)**

- There are many .... in Galway, e.g. at .... , to cater for the educational needs of the young population of Galway. There is an .... on the northern side of Galway at M 325 275 to attract industry into the city. It is located on the northern outskirts of the city to reduce pollution and congestion in Galway city. **(1 SRP)**

- There is a .... at M 294 251 to provide law and order for the city. There are also many .... in Galway, e.g. at M 300 256, to cater for all the people coming into Galway to work. **(1 SRP)**

- The different types of services and the .... have helped to make Galway a growing economic centre. **(1 SRP)**

3 Tourism

- Galway is the major .... on the map. The many tourist attractions bring visitors who spend their money in the city, helping to make Galway a growing economic centre. **(1 SRP)**

- There is a .... at M 305 264 and another one at M 312 246. These provide evidence of early settlement. **(1 SRP)**

- There is a holy well at .... and an old burial ground at M 284 242. These reflect early Christian settlement. **(1 SRP)**

- There are three castles in the city, e.g. at M 297 250. These were built for .... purposes. **(1 SRP)**

- Due to all of these attractions, Galway is the major tourist centre on the map, helping to make Galway a growing economic centre. **(1 SRP)**

Sample Question 2: Important centre of economic activity

With the aid of the Drogheda OS map (p. 200), explain three reasons why the town has become an important centre of economic activity.

« Background Information »

Drogheda is an important centre of economic activity. It is the main transport focus on the map, it is the centre of manufacturing on the map and it is the main tourist centre on the map.

Transport focus

1 variety of transport types ....

2 regional roads ....

3 railway lines ....

4 railway lines link up ....

5 Boyne estuary ....

Manufacturing centre

6 industrial estates. . . . .

7 access to estates . . . .

8 coastal town. . . . .

9 labour supply. . . . .

10 reservoirs. . . . .

Tourist centre

11 antiquities . . . .

12 golf course . . . .

13 tourist information centre . . . .

14 accessibility. . . . .

15 youth hostel . . . .

Sample Question 3: Historical development

With the aid of the OS map of Drogheda (p. 200), explain three different examples of historic settlement.

Insert the following terms into the blanks below:

ogham / landed gentry / soil, rocks and gravel / mounds / O 135 746 / standing stones / promontory / centres of devotion / places of worship / work / burial grounds / O 741 056 / abbey / Franciscans / burial chambers / medieval gates / holy wells / castle / transport and trade / tower / protection / foreign invaders / education / bailey / protect / demesne / economic strength and social standing / forest and tall outer protective wall / priory / planted / O 145 705 / R767 / monasteries / Norman / churches / motte / deciduous / bridge

« *Background Information* »

There is evidence of Bronze Age settlement, Christian settlement and defensive settlement on this map extract.

Christian settlement

- There are four . . . . on the map, two of which are located at O 129 755 and O 104 704. They are often associated with . . . . from the middle of the sixth century onwards. Often they were dedicated to a local saint or by St Patrick. They often became . . . . and people organised pilgrimages and other events around them. **(1 SRP)**

- There are also many .... on the extract. One of these is to be found at .... and one at O 115 764. They represent .... where groups of Christians gathered to pray. **(1 SRP)**

- The presence of graveyards and .... also provides evidence of early Christian settlement. Examples are to be found at .... and at O 115 755. Christians would have buried their dead at these locations. **(1 SRP)**

- There is also evidence of late Christian settlement on the extract dating from the twelfth century. At O 085 753 there is an .... and at O 083 755 there is a .... These were established by religious orders such as the .... They offered food, ... and help to the local population. **(1 SRP)**

Bronze Age settlement

- There is evidence of settlement dating from the Bronze Age, around 1400BC. At O 146 782 there are .... They indicate the location of .... and they often contain dead bodies and their possessions. **(1 SRP)**

- They are often used to indicate boundaries and some may contain .... writing which comprises notches, dots and lines. **(1 SRP)**

Defensive settlement

- The presence of a .... at .... and one at O 145 705 is evidence of an early defensive settlement on the extract. Castles are a feature of .... settlement in Ireland. Some were located on river banks such as the one at O 145 705, for water, ... **(1 SRP)**

- Towns often developed near castles as they offered .... Local people depended on the castle for .... as soldiers and servants. **(1 SRP)**

- A .... is located on the coast at O 160 763 and it was probably built to act as a lookout for .... , perhaps during Napoleonic times. It may also have been built to .... the mouth of the Boyne. **(1 SRP)**

- There is a .... fort at O 076 724, indicating another area of early defensive settlement on the extract. **(1 SRP)**

- There is an old house at O 126 767 which may have been a part of a .... This house may have been owned by the .... A typical Irish estate was centred on the big house which was the landlord's country residence. This symbolised his .... in the community. The house was often surrounded by a demesne, which was for the use of the house owners, and was not rented out. Often the house was protected from the elements by a .... **(1 SRP)**

- There is a .... forest at O 130 766. The trees were probably .... in the eighteenth and nineteenth centuries by landlords. They were planted to add to the beauty of the estate houses. Most houses were built along roads for easy access, as this one was. It is located on a third-class road with direct access to the regional road .... at O 126 964. **(1 SRP)**

■ There are a number of .... on the maps, e.g. at O 106 710 and at O 156 713, which were built for defensive purposes. A mound is a heaped collection of .... constructed for protection. **(1 SRP)**

■ At O 087 746 there is a .... in the town of Drogheda. This is a mound of earth topped by a wooden tower. The tower was linked to a .... or courtyard by a .... **(1 SRP)**

■ Drogheda also contains two .... at O 088 748. These gates offered protection to the inhabitants of Drogheda. They may have been opened during the day and closed at night. **(1 SRP)**

Sample Question 4: Functions of a city

With the aid of the Galway aerial photograph (p. 202), examine three functions of the city.

Transport function

1   bridging point . . . .

2   focus of routeways/traffic . . . .

3   car parks and commercial . . . .

4   industry . . . .

5   river . . . .

6   canal . . . .

Religious function

7   church/cathedral . . . .

8   central location . . . .

9   accessibility. . . . .

Residential function

10   planned/unplanned . . . .

11   terraced/inner city . . . .

12   link to services . . . .

13   semi-detached suburbs . . . .

14   link to manufacturing . . . .

15   conclusion. . . . .

Chapter 25

Graphs, Charts and Satellite Imagery

(a) Statistical Graphs and Charts

Insert the following types of graph into the blanks below:

> wind roses / bar charts / scatter graphs / divided / simple / choropleth / climograph / compound / triangle graphs / trend graphs or line graphs / radar charts / pie charts and doughnut charts / area graph / isolines / multiple

Type 1: ....

This is a circle divided into sectors. The circle represents the total amount, while the sectors indicate the fraction in each category.

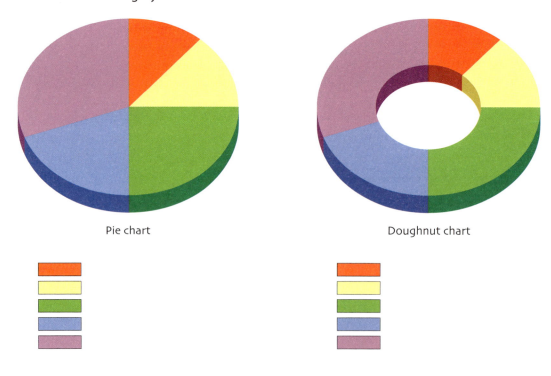

Pie chart   Doughnut chart

Type 2: ....

This is a chart comprising vertical or horizontal bars whose lengths are proportional to amounts or quantities.

There are four types:

a .... bar chart

Each bar drawn represents a single value.

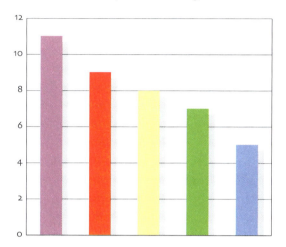

b .... bar chart

Many values are grouped together to enable comparisons.

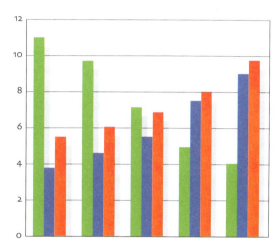

c .... bar chart

Different values are shown together on a single bar.

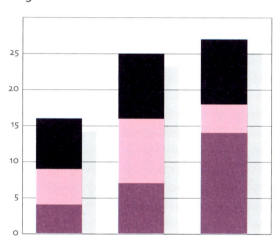

d .... rectangle

A horizontal bar that illustrates the percentages that make up the whole (i.e. 100 per cent).

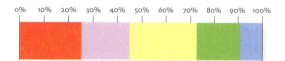

Type 3: ....

These are pyramid-shaped graphs with each of the three sides broken up into percentage scales. They are used to identify employment structure, soil composition, types of mass movements and the contents of water.

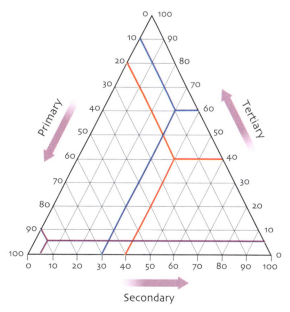

Type 4: ....

This is a graph that shows how a number of items are performing together, e.g birth rates and death rates and how they influence population growth over time. They can also be used to illustrate how other variables change over time.

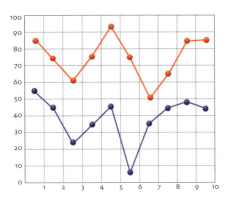

Type 5: ....

A diagram representing data to see if there is a relationship between two sets of measurements, such as how river speed and valley depth may be associated with each other. Two scales, one for each type of variable, are drawn at right angles to each other and each set of data is plotted. If the dots fall into a line pattern, an association or relationship may be indicated.

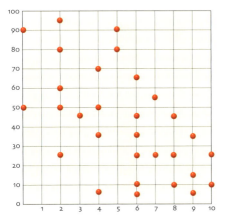

Type 6: ....

This is a graph which plots two or more quantities over a certain time period. Often, each quantity is shaded a different colour.

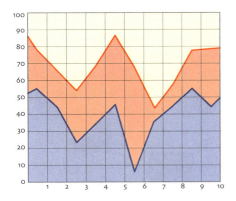

Type 7: ....

This provides information on the two most important elements of climate – temperature and precipitation. A climograph combines a vertical bar chart and a trend graph on the one diagram. The trend graph represents temperature while the vertical bar chart represents precipitation. Temperature is shown in degrees Celsius on the left-hand axis while rainfall is shown in millimetres on the right-hand side.

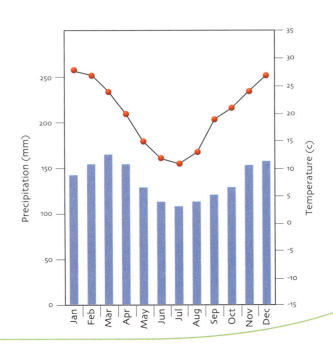

Type 8: ....

This is a graphic tool used by meteorologists to give a succinct view of how wind speed and direction are typically distributed at a particular location over time. The length of each arm is proportional to the amount of time the wind speed was observed from that direction.

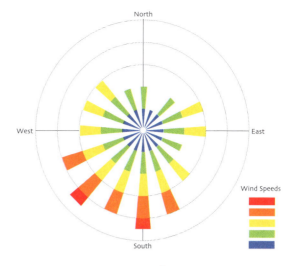

Type 9: ....

This is a line on a map that joins places having the same value or amount. The most common isolines are contours, isotherms and isobars.

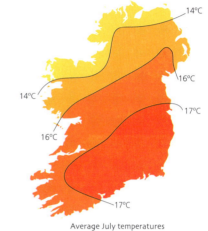

Average July temperatures

Type 10: ....

This is a map showing the distribution of a particular occurrence, such as the amount of annual rainfall, by graded shading to indicate the density per unit area. The greater the density of shading, the greater the occurrence in reality.

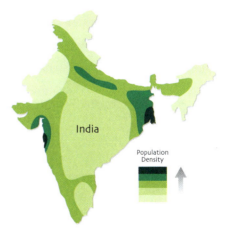

Type 11: ....

This is similar to a radar that detects planes departing from and landing at airports. It is polygonal. It is used to compare the values of different sets of variables.

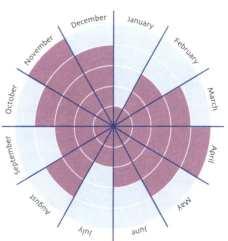

(b) Satellite Imagery

Insert the following terms into the blank spaces below:

island arc / delta / icebergs / deforestation / glacier / sandstorm / river delta / hurricane / volcano / glacier / bush fires / deforestation

....

....

....

....

....

....

....

....

....

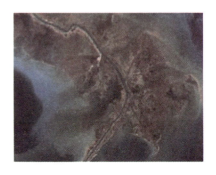

....

....

....

Section 4

The Human Elective (Patterns and Processes in the Human Environment)

Chapter 26

Population Change

(a) Population Density and Distribution

Sample Question 1

Describe and explain the differences between the terms 'population density' and 'population distribution' and the factors that affect them.

Population distribution

1 dispersal of people across the world . . . .

2 unevenly distributed . . . .

3 four distinct core regions . . . .

4 four distinct thinly populated regions . . . .

Population density

5 number of people per square kilometre . . . .

6 continental divisions . . . .

Factors affecting the global distribution and density of population

Physical factors

7 relief . . . .

8 climate . . . .

9 soils . . . .

10 resources . . . .

Socio-economic factors

11 levels of economic development . . . .

12 urbanisation...

13 industrialisation ....

14 politics and history..

15 can change over time and space..

(b) Density and Distribution in Ireland

Sample Question 2

Outline the factors which have influenced patterns of population density and distribution in Ireland, and how these patterns can change over time.

Insert the following terms into the blanks below:

potato blight / greater Dublin area (GDA) / wave of emigration / secondary and tertiary sectors / gley soils / well-drained / bridging points / well diversified economies / overdependent / Celtic Tiger era / primary sector / returning Irish emigrants / rural depopulation / commuter belt / strategic growth corridors / non-national workers / peat soils / infrastructure / upland or mountainous / decentralisation / primacy / favourable geographic location / famine / topography / coffin ships / urban areas / rivers / decreased dramatically / brown earth soils / Industrial Revolution / National Development Plans / lower population density / plantation towns / free trade policies / multinational companies / EEC (now EU) / rural-to-urban migratory trend

Physical factors

Relief

- The relief or .... in the province of Connacht, i.e. the west of Ireland, is predominantly .... , which repels settlement. As a result it has always had a .... than the other three provinces, which have a higher percentage of lowland area. **(1 SRP)**

Soils

- Soils in the province of Connacht are mainly .... , which have poor mineral content, and .... , which are prone to waterlogging. Both soils have limited agricultural potential and deter people from settling in the region. **(1 SRP)**

- The more fertile .... of Munster, Leinster and Ulster have attracted more settlement and as a result population density is higher, and this in turn affects the distribution of population around the country. **(1 SRP)**

Drainage

- People prefer to locate in .... regions and most of the dominant rivers in Ireland are located east of the Shannon. .... of these rivers have led to the development of many urban centres (i.e. towns and cities) throughout the country. **(1 SRP)**

- All cities with the exception of Kilkenny are located where ……………… enter the sea and therefore these rivers have a major impact on the distribution of settlement and population density in Ireland. **(1 SRP)**

Socio-economic factors

Levels of economic development

- Regions with …………………………………………… which have well developed sectors provide jobs and are more desirable locations. The province of Leinster, particularly the greater Dublin area (GDA), is one due to the exceptional growth during the …………………………………, and the same is true of Munster, though to a lesser degree. **(1 SRP)**

- The density of population in Leinster is much higher than that in the other three provinces, and has doubled in the last eighty years. Regions which are more underdeveloped, such as Connaght, and Ulster up till the Good Friday Agreement, have not increased their population density at the same rate. **(1 SRP)**

Urbanisation

- As Ireland began to develop economically in the 1960s, there was a shift from people working in the ……………………………… to the ………………………………………………… . Jobs in the secondary and tertiary are to be found in ……………………… , leading to increased urbanisation, a rural-to-urban migration and ………………………………………… , which led to significant changes in the distribution of population in Ireland. The population density also increased as the tide of emigration ceased. **(1 SRP)**

- Most of the exponential growth in population occurred in the ………………………………………… during the Celtic Tiger era. The area of the GDA includes Dublin, but also the counties in its ………………………………… , i.e. Kildare, Louth, Meath and Wicklow. Within the commuter belt a large number of rapidly growing urban centres have developed a short distance from Dublin city in ………………………………………… along the key routeways/motorways out of the city, e.g. M1, M3, M4, M7 and M11. **(1 SRP)**

- This rapid growth of the GDA has put many stresses on the physical and social environment, particularly in transport, as the ……………………… is not capable of meeting the public's demands. Government solutions to this problem include upgrading infrastructure under the ……………………………………… ………………… , the National Spatial Strategy devised in 2002 and the ……………………………………… campaign. **(1 SRP)**

Political and historical factors

- The ………………… of Dublin is partially due to its ……………………………………………… in relation to Ireland's former colonial power, Britain, and it became the administrative centre for English rule in Ireland under the Normans. After independence in 1922 it became the seat of government for the Irish Free State. Consequently its population density is well above the national average. **(1 SRP)**

- Plantations such as those in Ulster, Munster and Laois/Offaly have influenced the distribution of population in Ireland, particularly the former landlord estates (rural settlements) and ………………………………………… such as Bandon, Co. Cork (urban settlements). **(1 SRP)**

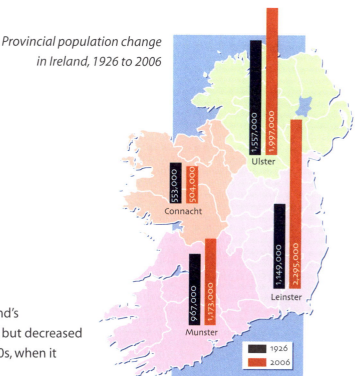

Provincial population change in Ireland, 1926 to 2006

Ulster 1,557,000 / 1,997,000
Connacht 553,000 / 504,000
Leinster 1,149,000 / 2,295,000
Munster 967,000 / 1,173,000

■ 1926
■ 2006

Change over time

■ At the time of the great .... Ireland's population had grown to over eight million, but decreased significantly for over a century until the 1960s, when it began to increase again.

Stage 1: The impact of the famine – population decline 1845–60

■ In the early nineteenth century the Irish people were .... on the potato crop as their main food source, and when the .... destroyed the crop in the years after 1845 widespread hunger, starvation, disease and death followed. **(1 SRP)**

■ Approximately a million people died from starvation in Ireland during the famine and a similar number emigrated in .... to the US and the UK. Consequently the population density .... during and after the famine, particularly in Connacht, where the population decreased by nearly 30 per cent. **(1 SRP)**

Stage 2: Century of emigration – population decline 1860–1960

■ The famine was the catalyst for a .... from Ireland which continued up to the 1960s. In Ulster the .... provided jobs and stemmed the tide of emigration, but the lack of economic opportunities in the other three provinces sustained the mass exodus of young people from the country, thus decreasing the population density. **(1 SRP)**

Stage 3: Economic growth – population increase 1960–present

■ Reasons for the increasing population density from the 1960s onwards were:

  ■ The .... of T.K. Whitaker during the Seán Lemass era successfully attracted foreign direct investment through ...., which led to job creation.

  ■ Entry into the .... in 1973 created a large export market. MNCs, mainly from the US, were attracted to Ireland as a means of gaining access to the EU market.

  ■ The emergence of the Celtic Tiger economy in the 1990s led to a wave of inward migration, both from .... and from ...., which increased the population density. **(1 SRP)**

- The key demographic features related to the distribution of population in Ireland during the Celtic Tiger era were the ...., which led to the exponential growth of the greater Dublin area, and rural depopulation, particularly in the west of Ireland. The global economic recession of 2008 has led to a slight decrease in population density in Ireland, as unemployment has soared and over 100,000 non-national workers have left the country. **(1 SRP)**

(c) Density and Distribution in China

Sample Question 3

With the aid of an international case study, outline how patterns of population density and distribution can change over time and the consequences this can have.

China and the one-child family policy

1   population explosion ....

2   fertility rate of 6..

3   population containment essential ....

The policy

4   set of regulations ....

5   penalties for non-compliance ....

Positive outcomes of the policy

6   reduced fertility rate to 1.8 in 2009 ....

7   reduced problems of overpopulation...

8   other benefits ....

Negative outcomes of the policy

9   4:2:1 problem...

10   Confucianism...

11   sex selection...

12   undocumented females...

13   abortions and infanticide ....

14   child abandonment..

15   criticisms of the policy ....

16   population distribution in China..

17   rural-to-urban migratory trend ....

Growth patterns

- For centuries wars, famines and plagues kept the global population in check.

- Around 1850, however, a new phase of population growth occurred where famine and disease could be controlled due to:

   1 Improved water supplies

   2 Better sewage disposal

   3 Increased agricultural yields thanks to improved technology

   4 Developments in healthcare, e.g. vaccines and antibiotics.

- The rapid decline in death rates among people who continued to have large families led to a doubling in the population in twenty-five years or less.

- In the late eighteenth century a scholar, Thomas Malthus, suggested that the world had reached its optimum population and that agricultural yields would be unable to keep pace with population increases, resulting in catastrophic consequences for the human race.

- Malthus did not see, however, that the carrying capacity of the world would increase enormously.

(d) Demographic Transition Model

Sample Question 4

With the aid of the demographic transition model, examine how changes in population occur.

Insert the following terms into the blanks below:

predictable set of population changes / urbanisation / basic medical supplies / explanation / high standard of living / tribal Africa / life expectancy / emancipation of women / subsistence / urban industrialised society / crop rotation / welfare state / low and undependable / infant mortality rates / natural decrease / debt crisis / equilibrium / work the land / famines / natural disasters / turning points / antibiotics / population explosion / natural increase / old-age pensions / selective breeding / highly developed / family planning / replacement level / democratic governments / neo-colonial exploitation / multinational companies / Eurocentric / terms of trade / liability / agricultural technology / industrialisation / the plague

Introduction

- The demographic transition model shows us that as a country develops it experiences a
  .... or 'demographic transitions'. In other
  words, the model sets out an .... for changes in population growth rates over time. It
  also allows us to analyse the relationship between population growth rates and levels of socio-
  economic development. **(1 SRP)**

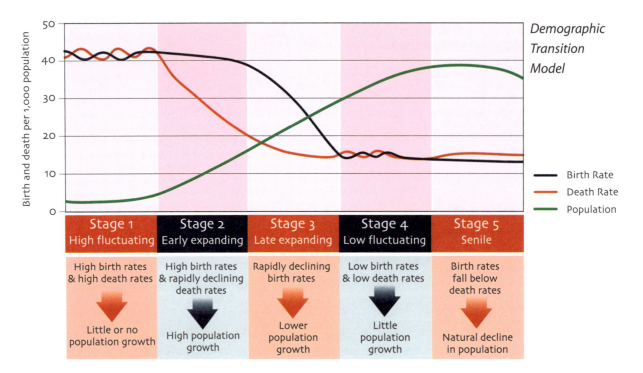

Stage-by-stage focus

Stage 1: High fluctuating stage (e.g. tribal Africa)

- This stage was experienced in Europe during medieval times and is currently seen in .... , where society is agriculturally based. Farming is .... in nature, technology is primitive and consequently food output is .... **(1 SRP)**

- The birth rates are high as parents are having large families to compensate for high .... and a low life expectancy. Children are perceived to be an economic asset and are needed to .... and to look after their parents when they get old. **(1 SRP)**

- The death rates are also high due to a lack of clean water, sanitation and basic medical care, resulting in epidemics of infectious diseases such as .... that devastated Europe's population in the middle ages. Undependable food output leads to frequent ...., such as that in Ireland in the 1840s and more recently in Ethiopia in the 1980s. Tribal, cultural and civil wars, religious persecution and .... also keep the death rate high. **(1 SRP)**

- The population during this stage fluctuates because both birth rates and death rates are high, so the high death rates cancel out the high birth rates, resulting in no overall natural increase or decrease. **(1 SRP)**

Stage 2: Early expanding stage (e.g. Mali)

- The industrial, agricultural and medical revolutions marked major .... in world population dynamics. These revolutions continue to have a similar influence on countries in the early expanding stage.

    1 .... improves the quality, quantity and distribution of food supplies. .... and the enclosure of land improves the productivity of farmland and .... improves the quality of livestock.

2 .... provides jobs that absorb a rapidly increasing workforce and initiate a rural-to-urban migratory trend. This leads to .... and thus increased levels of economic development.

3 Increased access to .... such as vaccinations, ... and antiseptics can eliminate many diseases, e.g. smallpox. **(2 SRPs)**

■ The demographic consequences of the these revolutions led to a .... where the birth rate remained high and the death rate fell rapidly, resulting in a rapid .... in population. **(1 SRP)**

Stage 3: Late expanding stage (e.g. Brazil)

■ This is the stage during which the key elements of an .... are established. In Europe the death rate continued to fall as urbanisation spread and living standards improved. Efforts were made by people to maintain a .... by restricting the size of their family, i.e. children came to be regarded as an economic liability. Guaranteed supplies of food from the New World colonies created a secure supply of food. **(1 SRP)**

■ In this stage the birth rate falls rapidly due to the following changes in the economy:

1 Technological advances such as tractors reduce the need for children to work the land.

2 .... are provided so parents don't need their children to look after them when they reach old age.

3 A .... may be set up to improve healthcare and consequently infant mortality rates improve. Parents realise that their children will survive to become adults. **(1 SRP)**

Stage 4: Low fluctuating stage (e.g. Ireland)

■ At this stage society is an affluent and .... urban, industrialised economy. The .... has significantly increased their social status. .... is practised, their standards of education have improved and many choose to work outside the home. As childcare costs increase, children are looked upon as an even bigger .... than in Stage 3 and consequently the birth rates fall to just above the replacement level. **(1 SRP)**

■ The death rate continues to fluctuate at a low level for the same reasons as in Stage 3. A state of .... exists whereby the birth rate and death are the same throughout the stage, i.e. there is no overall natural increase or decrease. **(1 SRP)**

Stage 5: Senile stage (e.g. Sweden)

■ Birth rates and death rates are both low but death rates are slightly higher than birth rates, leading to an overall .... These countries are not achieving their .... of 2.1 children per couple. Birth rates fall below replacement levels because family planning is practised and children have become very expensive (e.g. childcare) and thus are seen as an economic liability. **(1 SRP)**

■ Death rates remain low due to .... which invest heavily in health and education, with excellent medical services for the elderly, e.g. nursing homes. The result is that people live longer, having a .... of over eighty years. To counter population decline some countries try to give couples the incentive to have more children. Maternity leave in France is three years and three months (170 weeks). **(1 SRP)**

Conclusions

- Most highly developed countries are to be found in Stages 4 and 5, while underdeveloped or developing countries can be found in Stages 1, 2 and 3. Some commentators argue that developing countries, particularly in sub-Saharan Africa, are locked into Stages 2 and 3 due to .... driven by powerful ...., thus preventing socio-economic development. **(1 SRP)**

- It can be argued that this model is .... , focusing on the experiences of Britain, Germany and Belgium. It does not take into account the fact that developing counties don't control the .... and are locked into a .... that reduces their ability to invest in education and industrial development. **(1 SRP)**

(e) Population Structure, Fertility Rates and Mortality Rates

Sample Question 5

Examine how population structure, fertility rates and mortality rates can affect population characteristics of countries.

Population structure

1 pyramids show age and sex structure...

2 pyramidal shape ....

3 narrow base/wide top..

4 balancing sex structure ....

5 dependency ratio...

Fertility rates

6 vary over time and space..

7 factors affecting rates in developing countries ....

8 factors affecting rates in developed countries...

9 factors affecting rates, continued ....

Mortality rates

10 infant and child mortality rates ....

11 malnutrition . . . .

12 war/shanty towns . . . .

Solutions to high child mortality rates

13 improving primary healthcare . . . .

14 fair trade . . . .

15 political stability . . . .

16 impact of Aids . . . .

(f) Population Structure, Fertility Rates and Mortality Rates in Ireland

Sample Question 6

Outline how population structure, fertility rates and mortality rates can affect population change in a country that you have studied.

Insert the following terms into the blanks below:

urbanisation / child mortality rates / demographic transition model / pyramids / foreign direct investment / Catholic church / sex structure / mass emigration / increased / life expectancy / declined / replacement levels / natural decrease / immigration / tuberculosis / socio-economic development / birth rates / emancipation of women / childbearing / significant financial burden / workforce / contraceptives / low fertility rates / incentives / dependency ratio / economic recession / baby boomers / cost of living / living a lot longer / Celtic Tiger era / mass vaccination campaigns / old-age pensions / export-driven

Introduction

- Levels of economic development have had a major impact on Ireland's overall population. Its population decreased significantly during the periods of . . . . when the economy was underdeveloped and unemployment soared. On the other hand, the population increased during periods of economic prosperity such as the . . . .

Ireland's population structure

- Ireland's population structure has changed over time due to changing levels of . . . . as we have passed through the . . . . **(1 SRP)**

- Over time these changes have altered the shape of Ireland's population structure. Population . . . . are the best way to illustrate the age structure (proportion of people belonging to different age groups) and . . . . (ratio of males to females) of Ireland's population. **(1 SRP)**

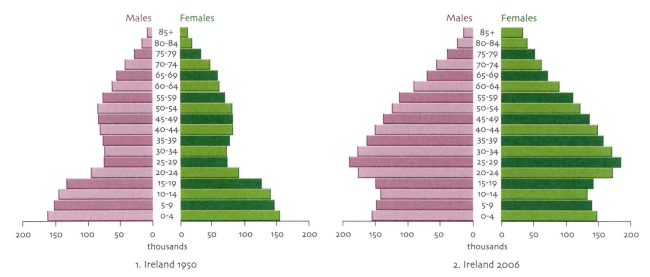

1. Ireland 1950   2. Ireland 2006

- Population pyramid 1 (1950): During this period Ireland was in Stage 3 of the 'demographic transition model' where .... were very high and death rates began to decrease. The broad base indicates a high birth rate while the narrow top indicates that .... is low, particularly in the 65+ age category. **(1 SRP)**

- Population pyramid 2 (2006): At this point Ireland has passed through Stage 4 and has entered Stage 5 of the demographic transition model, as birth rates failed to reach .... A much smaller percentage of Ireland's population is in the younger age categories, from 0 to 20, than in the next decade, i.e. from 20 to 30. This would indicate a decrease in the birth rate which would eventually lead to a .... in population. **(1 SRP)**

- The most efficient way of analysing the changes in Ireland's population structure is to focus on the changes in the fertility rates, mortality rates and the dependency ratio over time. **(1 SRP)**

Fertility rates

- Fertility rates in Ireland have changed radically from 1950 to the present. From the 1950s onwards fertility rates have steadily .... , from four children per mother to just under two children per mother. **(1 SRP)**

- Nevertheless, the last decade or so has seen a slight increase in the fertility rate from its lowest in 1994 at 1.85 births to 1.98 in 2006, but this is due mainly to the impact of .... and this will decrease slightly as immigrant workers and their families leave Ireland due to the current .... **(1 SRP)**

- Reasons for the decline in the fertility rate in Ireland are as follows:

   1 Increased .... meant that children were no longer needed to work in the agricultural sector and became an economic liability.

   2 The .... in Irish society has significantly increased their social status and they now marry a lot later in life, thus delaying .... and having fewer children. Irish women's average age of maternity has risen to their thirties.

   3 An increased number of women began to enter the .... and focused on the development of their careers. Consequently they have less time to spend rearing children, and childcare costs are perceived to be a ....

4 The decline in the influence of the .... meant that there was an increase in the uptake of artificial methods of family planning such as ....

5 A consequence of .... below the replacement level of 2.1 per couple in Ireland will be the impending decrease in the number of young people entering the workforce. Therefore women are needed to work and contribute to their government's income to decrease the ....

6 The modern Irish consumer society has led to an increase in the .... and high expectations regarding lifestyle which require women to work in paid employment. **(3 SRPs)**

Death rates and life expectancy

■ Death rates in Irish society have fallen from 13 per 1,000 in 1950 to 8 per 1,000 today, as Ireland has become a developed country. Life expectancy has increased by eighteen years over the same period as Irish people are .... **(1 SRP)**

■ Reasons for the decline in death rates and increases in life expectancy in Ireland since the 1950s are as follows:

1 Improved primary health care led to a reduction in .... and an increased life expectancy. Parents realise that their children will more than likely survive to become adults.

2 The implementation of .... , such as the successful Doctor Noël Browne campaign to eradicate .... , led to a radical decrease in death rates, particularly among young adults.

3 .... are provided so children are no longer needed to look after parents when they get old.

4 The emergence of an industrialised society as a result of .... from mainly US multinational companies has increased the gross domestic product, i.e. the wealth of the country. A successful .... manufacturing and services industry has led to an influx of money into the country, which the government used to develop the health and education sectors. **(2 SRPs)**

Dependency ratio

■ During the 1950s and early 1960s high birth rates and high unemployment led to a tide of mass emigration of the working population to the US, UK and Australia which .... the dependency ratio.

■ There has been a constant decline in the dependency ratio since the 1980s as the .... of the 1960s entered the 15+ age category and found jobs, stemming the tide of emigration. This decline is also due to a fall in the birth rates in the under-14 age category. This has created a narrowing of the base of the population pyramid while causing a bulge in the working age groups.

■ Over time, however, this will change, as the number in the 65+ age categories increases and the 15–64 categories decreases, thus increasing the dependency ratio.

■ Solutions to decreasing the dependency ratio are immigration and .... for couples to have more children. **(2 SRPs)**

Chapter 27

Overpopulation

- **Optimum population:** the number of people working with all the available resources of that area who will produce the highest standard of living and quality of life available to them.
    - Regions can have either a high or low optimum population.
    - Optimum population can change over time depending on the following factors:
        1. Technological improvements
        2. Emigration
        3. Changing population age and sex structure
        4. New discoveries of raw materials, e.g. oil or gas
- **Overpopulation** occurs when there are too many people in an area for the resources of that area to maintain an adequate standard of living.

(a) Causes of Overpopulation

Sample Question 1

Examine two causes of overpopulation in an area that you have studied, or outline how the overuse of resources can lead to overpopulation.

Sahel region in Africa

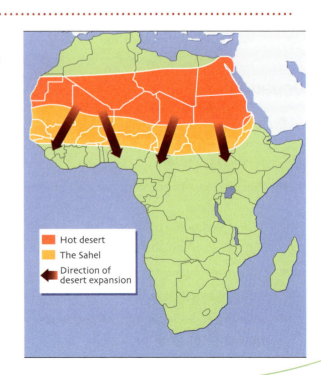

Hot desert

The Sahel

Direction of desert expansion

Cause 1: Overcropping

1   reasons for overcultivation . . . .

2   desertification in the Sahel . . . .

3   population increase . . . .

4   intensive agriculture . . . .

5   natural vegetation provides shade . . . .

6   salinisation . . . .

7   huge international debt . . . .

8   reduction in humus . . . .

Cause 2: Overgrazing

9   excessive number of livestock . . . .

10   damage to soil structure . . . .

11   helps reduce soil erosion . . . .

12   conversion to cash crops . . . .

13   high birth rates increased population . . . .

14   European colonisation . . . .

15   decreased food availability . . . .

(b) Causes and Effects of Overpopulation in the Sahel

Sample Question 2

Examine one cause and one effect of overpopulation in a region you have studied.

Insert the following terms into the blanks below:

kwashiorkor / nutrients / salinisation / migrated / fertilisers / topsoil / ability of the Sahel to produce food / cleared / sparse coarse grasses / wind erosion / shade / moisture / cash crops / evaporation / fallow / desertification / barrier / humus / international debt / fertility / monoculture / overcultivation / carrying capacity / refugee / over-reliant on aid / decline / incomes or food supplies / malnutrition / salts / rotation / swollen stomachs / poverty / spiral of land overuse / overpopulation / population explosion / shanty towns or bustees

One cause: Overcropping

- Overcropping or ………………………… is the growing of too many crops per hectare. The overgrazed soils become dry and dusty, resulting in a loss of soil fertility. Overcropping occurs for many reasons:
  - Farmers do not practise crop …………………… .
  - Farmers do not leave their land ……………… .
  - Farmers are unable to afford …………………… because most practise subsistence agriculture.

  (1 SRP)

- The Sahel region in Africa is being overcropped, causing …………………………………… . The Sahel is a semi-arid region covering just over three million square kilometres between the Sahara Desert to the north and the savannah and dense equatorial forests to the south. The Sahel passes through Burkina Faso, Chad, Mali, Mauritania, Niger and Senegal. In the past fifty years the Sahara has advanced into the Sahel at the rate of 2km to 5km per year. **(1 SRP)**

- Overcropping is also due to population increase. In 1961 the population of the Sahel was 19 million. By 2000 the population of the Sahel had increased to 50 million. This …………………………………………… resulted in an expansion of farmland and, as a consequence, overcropping. The population growth rate of 3 per cent per annum is greater than the …………………………………………………………………… . Annual food production is only increasing by a rate of 2 per cent per year. **(1 SRP)**

- These increased food demands were met by the introduction of intensive agriculture. Huge areas of natural vegetation were ……………… . The natural vegetation of the Sahel – ……………………………… ………………………… with thorn trees and shrubs – was altered and degraded. Soil erosion increased. Heavy seasonal rainstorms fell on exposed ground, washing away valuable ……………………… . …………………………………… also increased because there were fewer root systems to keep the soil in place. **(1 SRP)**

- Natural vegetation also provides …………………… cover for the soil. However, with the removal of this shade cover due to overcropping there is an increase in …………………………… . As a result, ………………… are drawn up to the surface. Soil salinity increases (the process of salinisation), hindering plant growth. **(1 SRP)**

- ………………………… forms a hard white crust which acts as a ………………… to nutrients entering the soil. The removal of plants also reduces the amount of ………………………… in the area. It may also mean less water being evaporated into the atmosphere, forming fewer rain-bearing clouds. Consequently, rainfall amounts ………………… , soil erosion increases and desertification occurs. **(1 SRP)**

- Many African countries have huge …………………………………………… . Farmers were encouraged to grow ……………………… for export. The repetitive growing of the same crop on the same piece of land on an annual basis reduces the soil's ………………… , causing soil erosion. The growing of the same crop every year is termed …………………………… . In order to maintain their output, farmers moved to new land and the process repeated itself. **(1 SRP)**

- The absence of vegetation cover also means there is less …………………… available to fertilise the soil. The soil loses its …………………………… and soil erosion occurs. This decrease in overall food availability will lead to an increase in overpopulation in a region. **(1 SRP)**

One effect: Desertification (the spread of deserts)

- Desertification has greatly increased suffering and ………………… in countries of sub-Saharan Africa such as Niger. Desertification has led to a decrease in the …………………………………………………… of land in the Sahel region. **(1 SRP)**

- An increase in the number of droughts and famines has led to .... problems within the region which only serve to exacerbate the problems. **(1 SRP)**

- People in refugee camps are .... from developed countries and lose their capacity to be self-sufficient. **(1 SRP)**

- Crops have failed and thousands of cattle have died of hunger. People have been left without adequate ...., which has caused an increase in .... , especially among the young. **(1 SRP)**

- Many children in the Sahel region die of diseases such as ...., a condition which results in thin, wasted limbs, ... and a complete lack of energy. **(1 SRP)**

- Many people in the worst-affected areas have no option but to move away in order to survive. Hundreds of thousands of people have .... southwards, contributing to .... and a further spiral of land overuse and desertification. **(1 SRP)**

- Those who decided to move to cities such as Niarney in Niger live in .... , which have developed at the edge of all big cities. The population increase in cities has increased the demand for firewood, causing deforestation of the limited number of trees that exist in urban hinterlands. This in turn contributes further to the .... and desertification. **(1 SRP)**

(c) Impact of Society, Income Levels and Technology on Overpopulation

Sample Question 3

Examine how any two of the following have impacted on or led to overpopulation:

1 society and culture

2 income levels

3 technology

Note: You need to have seven or eight SRPs on two of the following sections.

Impact of society and culture

1 high birth rates in developing countries ....

Empowerment of women

2 Cairo conference...

3 education ....

Culture

4 traditional roles..

5 women marry young..

6 discriminated against ....

Religious and political influence

Impact of income levels

High birth rates in developing countries

Low birth rates in developed countries

Focus on the Mezzogiorno

Impact of technology

Agricultural technology

Medical technology

Case study: USA

9 USA not overpopulated . . . .

10 unsustainable ecological footprint. . . . .

Intensive irrigation

Aerial crop-spraying

(d) Impact of Population Growth Rates on Development

Sample Question 4

Examine the impact of growth rates on development.

Insert the following terms into the blanks below:

> liability / the labour force / incentives / dependency ratio / enter the workforce / planning / increasing / modern schooling / urbanisation / unplanned / shanty towns / lifestyle / quality of life / provide an income / large families / drawbacks / policy / positive balance of trade / childcare / international debt / immigration / increased population growth / newly industrialising country / large cheap workforce / highly educated / birth spacing / replacement level / fewer children / agricultural / consumer society / inhibit / cost of living / poverty / moderate

Developing countries

Problems

- There is an intrinsic link between . . . . (high fertility rates) and . . . . (low wages). Poor people in developing countries have . . . . and as a result their income levels are consistently low. **(1 SRP)**

- A rapidly growing population in developing countries decreases income levels over time and increases the . . . . A high dependency ratio occurs when rapid population growth produces large numbers of children (up to 14 years of age) relative to the size of the working population (15–64 age group), i.e. . . . . **(1 SRP)**

- Most countries in sub-Saharan Africa have over 30 per cent of their entire population in the under-14 age category, ... the dependency ratio. **(1 SRP)**

- The result is that governments and families spend far more on children than children can quickly repay, as they do not . . . . Education costs a lot in the short term as . . . . replaces child labour, with the result that income levels in developing countries fall. **(1 SRP)**

- Rapid population growth has also led to increased .... as a result of rural-to-urban migration in developing countries. This in turn has led to the .... development of .... at the edge of large cities, e.g. São Paulo in Brazil. **(1 SRP)**

- The availability of a .... may slow the introduction of valuable new technologies as there is no pressure to integrate any of these new technologies. **(1 SRP)**

Solutions

- At a family level the ability to plan the number of children through ...., etc. can dramatically improve the quality of life. Governments can also achieve this through changes in healthcare and education .... , as in South Korea and Taiwan. **(1 SRP)**

- It does, however, take time for a government to introduce successful healthcare programmes, education programmes, new technologies, to upgrade infrastructure and achieve a .... **(1 SRP)**

- A massive increase in birth rates would .... a government's chances of successfully improving the .... for its people. In developing countries this has become more difficult as increased borrowing has led to a spiralling of .... **(1 SRP)**

- To conclude, it is clear that developing countries in which the population growth is .... will be more likely to increase their income and improve their overall quality of life and countries which have achieved this have become known as .... **(1 SRP)**

Developed countries

- In a developed country urban centres are fully developed, income levels are high, people are .... and birth rates begin to fall below the .... (2.1 children per mother). **(1 SRP)**

- Birth rates fall so significantly due to the following factors:

  - Children are perceived to be an economic ....

  - .... costs are seen as a significant financial burden.

  - Family .... is practised .

  - The social status of women has improved and they now marry a lot later in life, thus delaying childbearing and having ....

  - Women who .... and focus on the development of their careers have less time to spend rearing children

  - Increased urbanisation means that children are no longer needed to work in the .... sector.

  - The .... of the modern, developed world has led to an increase in the .... and high expectations regarding .... which cannot be achieved by having a large family. **(3 SRPs)**

- One of the potential .... of not achieving the replacement level will be an increase in the dependency ratio over time. Many developed countries have tried to overcome this potential problem by .... and .... for citizens to have larger families. **(1 SRP)**

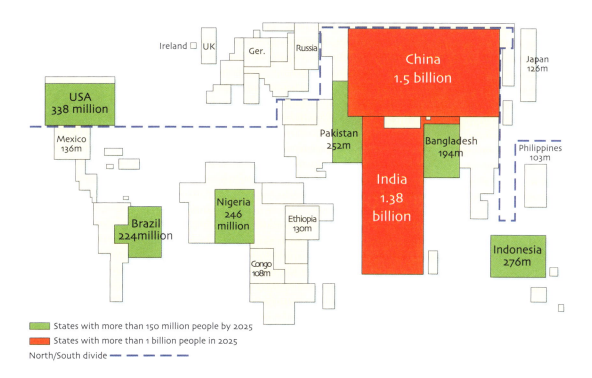

Ireland □ UK
Ger.
Russia
China
1.5 billion
Japan
126m

USA
338 million

Mexico
136m

Pakistan
252m
Bangladesh
194m
Philippines
103m

Nigeria
246
million
Ethiopia
130m
India
1.38
billion

Brazil
224million

Congo
108m

Indonesia
276m

🟩 States with more than 150 million people by 2025
🟧 States with more than 1 billion people in 2025
North/South divide – – – – – – –

Projected world population by 2025

Chapter 28
Migration

(a) Impacts of Migration

Sample Question 1

Outline the effects of emigration and immigration on Ireland.

Insert the following terms into the blanks below:

host countries / consumers / overall quality of life / unemployment / socio-economic decline / safety valve / well-paid employment / natural decrease / remittances / xenophobia / increased dependency ratio / below / overpopulation / increase productivity / brain drain / home market / mass emigration / donor country / rural depopulation / labour shortage / manufactured goods and services / professionals / skilled / repatriate / integrated / financial cost / racism / ghettos / birth rates / exploited / multi-ethnic / political migrants / push factor / foreign migrants

Emigration

- Emigration provided Ireland with a .... in the form of a solution to its oldest problem, ... Since the Great Famine of the 1840s unemployment has been the greatest .... to emigration. **(1 SRP)**

- Had emigration not been possible the high birth rates and spiralling unemployment problem would have increased pressure on Irish resources and .... would have resulted, thus reducing the .... **(1 SRP)**

- Ireland became a .... from the 1840s to the 1980s while the United States, the United Kingdom and Australia became the dominant .... for Irish emigrants. During most of this period Ireland had a .... in population despite having the highest .... in Western Europe. **(1 SRP)**

- Like many countries, Ireland benefitted from .... – money sent back by emigrants to help out the family at home. **(1 SRP)**

- An examination of Ireland's population pyramids between 1950 and 1988 shows a significant absence of people in the 16–40 age category. The absence of such people leads to an .... and limits a nation's ability to .... , and therefore income levels remain low. **(1 SRP)**

- The young people who leave are usually the most .... and the promise of .... is the dominant pull factor. This significant loss of skilled workers is referred to as a .... **(1 SRP)**

- People in the 16–40 age category are the key .... in any country and their absence decreases demand for .... and this reduces the size of the .... **(1 SRP)**

- The west of Ireland suffered the most during this period of .... and thus .... The average age of farmers in the west of Ireland increased dramatically during this period, increasing the dependency ratio and contributing to .... **(1 SRP)**

Immigration

- A .... in Ireland was created by the 'Celtic Tiger' and to ensure continued economic growth these jobs were filled by .... , predominantly from Eastern Europe. These migrants included both .... and the unskilled. **(1 SRP)**

- The cultural effects of immigration have led to a more .... , outward-looking, cosmopolitan society. **(1 SRP)**

- Some immigrants are not economic migrants such as those from Eastern Europe but .... from countries where they are oppressed, e.g. Nigeria. **(1 SRP)**

- Host countries can .... guest workers, i.e. foreign nationals employed on a fixed-contract basis can be sent back to their country of origin when they are no longer needed, even if their families have adjusted and .... **(1 SRP)**

- The .... of supporting refugees can be a serious strain on the host country's economy. **(1 SRP)**

- Ethnic hatred can become a problem as .... and .... create serious social issues and some native people resent the presence of foreigners. Language barriers and the development of .... only serve to widen the distrust between natives and foreigners. **(1 SRP)**

- A vast number of unskilled immigrants are .... and some are paid .... the minimum wage. **(1 SRP)**

(b) Impact of Changing Migration Patterns in Ireland

Sample Question 2

Examine the impact of changing migration patterns to and from Ireland.

Stages of migration patterns in Ireland

Stage 1 (1840–1960): Post-famine population decline

1 continued post-famine emigration ....

2 three million emigrated . . . .

3 1950s exodus . . . .

4 consequences of emigration . . . .

Stage 2 (1961–79): First economic boom

5 first programme for economic expansion . . . .

6 attracted modern industry/stemmed flow of emigration . . . .

7 joined EU, 1973 . . . .

Stage 3 (1980–90): Global economic recession

8 oil prices triggered world recession . . . .

9 brain drain . . . .

10 decline in births, 1980s . . . .

Stage 4 (1990–2006): Celtic Tiger era (second economic boom)

11 Celtic Tiger . . . .

12 quote from Paul Krugman (US economist) . . . .

13 mass immigration . . . .

Stage 5 (2007–present): Global economic recession

14 dramatic slowdown in the Irish economy . . . .

15 net out-migration for the foreseeable future . . . .

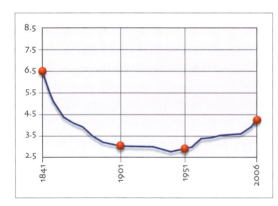

Population in Ireland, 1841–2006

(c) Migration Policy in Ireland and the EU

Sample Question 3

Outline the impact of changing migration policy in Ireland and the EU.

Migration policy in Ireland

1. unprepared for wave of inward migration. . . . .
2. European Economic Area . . . .
3. attract highly skilled workers . . . .

2007 policy: four categories of permit

4. green card/work permit. . . . .
5. intracompany transfer permit/spousal and dependent permit. . . . .

Key aspects of policy

6. green card/family reunification/recruitment expenses . . . .
7. five years/asylum seekers/students. . . . .
8. asylum seekers . . . .
9. refugee status . . . .

Migration policy in the EU

10. countries need migrants due to natural decrease . . . .
11. series of treaties . . . .
12. EU Council of Seville, 2002 . . . .

Key aspects of policy

13. common border control/shared responsibility for migrants. . . . .
14. Europol/Eurodac. . . . .
15. Fortress Europe . . . .
16. welfare payments. . . . .
17. Denmark . . . .

(d) Racial, Ethnic and Religious Issues Arising from Migration

Sample Question 2

Analyse the racial, ethnic and religious issues which arise from migration.

Insert the following terms into the blanks below:

native culture / ethnic cleansing / major challenges / racist intimidation / segregate / clearly identifiable / 'educate together' / Equal Status Act, 2000 / 'Troubles' / illegal / exploited / speak the language / cycle of poverty / worldwide / identity and traditions / locals and immigrants / two-way process / receiver country / immigrants / ethos / newly integrated multi-religious society / prejudice / mass extermination / conflict / ghetto / inferior / integration / multiculturalism / traditional hat / patronage of the Catholic Church / discrimination / multi-denominational / Sikh / natives / diaspora / apartheid

Racial issues

- Racism from migration occurs when tensions build up between .... can build up based on stereotypes. Racism is the belief that people are .... because of their skin colour, i.e. their biological physical appearance. **(1 SRP)**

- Fear of .... drives immigrants into one area within a city, which becomes a .... over time. This only serves to .... the locals and the immigrants even further and may fuel racist attitudes among both parties. **(1 SRP)**

- Some migrants are .... by their skin colour or other physical characteristics and may be viewed as outsiders as a result. In pre-1990s South Africa racial separation between blacks and whites was enforced by law in a government policy of .... **(1 SRP)**

- Migrants can be discriminated against as they may be .... and therefore .... by opportunistic employers. They may not be able to .... of the host country and may be paid less than the minimum wage, so that they become trapped in a .... **(1 SRP)**

Ethnic issues

- Ethnicity generally refers to the collective identity of a minority group within a larger host population. Most ethnic groups work hard to sustain the language, customs and traditions of their .... Ethnic groups set up organisations to preserve their .... **(1 SRP)**

- Those who emigrated from Ireland up until the 1990s to countries such the UK, the United States and Australia set up Irish folk, language, GAA and dancing clubs to protect their cultural identity. The spread of the Irish .... throughout the world has resulted in St Patrick's Day becoming a .... celebration. **(1 SRP)**

■ .... is the slaughter or expulsion of ethnic groups from a country or region. This occurred during World War II in the Nazis' .... of over four million people from minority groups such as the Jews and gypsies. **(1 SRP)**

Modern societies are more multicultural and multi-ethnic

Religious issues

■ The issue of religious freedom for a minority religion in the .... can pose some .... to the established majority religion. In Ireland, for example, Catholic schools with their Catholic .... have to deal equitably with religious diversity by accommodating different traditions within the school system. **(1 SRP)**

■ In a ...., matters of dress affiliated to a specific religion, e.g. the wearing of head-dress by Muslim women, may have to be accepted by schools. **(1 SRP)**

■ Religious differences may lead to .... such as occurred in Northern Ireland, where tension and distrust between Catholics and Protestants led to the .... , i.e. armed conflict, from the 1970s to the 1990s. **(1 SRP)**

Issues arising in Ireland

The turban issue

■ In relation to immigrants in Ireland, the Irish government's policy is one of .... rather than ....'Integration' as a policy required immigrants to adapt to Irish culture as a way of assimilating into society, while 'multiculturalism' in contrast gives distinct cultural groups equal status. **(1 SRP)**

■ In 2007 the Garda Síochána forbade a newly qualified recruit, a .... , to wear a turban during work hours as all gardaí had to wear the .... .This type of decision may create tension in the future as integration is a .... that places duties and obligations on both ethnic minorities and the state. **(1 SRP)**

The schools issue

■ The 2006 census revealed a large increase in non-Catholic children looking for school places. A serious issue arose in north Co. Dublin (Fingal County Council) as they could not provide enough school places for all the children enrolling. **(1 SRP)**

■ Ninety-eight per cent of primary schools in Ireland are under the ……………………………………… ……………………………… . According to the ………………………………………………… first preference for school enrolment was to be given to Catholics so that the ethos of the school would be protected. **(1 SRP)**

■ Some parents considered this to be a form of …………………………… and racism. ………………………………………… emergency schools were set up but it still segregates the …………… from the …………………… . Therefore more planning is needed if an ………………………………… philosophy is to be successfully adopted. **(1 SRP)**

Chapter 29
Settlement

« Definitions »

Site

The site of a settlement refers to **the land or area on which it is built**. Is it flat, gently sloping or at a dry point site or on a river's flood plain? The site might have been a defensive site for protection or a river site for a fresh water supply or transport, e.g. Dublin grew on a flat, lower-lying area on the banks of the Liffey.

Situation

The situation of a settlement describes its **location in relation to the surrounding area**, features, etc. An urban settlement might be situated in a river valley, on a coastal area, in a sheltered harbour, in a mountain gap, in close proximity to a railway line/station or at a focus of routeways, e.g. Naas has grown due to the influence of Dublin city and its location on a strategic road corridor.

Function

The function of a settlement is the **dominant activity or purpose** of the town:

- Navan = mining town
- Killarney = tourist town
- Tuam = religious town
- Rosslare = port town

Large towns and cities are multi-functional settlements, i.e. they have a variety of functions.

(a) Site, Situation and Function of Settlement in Ireland

Sample Question 1

Map question: With the aid of the Galway Ordnance Survey map (see p. 199), examine the site, situation and function of the settlement.

Insert the following terms into the blanks below:

Norman / situational / pollution / M 296 249 / N84 / tourist information centres / N6 / lowest bridging point / Corrib / rural areas / regional road / urbanisation / trading / fresh water / alluvium / sheltered harbour / bay / nodal / star-shaped forts / national primary road / beach / round tower / gently sloping / M 303 253 / hinterland / 100 metres / services / multi-functional / industrial estate / contours / northern bank / east–west / educational / M 294 251 / river crossings / required skills / long extended pier / tourist

Site

- The low-lying nature of the site is indicated by the close proximity to Galway Bay and by the fact that no ……………… reach over fifty metres above sea level in the city. The well spaced-out contours in the city also indicating that the site is ………………………………. **(1 SRP)**

- The site is located on the ………………………………………… of the Corrib river at M 296 249 in close proximity to where it enters Galway Bay at M 303 247. This in turn opens out into the Atlantic Ocean to the west of Galway Bay where the marked ferry route to the Aran Islands can be located at M 28 22. **(1 SRP)**

- The lowest bridging point at ……………… is where the …………………………… R336 crosses the Corrib River in a north-east/south-west direction. It is strategically important to the site development as it links the two main growth centres of the west bank and east bank of the river. The site has expanded outwards over time from these two banks due to increased ………………………… and urban sprawl, and there are now three bridging points of the river within the city. **(1 SRP)**

- There are two castles located on the eastern side of the river at M 296 250 and M 298 253. They are evidence of ……………… settlement during the middle ages dating from 1170 to 1300. The castle at M 296 250 is located less than ………………… east of the Corrib River, which would have been used for cooking, cleaning, transporting and as a source of food in medieval times. **(1 SRP)**

- The Normans used the site strategically for defensive purposes and for ……………. The continued importance of the site for defensive purposes would be indicated by the two star-shaped forts at M 312 247 and M 305 264. The close proximity of the castles to the bridging point would indicate that the Normans controlled …………………………… and river traffic, and therefore the trading system. **(1 SRP)**

Situation

- Lough Corrib, located on the north-west of the OS map, would have provided a constant supply of ………………………… for Galway city. This River Corrib flowing southwards from the lake at M 274 299 would have provided fresh water and ………………… for the surrounding flood plain. This flood plain would in turn have provided the city with a constant supply of food. **(1 SRP)**

- The city opens out into an easily accessible …………………………………… to the south, and this would have been a key ……………………… factor to the growth and development of the city, including fishing, defence and trading. **(1 SRP)**

- The city is ideally situated to serve as a market town for the surrounding …………………………. This has led to the development of a network of routeways on the OS map, with Galway city as a ………… point, as the focus of transport routes. **(1 SRP)**

- All the major roads on the map converge in the city. The .... , the N17, enters the map at M 354 310 and at the roundabout on the northern outskirts of Galway (M 321 272) becomes the .... and the R336. Galway is served by two national secondary roads, the .... which enters the map at M 320 310 and the N59, and by many regional roads, for example the R339 which enters the map at M 390 287. **(1 SRP)**

- There is a railway station at .... The railway line enters the map at M 390 261 and runs in an .... direction, allowing for effective transportation of people and goods. **(1 SRP)**

- All of these forms of transport link the surrounding hinterland to the city where .... are provided. Examples of these would be the hospitals at M 291 255 and at M 340 256 to cater for health, the seven post offices, e.g. M 313 258, which allow for sending mail, the Garda station at .... to provide law and order for the city and a fire station at M 297 247. **(1 SRP)**

Function

- The variety and density of functions have helped to make Galway city a .... settlement.

- Commercial/manufacturing function: There are many car parks in Galway, e.g. M 300 256, to cater for all the people coming into the city to work and for those going shopping. There is an .... on the northern side of Galway at M 325 275 to attract industry into the city. It is located on the northern outskirts of the city to reduce .... and congestion in Galway city. **(1 SRP)**

- Port/defence function: There is an intrinsic link between the ...., the development of trade and defence in the city. The presence of the .... River and the bay sheltered from the Atlantic Ocean made the city an ideal location for trade to develop. **(1 SRP)**

- The bay was also used for defence purposes. A .... is located at M 345 244 on the .... of the bay and would have been used by early Christian monks as a watch tower to defend themselves from attackers such as Vikings. Two star-shaped forts were built for defensive purposes, e.g. at M 312 247. The presence of the .... at M 302 248 in the Claddagh area would indicate that trade is still very important to the city today. **(1 SRP)**

- .... function: There is a university at M 288 258 and regional technical colleges at M 328 258 and at M 328 258, which would educate graduates with the .... to attract industry into the city. There are many primary and secondary schools, e.g. at M 308 264, to cater for the educational needs of the young population of Galway. There are no schools found in the .... of the map so the city would provide for the educational needs of those living in its hinterland. **(1 SRP)**

- .... function: Galway is the major tourist centre on the map. The many tourist attractions include two historical .... at M 305 264 and M 312 246, a holy well at M 306 256 and an old burial ground at M 284 242, reflecting early Christian settlement, and three castles are located in the city, e.g. at M 297 250, built for defensive purposes. **(1 SRP)**

- There is a .... at M 302 253 to provide information about all the activities available in the city and its hinterland. There is also a caravan and camping site at M 324 247, located on the bay, and a .... running along the bay in an east–west direction at M 27 23. **(1 SRP)**

(b) Rural Settlement Patterns

Sample Question 2

'Rural settlement in Ireland can be divided into dispersed, clustered and ribboned/linear.' Discuss.

Insert the following terms into the blanks below:

cul-de-sac driveways / road junction / roadside sites / commonage / clachan / open-field system / services / development plans / enclose / higher order of services / fencing and hedging / rural one-off housing / unsustainable / grouped close together / clusters / widely separated / plantation / bridging point / lower order of services / along the sides of roads / planning permission / individual buildings are scattered / bungalow blitz / hamlet / car ownership

Dispersed

- A dispersed settlement pattern develops when .... across a rural area in a random pattern. **(1 SRP)**

- Each individual farmhouse is surrounded by farmland and the farmhouses are therefore .... from each other. **(1 SRP)**

- The historic reason for the development of this settlement pattern was the .... of farming developed in the eighteenth century where farmers shared open grazing land called .... **(1 SRP)**

- Over time the original farmers began to .... land by .... and built their farmhouses in these enclosed areas, creating a dispersed settlement. **(1 SRP)**

- Since the 1960s a trend of .... has developed, but county councils are currently discouraging this as they regard this type of development as .... **(1 SRP)**

- Today this pattern can be seen on maps where farmhouses are located at the end of long .... which branch off from third-class roads. **(1 SRP)**

Clustered (nucleated)

- A clustered settlement pattern develops when buildings are .... in a rural area. **(1 SRP)**

- In the west of Ireland .... of houses are a sign of old farming systems. These were called .... A site may have been donated to a member of the extended family. **(1 SRP)**

- In some areas of the country, e.g. county Waterford, farmhouses were built in clusters during the .... era. **(1 SRP)**

- Some clusters were located at a small junction such as a .... or a .... of a river. Over time these clusters may have developed into a .... or small village with a .... Some may have developed into towns and cities with a .... **(1 SRP)**

Ribboned/linear

- A linear pattern of rural development occurs when a line of one-off buildings is built ....
.... **(1 SRP)**

- This pattern has developed in Ireland since the 1960s. It is where one-off houses form a continuous line up to 2km from villages and towns. It has become known as the .... **(1 SRP)**

- The main reasons for the ribbon development in Ireland are:

  1 Farmers could boost their income by selling these highly desirable ....

  2 .... such as water supply, sewerage, electricity and telephone lines were easily accessible from these sites.

  3 Local .... was easily granted from the county council for the development of these sites. **(1 SRP)**

- The knock-on effect of this, coupled with increased .... in Ireland, saw these sites becoming the dominant location for bed and breakfasts, petrol stations, etc. **(1 SRP)**

- The current national and county .... regard ribbon development as unsustainable due to increased costs of basic services, e.g. electricity, and the negative effect on the rural landscape. Local governments would prefer a more urbanised structure of development within towns, i.e. housing estates are more efficient. **(1 SRP)**

Linear rural settlement

(c) Planning Strategies in Rural Areas

Sample Question 3

Explain the process of planning strategies in rural areas.

Introduction

1 counter urbanisation ....

Planning strategies

Vulnerable landscape

Area under pressure from urban-generated housing

Structurally weak area

Open countryside

Ennis

Killaloe

Kilrush

Zoning in Co. Clare for rural housing

(d) Site Characteristics of Urban Settlement

Sample Question 4

Explain the characteristics of urban settlements, focusing on the Central Place Theory, hierarchy and hinterland.

Insert the following terms into the blanks below:

Galway / low / even out / goods and services / primate / weekly / existing services / lower order goods / interlocking / overlap / higher order goods / dominant urban centre / thresholds / minimum number of customers / level of demand / distance people are prepared to travel / travel further to larger centres / sizing and spacing / middle order goods / Dublin / hinterland / high / counteract / trade area / basic services / equal distance / relief / political boundaries / threshold population / Tralee / urban centre / hexagonal / centralised / rural depopulation

The Central Place Theory

- Walter Christaller devised this theory to explain the .... of settlements. He maintained that large, medium and small urban centres are linked to each other in a pattern. **(1 SRP)**

- The central place is the .... in a given area, which provides services for the surrounding area or .... Depending on their size, central places differ in the type of .... they offer, i.e. large centres offer a wide variety of services while small villages and hamlets will offer very .... **(1 SRP)**

- The Central Place Theory has three key concepts:

1 Range

- The range is the .... for a particular good or service.

- The range of different goods in the Central Place Theory are as follows:

  - .... and services are needed frequently so people are not willing to travel far for them, e.g. bread, milk.

  - .... and services are needed from time to time, so people are willing to travel a little further, e.g. supermarket, doctor.

  - .... and services are needed occasionally so people will travel wherever necessary for these, e.g. specialist services such as laser eye treatment. **(1 SRP)**

- Because people are willing to travel different distances for different goods and services, different sized urban centres have different .... **(1 SRP)**

2 Threshold

- The threshold is the .... needed to maintain a service. Each service has its own market area. A low threshold is needed for a corner shop, i.e. a small number of customers who may visit the shop on a daily basis. A high threshold is needed for a hospital, i.e. a large number of people who may only use it once every few years. **(1 SRP)**

3 Frequency of demand

- This refers to the ……………………………… for goods and services, i.e. whether these goods and services are required on a daily, weekly, monthly or occasional basis. In general frequency of demand is ……… for low order services such as daily needs but ……… for high order services such as a visit to a hospital. **(1 SRP)**

Urban hierarchy

- This is the grading or ranking in importance of urban centres in relation to each other in a given urban system. The 'urban hierarchy' of a country's urban system is arranged like a pyramid with the largest city on top:

  1 ……………… city

  2 cities

  3 towns

  4 villages

  5 hamlets

  6 rural dwellings. **(1 SRP)**

- An urban system is a set of urban centres within a region; these centres are part of an …………………… urban system that links communities together at local, regional and national level.

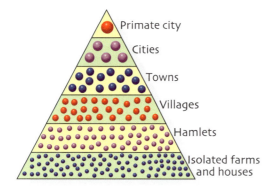

Focus on Ireland

Level 1: ……………… would be at the top of the pyramid as Ireland's primate city (higher-order services).

Level 2: This would include smaller cities such as Cork, …………… , Limerick (higher-order services).

Level 3: This would incorporate county towns, e.g. Mullingar, Portlaoise, ………… (middle-order services).

Level 4: This would include smaller towns and villages. Name a few in your county (middle-order services).

Levels 5 and 6: These would include hamlets and small villages. Name a few in your county (low-order services). **(2 SRPs)**

- The National Spatial Strategy (2002) was devised by the Irish government to balance the socio-economic growth of the country. It was a conscious effort to …………………… the sizing and spacing of settlements and to …………………… the dominance of Dublin city. **(1 SRP)**

Hinterland

- The hinterland is the ………………… surrounding the urban centre where customers live. The size of the hinterland is dependent on the size and number of services provided by the …………………… ……………………………………… . Hinterlands for higher-order services are large, while hinterlands for lower-order services are smaller. They may also ……………… where people live an ………………………………… from two similar-sized urban centres. **(1 SRP)**

- In his Central Place Theory, Christaller used the model of …………………… hinterlands, but this was assuming that no other factors influence them. In reality, the ideal model is affected by:

  1 Physical factors: He did not take into account the fact that …………… features, such as mountain ranges, or drainage features, such as rivers, would modify the ideal flat plain he had envisaged.

  2 Socio-economic factors: He also failed to account for …………………………………………, e.g. the north and south of Ireland, cultural and religious factors, and infrastructure, e.g. good roads may cause the boundary of a hinterland to change. **(2 SRPs)**

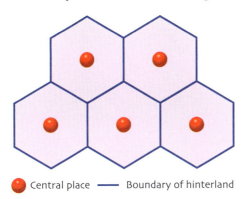

🔴 Central place —— Boundary of hinterland

Changes in population density and urban functions

- The process of urbanisation, i.e. the growth of cities and towns, has …………………… many functions which were once carried out in rural areas. The reasons for this are:

  - Urbanisation has increased the …………………………………………, which has led to the increased growth of urban functions in large towns and cities.

  - Urbanisation had also led to …………………………………………, whereby small towns and villages struggle to maintain ………………………………… .

  - The increase in the number of cars in rural areas allows people to ………………………………………… ………………………………… for low-order services.

  - The concept of daily grocery shopping has changed to ……………… shopping, as foods are increasingly processed to last longer. **(2 SRPs)**

(e) Functions and Services of Settlements over Time

Sample Question 5

With the aid of a case study, explain how functions and services of urban centres can change over time.

Case study: Galway city

1 dominant urban centre of the region ....

1: Defensive function

2 medieval times: Lynch's castle built ....

3 city wall ....

2: Port function

4 merchant city as international trade grew...

5 principal Irish port/infrastructure developed...

6 function declined in recent decades ....

3: Education function

7 university city in 1845 ....

8 attracted high-value foreign direct investment..

4: Manufacturing function

9 main manufacturing centre in the region ....

10 education and manufacturing/IT/medical ....

11 high-value well-paid jobs ....

12 increased residential function ....

5: Services function

13 multi-functional settlement ....

Focus on tourism

13 picturesque and lively/Irish traditions/Claddagh rings..

14 festivals/scenery and walking trails ....

15 Fáilte Ireland ....

Volvo Ocean Race in Galway City, 2009

Chapter 30
Urban Settlement

« Definitions »

- **Zoning:** when an area of land is used for a specific purpose.

- **Rezoning:** when zones are changed by local councils, e.g. an influx of people to a city due to provision of jobs might lead to rezoning from agricultural to residential land.

- **Functional zones** in cities:

  1 CBD – central business district in city centre.

  2 Commercial – offices, shops, etc.

  3 Residential – lower, middle and upper income.

  4 Industrial – light or heavy manufacturing.

  5 Recreation – parks and green areas.

(a) Land Use Zone Theories

Sample Question 1

Explain three theories of urban land use zones.

Insert the following terms into the blanks below:

environmentally friendly zones / fringe / shopping centres / social stratification / upper class / multi-functional / outwards / high density / industry / working-class people / focus for further development / terraced housing / middle-class people / growth point / expansion of towns and cities / more than one / car culture / industrial location / major routeways or sectors / private transport / polluted / commute / strategic routeways / change over time / city boundaries / concentric circles / renewal or redevelopment / no two cities are the same / nodal points / one large urban region / income / heavy manufacturing / more relevant in modern cities / physical landscape / port / accessible routes / CBD / guide to how cities develop / prevalent

255

Introduction

Urbanisation has led to the .... due to an increase in population since the Industrial Revolution. Many theories have been put forward as to how the patterns of development of cities .... This may involve physical, economic and cultural change. **(1 SRP)**

Theory 1: Concentric zone theory

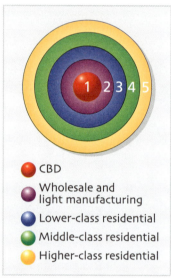

- Burgess, who devised this theory in 1924, claimed that cities are composed of .... , creating zones which grow .... from the centre.

- Some of his key assumptions were:

  - He believed that cities had well defined zones of residential areas linked to .... levels.

  - He believed that buildings got progressively younger towards the urban .... **(1 SRP)**

1 2 3 4 5

- CBD
- Wholesale and light manufacturing
- Lower-class residential
- Middle-class residential
- Higher-class residential

Zone-by-zone focus

- Zone 1: The .... in the city centre.

- Zone 2: Includes .... residences, i.e. multi-storey apartments. The poorest people, e.g. migrants, live in Zone 2. This zone also contains areas of .... It is also the zone of transition where land may be redeveloped and incorporated into the CBD.

- Zone 3: This zone comprises .... who are better off than Zone 2 people and live largely in ....

- Zone 4: This is where .... live in detached or semi-detached homes with gardens.

- Zone 5: This is where the .... lives, on the edge of the city. Many residents commute to work. **(2 SRPs)**

Conclusions

- Burgess's theory has some relevant aspects but it was devised prior to the .... in cities today.

- It does not take the .... into account. It assumes that the topography (relief) and drainage (rivers and valleys) are equal all over the city area.

- It also fails to take into account the changing factors associated with .... **(1 SRP)**

Theory 2: Sector theory

- Hoyt's theory, devised in 1939, took into account the concentric circles of Burgess's model, but claimed that .... extending outwards from the city also have an important bearing on urban land use and development. **(1 SRP)**

- Some of his key assumptions were:
  - He believed that wealthy people live in .... away from the industrial zone.
  - He believed that wealthier people could afford .... and therefore could live further away from the CBD.
  - He believed that particular land uses attracted other similar land uses. **(1 SRP)**

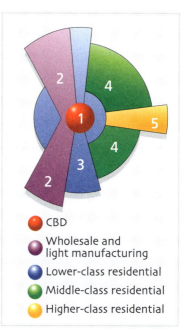

CBD

Wholesale and light manufacturing

Lower-class residential

Middle-class residential

Higher-class residential

Zone-by-zone focus

- Zone 1: CBD.

- Zone 2: This extends outwards from the CBD along major routeways and contains industry.

- Zone 3: This extends outwards from the CBD next to the industrial zone and can be .... as a result. This is a residential area where lower-income people live.

- Zone 4: This is a residential area for middle-income people.

- Zone 5: This is a residential area for high-income people. From the 1930s to the 1970s only wealthy people could afford to .... and therefore they moved to the edge of the city in environmentally friendly neighbourhoods. **(2 SRPs)**

Conclusions

- Hoyt tended to base his theory on .... out from the city centre and on .... in cities, i.e. people of similar incomes lived in the same area. **(1 SRP)**

- Some critics believe he did not take into account the that zones may be .... and are never as clear-cut as shown on the model. Neither did he take into account urban .... schemes. **(1 SRP)**

Theory 3: Multiple nuclei theory

- Harris and Ullman envisaged that most large cities had .... CBD, i.e. cities grew around a number of different .... or business centres.

- Some of their key assumptions were:

  - They believed that each business centre acted as a ....

  - These centres would themselves attract growth, becoming a ....

  - All centres would then grow outwards until they all merged into .... **(1 SRP)**

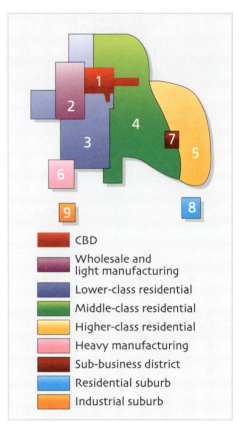

Zone-by-zone focus

- Zones 1 and 7: These are the CBD and sub-CBD respectively.

- Zone 2: This is the manufacturing zone.

- Zone 3: This is the lower-income residential zone and, as in Hoyt's theory, is located next to the industrial zone.

- Zone 4: This is the middle-income residential centre.

- Zone 5: This is the upper-income residential centre.

- Zone 6: This is the .... zone located next to the lower-income residential area.

- Zone 8: These are commuter towns outside the ....

- Zone 9: This is an industrial suburb. **(2 SRPs)**

Conclusions

- Some aspects of the multiple nuclei model are .... than Burgess's and Hoyt's models:

  - In modern cities alternative business districts such as .... have become individual growth centres.

  - Heavy industry will locate near a ....

  - Social stratification is .... in cities. Higher-income housing will locate in more desirable sites.

  - Retailing will develop on busy .... **(2 SRPs)**

Overall conclusions

- The advantage of these models is that they give us a .... in relation to strategic corridors or routeways, social stratification, industry and alternative business districts. **(1 SRP)**

- The disadvantage of these theories is that they fail to realise that .... and that other issues have influenced they way cities develop, such as the renewal and redevelopment of the inner city. **(1 SRP)**

(b) Social Stratification

Sample Question 2

Outline, with the aid of a case study, how social stratification occurs in cities and how this might affect land values.

1 land values ....

Social stratification

2 economic background ....

3 separated by wealth ....

4 factors influencing house purchases..

How house price and design can reflect social segregation

5 lower income/middle income/upper income ....

6 access to education ....

7 integration ....

8 new planning laws ....

How land values are affected by social stratification

9 property values..

10 poor planning strategies ....

11 change over time ....

....

12 'Nimby' attitude......................................

....

13 age-based stratification ....

....

14 residential segregation in Dublin ....

....

15 Dublin docklands ....

....

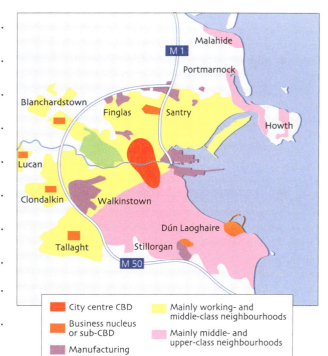

Social stratification in Dublin city

(c) Urban Sprawl

Sample Question 3

'Urban sprawl is putting pressure on rural landuse.' Discuss.

Insert the following terms into the blanks below:

soulless suburbs / Central Park / alternative poles for development / traffic congestion / yuppies / rural environment / National Spatial Strategy / commuter culture / historic monuments / urban areas / urban environments / recreation / planners / permanent fixtures / over 80 per cent / urban expansion / pressure / river flood plains / the Phoenix Park / local identity / social consequences / rural environments on the urban fringe / commuter traffic jams / compulsory purchase orders / pollution / ecological awareness / needs of the urban population / green belts / redeveloping and renewing / hedgerows and wetlands / balanced sustainable development / agricultural land / urban sprawl / overspill towns

Green belts

- As cities expand, green belts within cities or .... come under increased pressure to change their use. They are normally changed to urban industrial or urban residential use to serve the growing needs of the city. This process is called .... **(1 SRP)**

- Today in Europe .... of its half a billion inhabitants live in .... This figure is increasing all the time, thus putting increased pressure on rural areas in green belts and on the fringes of the city. **(1 SRP)**

CBD   Motorway
Inner city   Rail routes
Suburbs   Business and shopping centres
Satellite towns
Suburban rural area   Factory

The expansion of cities

- Open space on the fringe of large towns and cities is predominantly agricultural land. Pressure from rapid urbanisation forces local authorities to use .... to rezone land for residential and industrial use. **(1 SRP)**

- Open space areas in cities and large towns are called .... and consist of parks and areas of woodland. An example of these within a city would be .... in Dublin city and .... in New York City. **(1 SRP)**

- The functions of green belts are:

  1 To break the monotony of ....

  2 To improve the quality of ....

  3 To provide urban ...., i.e. sports fields, areas for leisure walks, etc. **(1 SRP)**

- Urban .... value these parks and woodland areas and therefore they have become .... of the city landscape. **(1 SRP)**

- Nevertheless, urbanisation continuously places more and more .... on existing green belts and farmland for .... **(1 SRP)**

Problems of urbanisation affecting rural areas

- .... is lost as green belt areas are built up with roads, industry and housing.

- Ground bulldozed for new developments has led to the destruction of .... and therefore the destruction of habitats.

- Some .... can be destroyed, e.g. the construction of the M3 motorway through the Skryne Valley close to the Hill of Tara.

- The renaming of places and townlands by developers can lead to a loss of .... The new names are generally unrelated to the history of the area.

- The construction of housing estates on .... can have devastating consequences downstream, e.g. in Clonmel.

- There are often also .... of urban sprawl, including long hours sitting in .... , increased CO_2 emissions, visual .... from soulless suburbs, and inner-city decline. **(3 SRPs)**

Conclusions

- Urban development should be a form of ...., i.e. it should involve the maintenance of natural rural areas as well as the economic development of the city. **(1 SRP)**

- Local authorities must combine .... with an understanding of the .... **(1 SRP)**

- Some countries have attempted to reduce urban sprawl by:

  - .... inner city areas, making them more attractive to live in, e.g. the Temple Bar area in Dublin city.

  - Local authorities actively encouraging young professionals (..................) to live in the CBD and the zone of transition.

  - Seeking .... , i.e. developing other centres. The Irish government's ...., devised in 2002, was an attempt to ease the pressure of urban sprawl on Dublin city, whose growth was exponential during the Celtic Tiger era. **(1 SRP)**

Focus on the impact of Dublin city's growth

- Unplanned urban sprawl of Dublin city in the 1970s led to the development of planned .... (Blanchardstown, Tallaght and Clondalkin), which expanded the city into the surrounding countryside to over fifteen kilometres beyond the city centre. **(1 SRP)**

- During the Celtic Tiger era the competition for land and high cost of living in the city forced people to look for homes up to 100km from the city centre, putting pressure on the surrounding .... This created a .... where people had no choice but to travel long distances to and from work, increasing .... and pollution in rural towns located on the strategic road corridors out of the city. **(1 SRP)**

Chapter 31

Problems with Urbanisation

(a) Traffic Problems

Sample Question 1

With the aid of a case study, outline the problems of urban traffic and their solutions.

Introduction

1 cars have high levels of efficiency..

2 narrow, unplanned streets/wide, planned grid pattern ....

Problems with traffic movement

3 rush hour...

4 commuters/children dropped and collected from school..

Solutions

5 ringroads and bypasses/more road space...

6 efficient public transport/better traffic management..

Case study: Dublin city

7 urban sprawl ....

Problems

8 unplanned street network...

9 traffic congestion during school time..

10 increased population ....

11 M50 became urban spine ....

Solutions

12 Transport 21/DART...

13 port tunnel/Luas..

14 quality bus corridors (QBCs)/computerised traffic signals (SCATS)...

National Development Plan 2007–13

15 new Luas lines/two underground lines ....

16 integrated ticketing system/barrier-free tolling ....

17 Dublin councils encourage infill development ....

Traffic congestion at the port tunnel in Dublin

(b) Inner City Decline and Urban Sprawl

Sample Question 2

With the aid of a case study, discuss the problems associated with inner city decline and urban sprawl.

Insert the following terms into the blanks below:

primary / absence of community / basic facilities / wealthier / little recreation space / 40,000 jobs / roll-on/roll-off / unemployed / urban housing crisis / urban sprawl / multi-storey tower blocks / Grand Canal Theatre / high cost of land / Le Corbusier / industrial estates / suburban areas / commuter culture / outbound / vast urban environment / traffic congestion / social welfare dependency / migration / cell-like individual apartments / insecurity / yuppies / a lack of identity / planned overspill towns / elderly / road systems / Wright Plans in 1967 / poor quality / self-contained communities / green belts / Urban Renewal Act, 1986 / 11,000 housing units / inbound / local community / inner city decline / dominant distribution centre / deindustrialisation / secondary and tertiary / sustainable socio-economic / Historic Area Renewal Project (HARP) / younger people

Case study: Dublin city

- Rapid urban growth in cities has resulted in the movement of people from the inner city communities to new homes in the suburbs, thus creating .... and ....
  (1 SRP)

Inner city decline

- Local authority policies, poor quality housing and closure or movement of inner city industries has led to a large-scale movement of .... away from the inner city. **(1 SRP)**

- Push factors to this migration out of the inner city were that dwellings were of ...., there was .... , increased traffic volumes made the streets noisier and unsafe for children and unemployment had risen as industry moved out of the city centre and the zone of transition. Consequently, mainly .... people and the .... were left in the inner city. This very high percentage of .... in inner city areas created massive social problems, such as crime and drug abuse. **(1 SRP)**

- A Swiss-French architect and urbanist called .... sought efficient ways to house large numbers of people in response to an .... He believed that his new, modern architectural forms of large blocks of ...., stacked one on top of the other, would solve this problem. **(1 SRP)**

- In the 1970s local council initiatives re-housed Dublin's large inner city communities in poorly designed .... in the suburbs, e.g. Ballymun. Many of these high-rise buildings lacked ...., such as lifts, and the lifts of those that had them were never fixed when they broke down. **(1 SRP)**

- Chronic traffic congestion and the .... in the city centre forced industries to locate outside the centre, most notably in .... near city ring roads, e.g. Sandyford in Dublin. This increased unemployment in the inner city. **(1 SRP)**

Urban sprawl

- As a country develops economically there is a shift of people working in the .... sector, to the .... sectors, most of which are found in urban areas. On a global level, there is a large-scale .... of people from rural to urban areas. **(1 SRP)**

- Car ownership increases dramatically as a society becomes .... Improved .... allowed more people to live in .... and use their car to get to work. **(1 SRP)**

- Most offices and department stores are located in the city centre, which creates a .... of driving .... to the city centre in the morning rush hour and .... in the evening rush hour. **(1 SRP)**

- The expansion of suburbs has caused the edges of suburbs and commuter towns to merge with the city, creating a .... **(1 SRP)**

- Industry has been forced to locate on the edges of cities, particularly near ring roads, and this has increased .... even further. **(1 SRP)**

- In some lower-income suburbs, there is an .... as whole families moved from the inner city and were separated into different suburban areas. The family support so valued in the inner city was lost, creating .... and .... **(1 SRP)**

Solutions

- The goal of the .... was to create .... in Tallaght, Blanchardstown and Clondalkin. These towns were to be .... where residents would live and work, thus reducing the number of commuters into the city centre. .... for recreation were to be created between these towns and Dublin city. **(1 SRP)**

- The .... was designed to renew inner city areas and reduce urban sprawl. The .... revitalised the Smithfield area of Dublin city by renovating and replacing new houses. This led to an influx of .... , young business professionals whose preference is to live in the city centre. **(1 SRP)**

Focus on the redevelopment and renewal of the Docklands

- Up till the 1950s Dublin port was the .... in the state. The introduction of .... ferries at Dublin port in the 1950s led to a rapid .... and the area became socially deprived.

- In 1997 the Dublin Docklands Development Authority (DDDA) was established to create a .... and environmental renewal of the 520-hectare Docklands site.

- The thrust of the plan involved the creation of up to .... and .... It was to be accessible through the DART, Luas and port tunnel transport systems.

- A key development in this project was the active involvement of the .... , and their quality of life became central to the project.

- The as-yet-uncompleted project will produce many landmark buildings, such as the .... and the proposed 'U2 Tower'. **(2 SRPs)**

Grand Canal Theatre

(c) Urban Growth and the Environment

Sample Question 3

Discuss the interrelationship between urban growth and the environment.

Urbanisation

1 increased urbanisation creates environmental problems . . . .

2 burning of fossil fuels . . . .

Air pollution

3 Air Pollution Act, 1987 . . . .

4 health problems prior to this act . . . .

5 lead petrol phased out . . . .

6 CO_2 increase during Celtic Tiger era . . . .

7 Kyoto Protocol . . . .

8 still rely heavily on cars . . . .

Steps to improve air quality in the urban environment

9 natural gas replaced coal/public transport upgraded . . . .

10 low-sulphur diesel/better insulation standards . . . .

Heritage issues in urban areas

11 Heritage Council . . . .

12 register of protected structures . . . .

13 national heritage plan/county development plan . . . .

14 archaeological excavations prior to planning . . . .

15 heritage officer . . . .

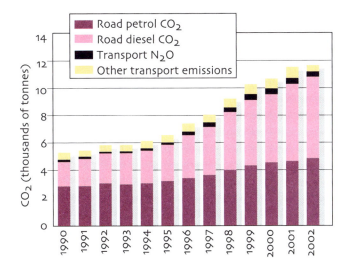

Greenhouse gas emissions from transport in Ireland, 1990–2002

(d) Developing World Cities

Sample Question 4

Examine the problems associated with developing world cities.

Insert the following terms into the blanks below:

unplanned squatter settlements / human waste / socio-economic problems / typhoid / massive housing shortage / one-third of urban dwellers / chronic traffic congestion / rapidly / pavement dwellers / open sewers / 48 million people / corrugated metal / tree branches / agricultural / old, worn tyres / liable to flooding / demographic transition model / self-constructed housing / financial resources / urban areas / lack of funding / contaminate / five years / subsistence level / eviction / social welfare benefits / pull factor / gender-biased / street trading / monsoon season / secondary and tertiary

Introduction

- As poorer countries have begun to develop economically there has been a shift from subsistence .... activities to .... activities. Jobs for secondary and tertiary sectors are mostly to be found in ...., resulting in a rural-to-urban migratory trend. **(1 SRP)**

- Developing countries are in Stage 3 of the .... and population growth is increasing ...., serving only to worsen the problem. **(1 SRP)**

- In cities the key .... is the opportunity to find jobs. This has led to rapid growth of urban populations, thus creating serious .... **(1 SRP)**

Housing problems

■ The flood of rural migrants to cities in developing countries has created a ……………………………… ………………………… and most authorities have failed to provide adequate housing, predominantly due to the ……………………………. **(1 SRP)**

■ An estimated ………………………………………………………… in developing world cities cannot find adequate accommodation and have to either sleep rough as ……………………………………… or build their own hut. **(1 SRP)**

Shanty towns

■ These ………………………………………………………… are located on the outskirts of cities. The inhabitants face the constant threat of ………………… as they do not own the land they reside on. **(1 SRP)**

■ Nobody knows how many people live in any one shanty town and most figures are just estimates. Nevertheless, in São Paulo in Brazil an estimated 25 per cent or ………………………………………… live in shanty towns (*favelas*). **(1 SRP).**

■ Homes are of very poor quality construction:

  ■ Walls are made of spare pieces of …………………………………………, plywood and plastics.

  ■ Poles cut from ………………………… are used as frames for the houses.

  ■ Roofs are sometimes stabilised by …………………………… . **(1 SRP)**

■ Many shanty towns are built on land ……………………………………… , such as a tidal bay. In Ecuador houses are connected by raised wooden footpaths. **(1 SRP)**

Lack of basic services

■ Shanty towns are units of irregular ……………………………………………………… that are typically unlicensed and occupied illegally. Most shanty towns lack basic services, such as water supplies, rubbish removal and sewerage disposal. ……………………………… are commonplace and the stench of ……………………………… is ever present. **(1 SRP)**

■ During the ………………………………………… , canals and sewers overflow and ……………………………… the water supply, resulting in outbreaks of waterborne diseases such as ……………………… and cholera. **(1 SRP)**

■ Educational services are also inadequate and one-third of children in India do not complete ……………………………… in school. Most schools are still ……………………………… . **(1 SRP)**

Unemployment

■ Most employment in shanty towns is at a ……………………………………… where people just make enough to survive, especially as no ………………………………………………… exist. **(1 SRP)**

■ Most shanty town dwellers do basic jobs such as ……………………………… and shining shoes. **(1 SRP)**

Traffic congestion

■ Governments of developing countries do not have the ……………………………………… to develop the level of transport infrastructure needed to solve ……………………………………………… . **(1 SRP)**

■ Dublin city, for instance, struggles to cope with traffic congestion in a city of only 1.2 million people, so we can only imagine the problems facing planners in cities of 10–20 million people. **(1 SRP)**

An unplanned shanty town

(e) Urban Planning Strategies

Sample Question 5

With the aid of a case study, outline the effectiveness of urban renewal schemes in solving urban problems.

The Ballymun regeneration project

1 flats complex constructed due to housing shortage . . . .

2 urbanist Le Corbusier . . . .

Problems with the housing complex

3 break-up of community . . . .

4 tower blocks poorly maintained/substandard insulation . . . .

5 poor housing management/poor infrastructure. . . . .

6 devastating results. . . . .

The regeneration project

7 Ballymun Regeneration Limited (BRL)/€2.5 billion . . . .

8 demolition of towers/new houses built . . . .

9 town centre constructed/fully serviced . . . .

10 new urban parks/new job opportunities . . . .

11 development of community programmes . . . .

12 social support services/centres for education and training. . . . .

13 development of new routes/science and technology parks. . . . .

14 community consultation . . . .

15 new air of optimism in the community . . . .

The Ballymun regeneration scheme: new houses and low-rise apartments (left) are replacing the old high-rise apartments (right)

(f) Future of Urbanism

Sample Question 6

Outline the issues associated with the future of urbanism.

Insert the following terms into the blanks below:

Canary Wharf / Kuala Lumpur / increasing sense of insecurity / design architects / free private space / complex spaces / divisive / individual neighbourhoods / lower classes / surveillance / surplus / negative effects on both groups / wealth-creating activities / poor / feel-good, feel-safe / financial investment groups / social divisions / the Docklands / ethnic minorities / widening / locally generated viewpoint / rich / dull, dreary and heavily polluting / futuristic buildings / economic stimulants / deter criminal activity / privacy / public–private partnership / La Défense / government aid / high-rise, glass-fronted and imaginatively designed / organic planning

Introduction

■ Modern cities and cities of the future are . . . . where webs of technologies bind spaces and people together while, on the other hand, social and employment activities are . . . . **(1 SRP)**

The dual city

- This refers to the .... within urban areas between rich and poor. This gap seems to be .... and a larger and larger proportion of a city's population is cut off from .... The poor group, or ...., are considered to be .... to the needs of a modern urban society. These include .... and the elderly. **(1 SRP)**

- This future of extremes has ...., i.e. a growing sense of despair due to exclusion among the poor, and an .... and racism among the rich. **(1 SRP)**

- The eventual result, which can be seen already in modern cities, is that the .... will live and interact among themselves and the .... will do likewise. **(1 SRP)**

Mega-projects

- Urban mega-projects represent a new form of urban living which is being rapidly introduced. **(1 SRP)**

- A combination of .... and .... promote this type of project, such as the construction of casinos, large shopping centres and hotels. **(1 SRP)**

Flagship developments

- These amount to the redevelopment of a large section of the city, where .... office buildings are to be found. **(1 SRP)**

- Developments such as .... in London, ... in Dublin and .... in Paris are all examples of flagship developments. Most of these large projects are built via .... **(1 SRP)**

Petronas Towers, Kuala Lumpur, Malaysia

- Cities are using such flagship developments to promote inward investment and business opportunities. The Petronas Twin Towers in .... , Malaysia are a good example of a flagship development. **(1 SRP)**

Industry

- The image of industry in modern, forward-looking cities is changing rapidly. It is no longer thought of as .... Modern industry promotes itself with .... of mirrored glass, landscaped gardens and high technology. **(1 SRP)**
- Mega-projects and flagship developments act as .... to attract inward investment and thus consumer spending. **(1 SRP)**

Social control

- .... with CCTV cameras has become very popular in modern cities, and its function is to .... and create a .... factor among consumers and residents. **(1 SRP)**
- There are, however, issues relating to people's .... Some people think that soon there will be no .... left in cities of the future. **(1 SRP)**

Sustainable neighbourhoods

- Many geographers believe flagship developments and mega-projects do not necessarily lead to long-term success and believe that a more practical way forward is for .... to deliver solutions to their own problems with the help of .... **(1 SRP)**
- Some geographers prefer the idea of .... , which favours the .... for future developments. **(1 SRP)**

Section 5

The Economic Elective (Patterns and Processes in Economic Activities)

Chapter 32

Introduction

- Economic activities are unevenly distributed over the earth.

- There are huge gaps in wealth between the developed (rich) and developing (poor) worlds.

- The developed world includes only 15 per cent of the world's population but possesses 80 per cent of the world's wealth.

- In developing countries 1.2 billion people live on less than a dollar a day.
  On a global scale countries may be classified into:
  MDCs – Most Developed Countries
  NICs – Newly Industrialised Countries
  LDCs – Least Developed Countries

Characteristics of Most Developed Countries (MDCs)

MDCs include the EU, USA, Japan, New Zealand, Australia.

- High GNP per capita

- Capital-intensive primary sector

- Capital-intensive secondary sector

- A highly developed tertiary sector employing over 50 per cent of the labour force

- Well-developed infrastructure with easy access to world markets

- A highly educated and skilled workforce

- A wealthy home market

- They are often former colonial powers that exploited their poorer colonies.

Characteristics of Newly Industrial Countries (NICs)

NICs include Brazil, Taiwan, South Korea, China, India.

- Agriculture is of a subsistence nature but the numbers involved have decreased due to developments such as the Green Revolution.

- Any surplus output is exported as a cash crop.

- MNCs often locate their production plants in NICs, which has helped to industrialise them.

- Infrastructure is being developed.

- Communications are improving and many back-office services such as call centres have located here, helping to develop the tertiary sector.

Characteristics of Least Developed Countries (LDCs)

LDCs include Burma, Ethiopia, Peru and most of sub-Saharan Africa.

- Agriculture is subsistence farming, with over 60 per cent of the population employed in the sector.

- Drought, infertile soils and soil erosion are major problems.

- MNCs often control large tracts of fertile land.

- Infrastructure is poor, hindering efforts to attract FDI (foreign direct investment).

Chapter 33

Economic Development

(a) Gross National Product

Sample Question 1

Outline how gross national product (GNP) can be used as a measure of economic development.

Explanation

1   gross domestic product . . . .

2   gross national product . . . .

3   purchasing power parity . . . .

4   per capita income . . . .

5   Industrial Revolution . . . .

6   GNP can vary . . . .

Problems of using GNP

7   fails to show distribution of income. . . . .

8   ignores voluntary work. . . . .

9   ignores subsistence production . . . .

10 produces no net change . . . .

11 no account of quality of goods . . . .

12 does not measure damage done to environment . . . .

13 sustainability of growth . . . .

14 does not take into account the black market . . . .

15 comparing GNP figures . . . .

(b) Human Development Index

Sample Question 2

Outline how the human development index (HDI) can be used as a measure of economic development.

Human development index

1 high levels of GNP ....

2 the human development index..

3 concerned with three elements ....

4 life expectancy ....

5 adult literacy rate ....

6 standard of living ....

7 score of between 0 and 1..

8 high/medium/low development ....

9 high level of GNP ....

10 wars..

11 national debt ....

12 structural adjustment programmes...

13 financial aid only given...

14 Zimbabwe ....

15 politics ....

16 water availability..

17 Aids ....

Chapter 34

Levels of Development Change over Time

(a) Economic Development Change over Time

Sample Question 1

'Economic development can change over time and space.' Discuss.

Insert the following terms into the blanks below:

large movement of people / economic well-being / economic organisation / FDI / drought and desertification / colonialism / structure / development gap / war and political instability / dynamic / positive balance of trade / technology / economic well-being / economy / a health crisis / overdependency on the primary sector / economic development

Change over time

- Economic development is a .... (constantly changing) process that results in significant changes in levels of development over time. It affects the make-up of a region's economy and therefore its levels of prosperity. **(1 SRP)**

- The following changes are needed for a region to become economically developed over time:

  1 A change in the .... of a country's .... from overdependence on the primary sector (e.g. agriculture), and diversification into the secondary sector (e.g. manufactured goods) and tertiary sector (e.g. financial services). **(1 SRP)**

  2 An increase in its levels of .... , e.g. machinery and computers, can increase productivity. **(1 SRP)**

  3 A change in its .... , i.e. shifting from a subsistence economy to a commercially intensive economy. **(1 SRP)**

  4 Improvements in the .... of the country by investing in health, education, housing, etc. **(1 SRP)**

  5 Changes in the volume and value of its trade to achieve a .... This is done by increasing the volume and value of exports by shifting from low-value, primary, unprocessed raw materials, e.g. coffee, to high-value industrial goods and services, e.g. financial services. This results in an influx of money into the country which can be used to develop its economy. **(1 SRP)**

Spatial variation

- Spatial variation refers to uneven patterns of .... among different countries. **(1 SRP)**

- On a global level, an uneven rate of development since the Industrial Revolution has led to a major '......................................' between the rich north and the poor south which continues to widen. **(1 SRP)**

Statistics

Development gap: ratio of living standards between north and south

YEAR	NORTH	:	SOUTH
1750 (prior to colonial period)	3	:	1
2010 (neo-colonial period)	90	:	1

- Many of the poorer countries have experienced major difficulties in advancing their levels of economic development. Factors inhibiting the development of some countries are:

  1 In the past .... created a dominant–dependent relationship which widened the inequality between rich and poor countries. This stunted the growth of the colonies and prevented economic development. **(1 SRP)**

  2 .... deters foreign direct investment (FDI), i.e. multinational companies will not locate in unstable countries. **(1 SRP)**

  3 A '.............................' linked to HIV/Aids has resulted in many deaths in countries severely affected by the virus and poor countries have been hit most severely, particularly those in sub-Saharan Africa which do not have the resources to combat the problem. **(1 SRP)**

  4 .... inhibit agricultural production, which reduces export earnings and therefore income levels are reduced. **(1 SRP)**

  5 There is an .... for export earnings and this prevents a country from attaining a positive balance of trade. **(1 SRP)**

  6 .... cripple a country's opportunity to spend money on developing its economy in areas such as infrastructural improvements and government grants to entice FDI. It also prevents money being spent to improve people's quality of life, in areas such as health and education. **(1 SRP)**

- Some former developing countries have shown more positive trends, linked mainly to a significant increase in ...., which has helped to build a manufacturing base in their countries. This FDI involves the setting up of branch plants of multinational corporations, focusing on low-wage labour and mass-producing basic industrial goods. **(1 SRP)**

- This has led to a .... from the primary sector to the secondary and tertiary sectors, helping to raise levels of prosperity. Examples include Taiwan, Singapore and South Korea. These have become known as newly industrialised countries (NICs). **(1 SRP)**

(b) Economic Development in Ireland

Sample Question 2

Explain the changes in patterns of economic development in Ireland spatially and through time.

Insert the following terms into the blanks below:

service / Dublin / west / manufacturing gap / Dublin region / 1926 / east–west development gap / industrial development / services / world economic recession / Dublin / gains / IFSC / widened / slowed / over 50 per cent of all services / third-level institutions / Galway / footloose international services / Celtic Tiger / GDA / communications / back office services / fewer / Irish industries / reduced / protectionism / Cork / Limerick / free-trade economy / services / 10 per cent / MNCs / dominant services centre / centralisation / one-third / manufacturing / 450 companies / reduced / branch plants / new industries / call centre services / footloose / IMF/EU bailout

Stage 1: 1922–60

Manufacturing industry (secondary sector)

■ In .... only .... of the Irish workforce was employed in .... , and .... of this was in Dublin. The government followed a policy of '...........................' by putting tariffs on imported goods to protect Irish industries from cheaper imports. **(1 SRP)**

■ Result: Most industries preferred to locate in the .... , creating an east–west divide. **(1 SRP)**

Services industry (tertiary sector)

■ .... industries began to develop in major urban centres which had established a large manufacturing sector. .... , being the biggest urban centre, dominated the services sector. **(1 SRP)**

■ Result: This widened the .... in relation to the services sector. **(1 SRP)**

Stage 2: 1960–80

Manufacturing industry (secondary sector)

■ A change in government policy to a .... was used to attract foreign .... These branch plants of MNCs were .... and preferred to locate in low-cost locations in the .... of Ireland to mass-produce basic industrial goods. **(1 SRP)**

■ Result: The .... between the east and west was reduced due to large employment gains in the west. **(1 SRP)**

Services industry (tertiary sector)

■ Employment in .... grew rapidly during this period due to increasing .... and higher income levels. .... and other key urban centres such as .... , ... and .... attracted most of the high-value office employment such as banking and financial services. **(1 SRP)**

■ Result: In the services sector there were .... in both east and west but only in urban centres. **(1 SRP)**

Stage 3: 1980-90

Manufacturing industry (secondary sector)

- There was a .... during this period and this resulted in .... MNCs being attracted to Ireland, while many .... were closed or their workforces .... Many traditional .... had to close, causing many job losses. **(1 SRP)**

- Result: Industrial employment in the west .... down, but yet performed better than urban regions such as Cork and Dublin, and this further .... the industrial divide between east and west. **(1 SRP)**

Services industry (tertiary sector)

- The world economic recession of the 1980s did not hit the services sector to the same degree as the manufacturing sector, and it continued to grow, albeit at a slow pace. The setting up of the .... in 1988 led to the .... of services in Dublin and as a result it became the .... and thus the decision-making centre in Ireland. **(1 SRP)**

- Result: The development gap between east and west .... once more as the west relied on Dublin for many high-value services. **(1 SRP)**

Stage 4: 1990-2008

Manufacturing industry (secondary sector)

- During this .... period, manufacturing employment boomed due to a new wave of FDI. .... were attracted to Ireland thanks to the following factors:

  - Proximity to ...., which provide a well-educated workforce for research and development

  - Well developed ....

  - Access to high quality transport and .... **(1 SRP)**

- Result: These new, high-tech footloose industries located in urban centres due to the factors above, and as a result most MNCs located in the ...., widening the east–west divide. **(1 SRP)**

Services industry (tertiary sector)

- All regions benefitted from the strong growth in the services sector but the GDA, centred around the IFSC, gained most from the boom in .... By 2006 the IFSC had over .... employing more than 11,000 workers. It is one of the fastest growing services centres in the world. Dublin also became the location for many .... and .... of large international companies, e.g. Dell. **(1 SRP)**

- Result: The GDA contains .... employment in Ireland, which widens the 'development gap' between east and west. **(1 SRP)**

The Present

- The worldwide economic downturn which started in 2008 and the crisis in the Irish banking system put a stop to the boom. Some multinational companies withdrew from Ireland, and confidence in the Irish economy is now low after the .... **(1 SRP)**

(c) Brazil: Case Study of a Developing Country

« Background Information »

- **Fifth largest country in the world**
- **Population:** 188.9 million (253.1 million by 2050)
- **Capital:** Brasilia
- **Population Density per km²:** 22.2
- **Average annual growth rate, 2010–15:** 1.087 per cent
- **Life expectancy:** Men – 68.8 years; Women – 76.1 years
- **Fertility rate:** 2.2
- **Urban population:** 84.2 per cent
- **GDP per head:** $5,650
- **Agriculture** employs 21 per cent of the population.
- **Industry** employs 21 per cent of the population.
- **Services** employ 58 per cent of the population.
- 7.9 per cent of GDP is spent on **health**.

Sample Question 3

Examine the impact of colonialism and/or globalisation on a developing country you have studied and how it has adjusted to the global economy.

Colonialism

1 colonised by the Portuguese ....

2 slaves were imported ....

3 independence in 1822 ....

4 exporting rubber ....

5 primary exports ....

6 import substitution ....

Globalisation

7 Brazilian miracle ....

8 multinationals ....

9 military rule ....

(d) France: Case Study of a Developed Country

« Background Information »

- **Population:** 60.7 million
- **Capital:** Paris (population 10 million)
- **Sixth largest economy in the world**
- **GDP:** $2,248 billion.
- **GDP per capita:** $37,040
- **Human Development Index rank:** 14
- **Seventh biggest exporter in the world**
- **Unemployment rate:** 10 per cent
- **Population growth per annum:** 0.39 per cent
- **Fertility rate:** 1.9
- **Life expectancy:** Men – 77.1 years; Women – 84.1 years
- **Urban population:** 79.7 per cent
- France enjoys an **excellent geographic location** on the western edge of Europe.

Sample Question 4

Examine the development of one or two of the following in relation to a developed country you have studied:

1 Tertiary economic activities
2 Industrial region in decline
3 Footloose industries
4 Mass tourism.

Note: You need to have at least fifteen SRPs altogether.

1 Tertiary economic activities

Insert the following terms into the blanks below:

> galleries / museums / research and development / health service / services / tourism / excellent transportation sector / theatres / educational sector / communication systems / government / tourist industry / single largest employer / financial services / 80 million tourists / head offices / roads / 74 per cent / French national rail network / centre of culture

- Tertiary economic activities refer to the provision of .... such as .... , medical, financial and educational services. **(1 SRP)**

- As income in an economy increases, demand for tertiary economic activities increases. .... of the French workforce is employed in tertiary economic activity. It is the fastest growing sector of the French economy, with a growth rate of over 2 per cent per annum. **(1 SRP)**

- France has an .... which focuses on Paris. The TGV (Train à Grande Vitesse) links Paris to cities all over the country, including Lyons, Strasbourg and Lille in the Nord-Pas-de-Calais. The TGV also links Paris with London via the Channel Tunnel. **(1 SRP)**

- The .... is managed by SNCF. The SNCF also operates inner-city routes and suburban services. **(1 SRP)**

- The French have excellent .... Charles de Gaulle airport in Paris is the seventh busiest in the world. Over 1,500 planes arrive at and depart from the airport daily. **(1 SRP)**

- France has over 950,000km of .... These are vital for the import of raw materials and the export of processed goods.**(1 SRP)**

- The French are very proud of their .... Of their GDP, 5.7 per cent is invested in education. Education is essential to equip the French workforce with the skills required in a competitive world environment. Paris is home to the Sorbonne, a world-famous university. **(1 SRP)**

- The French have an excellent .... France is an ageing society so spending on care for the elderly is increasing. Over 11 per cent of GDP is spent on the health service. Life expectancy in France is 80.7 years, the ninth highest in the world. France has one of the lowest infant mortality rates at 4.3 per 1,000 live births. **(1 SRP)**

- France is a leading provider of .... Paris is home to the Paris Bourse, the second largest stock exchange in Europe and the fifth largest in the world. The major insurance companies are located in Paris. **(1 SRP)**

- Paris is the seat of .... and as such dominates the tertiary sector. The government is the .... in the economy. **(1 SRP)**

- Paris is home to the .... for most of the large French companies. Nearly all .... is carried out in Paris and La Défense is the financial services centre of France. Paris contains most of the country's universities and other educational centres. Paris also contains the headquarters of all the major French banks. **(1 SRP)**

- France has a major .... It is centred on Paris and the Mediterranean coastline of the south of France, with its hot, dry summers and mild, moist winters. **(1 SRP)**

- Almost .... visit France annually, spending almost $43 billion in the economy. **(1 SRP)**

■ They come to see the many ...., ... and .... , many of which are in Paris. Paris is known around the world as the .... It is home to the Louvre, an art gallery, the cathedral of Notre Dame and the royal palace of Versailles. **(1 SRP)**

2 Industrial region in decline

1 major industrial economy ....

2 Nord-Pas-de-Calais...

3 iron and steel industries...

Reasons for industrial decline

4 coal seams...

5 new alternative forms of energy ....

6 small iron and steel plants...

7 textile plants..

8 unemployment and deindustrialisation..

9 conversion poles...

Redevelopment of Lille

10 major urban centre ....

11 Eurostar ....

12 World Trade Centre ....

13 technopoles ....

14 out-migration ....

15 secondary and tertiary activities dominate...

3 Footloose industries

Insert the following terms into the blanks below:

excellent infrastructure / excellent telecommunications / free to locate anywhere / ideal physical environment / decentralisation / out-migration / light industries / peripheral regions / Provence-Alpes-Côte d'Azur / centres of education

- A footloose industry is an industry .... No single locational factor dominates its ideal location. Footloose industries tend to be .... such as computer assembly, with inputs and outputs that are easy to transport. **(1 SRP)**

- They act as an aid to ...., helping to reduce the pressure on core regions. They often set up in .... and help to reduce .... **(1 SRP)**

- The .... (PACA region) attracts footloose industries for the following reasons: **(1 SRP)**

  1 .... : The region is served by the TGV and autoroutes which allow for the easy movement of imports and exports. There are international airports in Marseille and Nice. Marseille, on the Mediterranean coast, is a major port which also facilitates imports and exports. **(1 SRP)**

  2 .... : PACA possesses a young, skilled workforce. The region contains a large number of universities and other third-level institutes. **(1 SRP)**

  3 .... : Broadband, combined with a fibre-optic network, allow for easy communication between all of France and the rest of the world. **(1 SRP)**

  4 .... : PACA is situated along the Mediterranean coast which is ideal for water sports. The region also has a Mediterranean climate which guarantees hot, dry summers and mild, moist winters. The region contains the Maritime Alps and is close to the Italian Alps, which are ideal for hiking in summer and skiing in winter. **(1 SRP)**

4 Mass tourism

Insert the following terms into the blanks below:

French Riviera / casinos / very accessible / climate / swampy / intensive / tertiary economic sectors / summer droughts / new marinas / improved access / coastal resorts / Mediterranean climate / 1960s / out-migration / rich culture / GDP / Alps / farm incomes

- Tourism is a major tertiary economic activity in France and a huge contributor to the country's .... Almost 80 million tourists visit France every year and tourist receipts amount to almost $43 billion. **(1 SRP)**

- The .... in the south of France is a major tourist attraction for the following reasons:

  1 .... : The region has a Mediterranean climate which guarantees high atmospheric pressure every summer. This climate boasts hot, dry summers and mild, moist winters. **(1 SRP)**

  2 The region has a very .... with many ancient Roman ruins. The Roman towns of Nîmes and Arles attract thousands of tourists. **(1 SRP)**

  3 The nearby .... attract sport enthusiasts with hikers in summer and skiers in winter. **(1 SRP)**

  4 The coastal cities of Nice and Monte Carlo are famous for their .... **(1 SRP)**

5 The region is .... – it is served by the TGV, an airport at Marseille and excellent autoroutes. **(1 SRP)**

■ Farmers used to produce a cheap table wine (vin ordinaire) which they relied on for income. Due to poor farm income, there was massive .... It used to be a .... area and because of its hot .... mosquitoes thrived. **(1 SRP)**

■ However, all changed in the ...., when it was decided to develop the area. The development included:

　■ The development of new .... with their own waste-treatment plants. **(1 SRP)**

　■ The construction of .... and the development of green areas. **(1 SRP)**

　■ Investment in new motorways and high-speed trains for .... **(1 SRP)**

■ The project was a success.

　■ Farming is now very .... to cater for the needs of the tourist. **(1 SRP)**

　■ .... have increased, helping to reduce out-migration from the region. **(1 SRP)**

　■ The problem of .... is now solved by taking irrigation water from the Canal du Midi. **(1 SRP)**

　■ Employment in the ...., such as banking, has increased. **(1 SRP)**

Chapter 35

Globalisation and Multinational Companies

(a) Globalisation

Sample Question 1

Assess the causes which have led to the growth and development of globalisation.

Insert the following terms into the blanks below:

deforestation / Citigroup / tariffs and quotas / GDP / Geneva / production plants / integrated / trading blocs / fair trade / faster / communicate / Ireland / stock markets / International Financial Services Centre / world / mass-produced / borrow / capital and technology / China / foreign direct investment (FDI) / economic resources / International Monetary Fund / cheap / refrigerated containers

Globalisation

- Globalisation is the free movement of .... and factors of production across international borders, forming an increasingly .... economy. **(1 SRP)**
- Examples of globalisation would be:

    - .... in the Amazon Basin not only affects local climate but also global climate.

    - Information and ideas move around the globe much .... than before.

    - Goods and services in one corner of the globe are now available in all parts of the .... **(1 SRP)**

Causes of globalisation

1 **Improved Communications**

- The availability of ...., rapid and reliable communications allows people across the globe to communicate wherever they are. **(1 SRP)**

- The internet, mobile phones, email and TV channels allow MNCs in one country to .... directly with their headquarters in another country. **(1 SRP)**

2 Improved transportation

- Developments such as .... allow for the movement of large volumes of goods across the globe. **(1 SRP)**

- Fresh flowers, fresh fruit and other exotic goods are now available in .... on a daily basis due to improved transportation. **(1 SRP)**

3 The role of multinational corporations

- MNCs are very large organisations such as Dell, Ford and Nike, who have .... all over the world. Their annual sales, in billions of dollars, are greater than the .... of many developing countries. **(1 SRP)**

- .... MNCs favours globalisation. It allows them to export all over the world free from .... **(1 SRP)**

- They favour ...., the establishment of offices and factories in many different countries. **(1 SRP)**

- Research of a new product and its development may occur in a core area in Europe where .... are available. The goods may be .... in a low-cost economy, such as China or India, and then sent back to the European market to be sold for a profit. **(1 SRP)**

4 The growth of global banking and integrated financial markets

- Billions of dollars, pounds sterling and euro are traded daily on the world's .... The four most important in the world are located in the United States, ..., Japan and the United Kingdom. **(1 SRP)**

- The USA and the UK are home to three of the world's largest banks – the Bank of America Corporation, ... and HSBC Holdings. The stock exchanges and the banks enable the MNCs to .... vast sums of capital to enable them establish production plants across the world. Dublin is now part of this process with the development of the .... **(1 SRP)**

5 WTO and IMF

- The World Trade Organisation (WTO), based in .... , and the .... (IMF) favour free trade. **(1 SRP)**

- They encourage countries to reduce tariffs and quotas and to boost their foreign earnings through the development of export-led growth. **(1 SRP)**

- .... such as the EU and NAFTA seek to promote .... between their member states. **(1 SRP)**

(b) Multinational Corporations

Sample Question 2

Define multinational or transnational corporations and outline the reasons they locate in so many different countries. In your answer, refer to advantages and disadvantages of globalisation.

1 definition ....

Reasons for locating in different countries

2 cheap labour ....

3 access to raw materials...

4 access to the economic triad ....

5 reacting to global economic factors ....

6 taking advantage of the product life cycle ....

7 introductory stage ....

8 growth stage ....

9 maturity stage ....

10 decline ....

Advantages of globalisation

11 increased trade between countries ....

12 global mass media links the world together..

13 cultural barriers are reduced ....

Disadvantages of globalisation

14 an economic problem in one country...

15 more civil wars..

16 increased environmental pollution ....

(c) Case Study of a Multinational Company: Dell

Sample Question 3

With reference to one multinational company (MNC) you have studied, examine how its distribution is influenced by global factors.

Insert the following terms into the blanks below:

Asia, Pacific and Japan / product development / the Multiplier Effect / global recession / direct computer systems / tariff-free exports / higher tax revenues / IDA Ireland / Hewlett Packard / three regions / young and well educated / Michael Dell / labour costs / spend their incomes / corporation tax / 1990 / Round Rock, Texas / indirectly / compulsory redundancies / competitive / Europe, the Middle East and Africa (EMEA) / two locations / grants / 1984 / the Americas / outsourcing / 85,000 / European Union / Shannon Airport / 3,000 workers directly

Dell

- Dell was founded in .... by .... Its global headquarters are in .... **(1 SRP)**

- Dell is one of the three largest computer manufacturers in the world, employing .... people in approximately ninety countries. **(1 SRP)**

- Dell is the world's leading .... company with customers in 180 countries. Every day 100,000 systems are shipped globally – more than one every second. **(1 SRP)**

- For purposes of global distribution, Dell has divided the computer world into .... :

1 ....

Its regional headquarters are in Bracknell in the UK. It has a manufacturing facility in Lodz, Poland, with regional offices in about thirty countries. **(1 SRP)**

2 ....

Dell's regional headquarters are in Singapore. It has manufacturing plants in China, Malaysia and India, and regional offices in thirteen countries. **(1 SRP)**

3 ....

Dell's worldwide headquarters are located in Round Rock, Texas. The company has four manufacturing plants in the US and Brazil. It has regional offices in nine countries. **(1 SRP)**

Dell in Ireland

- Dell set up in Ireland in ....It has .... in Ireland, in Limerick and in Cherrywood, Co. Dublin. **(1 SRP)**

■ Dell chose Ireland for a number of reasons:

1 As a member of the ...., exporters from Ireland enjoy .... into the rich European market.

2 Dell was attracted by the Irish government's low .... rate of 12.5 per cent. This rate compares favourably with 30 per cent in Germany and 39.5 per cent in the US.

3 Ireland's .... workforce also attracted Dell to Ireland. The workforce was also English-speaking and IT-literate.

4 Excellent support, in the form of .... from the government and .... also encouraged Dell to locate in Ireland. Dell received €55 million in grants from the government.

5 The proximity of .... was another major attraction, allowing easy access to Dell's headquarters in Texas and other Dell manufacturing plants and regional offices worldwide. **(3 SRPs)**

■ Dell is one of the largest employers in Ireland, employing over .... between its two locations and many others .... in support services. The workers employed directly and indirectly .... in the Limerick and Dublin regions, benefitting the local economies. **(1 SRP)**

■ The government also receives .... which can be invested in other sectors of the economy. These knock-on benefits are termed .... **(1 SRP)**

Global Restructuring

■ In 2009, in the wake of the .... , Dell announced radical cutbacks in its Irish operation, moving all manufacturing in the EMEA region to its new plant in Lodz, Poland, where .... are considerably lower than in Ireland. This involved 1,900 .... in its Limerick operation. **(1 SRP)**

■ The remaining employees in Limerick continue to co-ordinate EMEA manufacturing, logistics and supply-chain activities across a range of functions including ...., engineering, procurement and logistics. **(1 SRP)**

■ The job losses were part of a global restructuring plan carried out in order to make Dell more .... and to regain its status as the world's number one supplier of PCs. .... is currently the world's number one PC provider. **(1 SRP)**

■ Dell's restructuring programme has led to the .... of its manufacturing to lower-cost locations around the world: Lodz for the EMEA region; Penang in Malaysia and Xiamen in China for the Asia, Pacific and Japan region; and Eldorado do Sul in Brazil for the Americas region. **(1 SRP)**

(d) Factors Affecting Industrial Location

Sample Question 4

List and explain the factors affecting industrial location.

Raw materials

1 key inputs ....

2 easy access to the resource material ....

Labour

3 often the defining factor ....

4 large educated workforce ....

5 an industrial tradition ....

Transport

6 near major roads...

7 peripheral regions ....

Markets

8 close as possible to their markets...

Energy

10 in the past ....

11 proximity to coalfields ....

Capital

12 an injection of funds ....

13 role of capital has increased ....

The role of government

14 grants and incentives ....

15 decentralisation ....

Services

16 telecommunications, electricity and water services..............................

17 Intel ....

Chapter 36

Ireland and the European Union

« Background Information »

- The European Union (EU) comprises **27 member states**. The population of the EU is almost **500 million**. The members of the EU have established common institutions to which they delegate some of their sovereignty so that decisions on matters of common interest can be taken democratically at a European level.

(a) Advantages of EU membership for Ireland

Sample Question 1

List and explain the advantages of European Union membership for Ireland.

Ireland's EU membership

1 1973 ....

2 reduced dependence on the UK market ....

2 Ireland's exports ....

3 multinational corporations (MNCs) ....

4 improvements in infrastructure. ....

5 increased levels of employment ....

6 increased GNP ....

7 Common Agricultural Policy. ....

8 Guidance Fund ....

9 Common Fisheries Policy. ....

10 Total Allowable Catch ....

11 equal pay. ....

12 consumer protection. . . . .

13 environmental protection . . . .

14 encouraging tourism. . . . .

15 transformation. . . . .

(b) Common Agricultural Policy

Sample Question 2

Outline the impact of the Common Agricultural Policy (CAP) on Ireland's economic development.

Insert the following terms into the blanks below:

eastern expansion / farms / 5 per cent / structural / 45.4 per cent / larger and more efficient / tariffs / chemical / intervention price / reduced / overproduction / loss / agriculture / self-sufficient / 1.6 per cent / price support system / funding / reforms / overproduction / Rural Environmental Protection Scheme / Border, Midlands and West / reduced / direct payments / set-aside / quotas / diversifying / primary / prices / decoupled / single farm payments / 1962 / size / €31 billion / export / market price / improvements / guaranteed / 24 per cent / pensions / protect / food mountains / pollution / overgrazed / standard of living / environmentally / incomes / modern / over-reliant / full-time farmers

Impact of the Common Agricultural Policy (CAP) on Ireland

■ The CAP was introduced in . . . . .It sought to make the EU . . . . in food production by increasing output. It attempted to ensure a reasonable . . . . for the farming community. It also attempted to ensure fair . . . . for consumers. It also imposed . . . . on imports from outside the EU. Farming in Ireland is very influenced by the CAP. **(1 SRP)**

■ Its primary aim was to intervene in the market to purchase farm output when the . . . . for agricultural goods fell below a certain level. This target level was called an . . . . When the market price for a good fell below this the EU purchased the entire production at the intervention price. The EU provided a . . . . market for Irish farmers. **(1 SRP)**

■ While this development . . . . the EU's dependence on food imports, it resulted in the formation of '. . . . . ', ' beef mountains' and 'milk lakes' due to . . . . Surplus production was often sold at a . . . . on world markets, greatly damaging producers in developing economies. **(1 SRP)**

■ The cost of the CAP as a proportion of the EU budget is huge. In 2006 the CAP accounted for . . . . of the EU budget. However, only . . . . of the EU labour force is employed in . . . . .It only accounts for . . . . of the EU's GDP. The costs of maintaining 'lakes' and 'mountains' were rising. **(1 SRP)**

- Up to 1992 CAP favoured the .... farmers of the east of Ireland. This was all to change with major CAP .... More incentives were now available for smaller farmers, especially in the .... region. **(1 SRP)**

- Under the new reforms the EU agreed to abandon the ...., which meant .... payments for Irish farmers. These guaranteed prices were replaced with .... to Irish farmers if prices fell below a certain level. Cereal farmers in the south-east were forced to reduce the number of hectares devoted to cultivation in the '....................' programme. Milk .... were also increased. **(1 SRP)**

- In 1995 the EU introduced rural development aid with the aim of .... farm incomes and making Irish and European farmers more competitive. In 2003 and 2004 the EU '.......................' subsidies from production levels. Instead, payments were linked to environmental awareness, animal welfare and food safety. These are called .... **(1 SRP)**

- Irish membership of the EU increased farmers' .... and transformed living standards. Between 1973 and 2003 Ireland received .... in price supports and direct payments. Farmers also benefitted from higher prices on the EU markets due to tariffs on imports and .... subsidies. **(1 SRP)**

- Irish farming has also benefitted from the .... funds. These funds resulted in farm .... which led to increased output and more .... friendly methods of farming. **(1 SRP)**

- In 1973 farming employed .... of Ireland's workforce. Farmers over 55 years old were offered attractive .... to retire. Farm income increased as a result. In 2007 only 7 per cent were employed in farming. While the number of .... has declined farm .... has increased. Farm management and technology skills also improved. **(1 SRP)**

- Over 50,000 Irish farmers have also gained from the .... (REPS). Before its introduction, farmers used intensive farming methods. .... fertilisers resulted in water .... due to run-off. Mountainsides were .... **(1 SRP)**

- Traditional and older attractive farm building have been replaced by more .... structures. Under the REPS scheme farmers are paid to .... the landscape. The scheme helps to reduce .... and the harmful effects of intensive farming. **(1 SRP)**

- However, Irish farmers are still .... on EU subsidies, so much so that Irish agriculture is very vulnerable to any planned changes in EU subsidies. **(1 SRP)**

- The .... of the EU has serious implications for Ireland and the CAP. These new members are reliant on .... economic activities. In order to develop their primary sector they will depend on support from the CAP and so less .... will be available for Irish farmers. **(1 SRP)**

(c) Common Fisheries Policy

Sample Question 3

Outline the impact of the Common Fisheries Policy (CFP) on Ireland's economic development.

Aims

1 1983/conserve fish stocks ....

2 modernisation of the fleet. . . . .

Measures

3 Total Allowable Catch (TAC) . . . .

4 quotas. . . . .

5 record of landings . . . .

6 reduction in the EU fleet . . . .

7 focus on hunting new species . . . .

Enforcement and compliance

8 TACs. . . . .

9 checking fishing register . . . .

10 international agreements . . . .

Impact of the CFP on Ireland

11 TACs. . . . .

12 free access to Ireland's water . . . .

13 important spawning area . . . .

14 EU Funding . . . .

15 €335m is being invested. . . . .

16 new species . . . .

17 2002 reforms . . . .

(d) Common Regional Policy

Sample Question 4

Outline the Common Regional Policy (CRP) and how it has impacted on Ireland's economic development.

Insert the following terms into the blanks below:

inequalities / unemployment / May 2004 / less than 90 per cent / regional inequalities / retrain / Structural Funds / marginalised groups / €30.5 billion / rail link / Cohesion Fund / sustainable jobs / Objective 2 status regions / Territorial Co-operation objective / financial assistance / Celtic Tiger / Objective 1 status / extend / 140 per cent / GDP / rural development / 64 per cent / environment / A1 route / people / rolling stock / discrimination / Regional Competitiveness and Employment objective / Objective 1 status regions / Dublin port tunnel / motorway / sustainable development / Western Rail Corridor / Objective 3 status regions / Border, Midlands and West / Convergence / M1 motorway / primary / upgrading / Atlantic Corridor / Heuston Station / labour market

The Common Regional Policy (CRP) of the EU

■ While the EU is one of the richest trading blocs of the world, there are huge .... among its members. The entry of ten new member states in .... has only served to widen the gap between the rich and poor regions of the EU. **(1 SRP)**

■ The CRP was introduced in 1975 to reduce .... between member states. It comprises four .... and a .... Ireland will have received €30.5 billion from the Structural Operations funds (i.e. Structural Funds and Cohesion Funds) between 1975 and 2013. **(1 SRP)**

Point to note

Structural Operations includes both Structural Funds and the Cohesion Fund.

Structural Funds

■ Structural Funds were established in 1975 to give .... to countries and regions which were lagging behind economically, i.e. those whose .... was below the EU average.

■ **Structural Fund 1**: The European Regional Development Fund (ERDF) invests in projects to protect the .... , to reduce a region's dependence on .... economic activity and to create .... **(1 SRP)**

■ **Structural Fund 2**: The European Social Fund (ESF) is the EU's financial instrument for investing in .... Its aim is to help prevent and fight ...., to make Europe's workforce and companies better equipped to face new challenges and to prevent people losing touch with the .... €375 million will be invested in the ESF between 2007 and 2013. **(1 SRP)**

■ The objectives of the ESF up to 2013 are:

  1 To introduce programmes to .... workers.

  2 To support increased participation by .... in the labour force.

  3 To promote equality and prevent .... in the workforce. **(1 SRP)**

■ **Structural Fund 3**: The European Agricultural Guidance and Guarantee Fund (EAGGF) includes the Common Agricultural Policy (CAP) and the European Agricultural Fund for Rural Development (EAFRD). Its function is to improve agricultural structures and support .... **(1 SRP)**

- **Structural Fund 4**: The European Fisheries Fund provides financial support for fishing communities as part of the Common Fisheries Policy (CFP) and also promotes .... within the industry. **(1 SRP)**

Statistic

EU expenditure from Structural Funds:

2000–06: €231 billion

2007–13: €336 billion

Cohesion Fund

- The Cohesion Fund was established in 1993 to give additional funding for transport, environmental and infrastructure projects in existing and new member states where GDP was .... of the EU average, i.e. Ireland, Greece, Spain and Portugal. Between 1993 and 2006 Ireland received €2 billion through the Cohesion Fund. **(1 SRPs)**

Funding Structures

- The status of regions for funding:
  - .... : These received over 75 per cent of funding as these countries or regions had a GDP per capita of less than 75 per cent of the EU average. **(1 SRP)**
  - .... : These are countries or regions which are undergoing an economic decline due to structural problems. These regions include northern England and central France. **(1 SRP)**
  - .... : These are the core regions within the EU, most of which have GDPs of over 115 per cent of the EU average and thus receive very little funding. **(1 SRP)**
- Since 2004 there has been a change in the structure of funding provision. The following three categories now apply:
  - .... regions, which are similar to the original Objective 1 and 2 status regions. They include regions with a GDP per capita below 75 per cent of the EU average, and focus on accelerating economic development.
  - .... Its aim is to reinforce competitiveness and attractiveness outside the Convergence regions.
  - .... This is a new initiative which focuses on three strands:
    (a) cross-border co-operation,
    (b) transnational co-operation,
    (c) inter-regional co-operation. **(3 SRPs)**

Impact on Ireland

- Ireland has gained enormously from the CRP.
  - On joining the EU in 1973 Irish GDP was less than two-thirds of the EU average, at ....

- From 1975 to 1999 Ireland was designated an .... region, which meant it received priority funding from the EU Structural and Cohesion Funds

- With the aid of these funds, the GDP of Ireland's '.............................' economy increased rapidly and it had reached the EU average by 2000.

- Therefore from 2000 to 2006 only the newly formed .... (BMW) region in Ireland maintained its Objective 1 status as it economically lagged well behind the prosperous east and south regions.

- By 2006 Ireland's GDP had reached .... of the EU average. It lost its Objective 1 status and as a result no longer receives priority funding.

- Nevertheless, Ireland will have received .... from Structural Funds and the Cohesion Fund by 2013. **(3 SRPs)**

National Development Plans (NDP)

- The government, in order to ensure effective use of structural funding, had to submit a National Development Plan (NDP) to the EU before the funds would be handed over.

NDP 1: 2000–06

- The first NDP invested €57 billion of public, private and EU funds. Investment was made in education, transport, health and many other areas throughout the country.

NDP 2: 2007–13

- This aims to invest just under €184 billion as follows, but the EU will only fund €3 billion of this:

  - €54.6 billion for improvements in economic infrastructure

  - €49.6 billion for social inclusion (children, etc.)

  - €33.6 billion for social infrastructure (health, etc.)

  - €25.8 billion for human capital (schools, training, etc.)

  - €20 billion for enterprise, science and innovation. **(2 SRPs)**

Road improvements under the NDP

- Great progress has been made on upgrading Ireland's .... network.

- The .... extending from Dublin to Belfast has been completed with the motorway/dual carriageway that crossed the border to become an upgraded .... to Newry.

- Work is also in progress on .... the now-complete M50. One of these projects involved the building of the ....

- However, little progress has been made on the .... Parts of the Corridor are at the planning stages. The Atlantic Corridor is designed to link Letterkenny to Waterford, via Sligo, Galway, Limerick and Cork. **(2 SRPs)**

Rail improvements under the NDP

- There has been huge investment in new .... There are plans to .... the Luas network.

- .... has been upgraded, as well as many of the suburban stations.

- There are plans to develop a .... to Dublin Airport.

- Work has begun on the re-opening of the .... between Limerick and Sligo. **(2 SRPs)**

Chapter 37
Environmental Impacts

(a) Renewable Resources

Sample Question 1

Explain the term 'renewable resource'. In your answer refer to one type of renewable resource which is being used in Ireland.

« *Definitions* »

Renewable energy resources are resources that will never become exhausted.

« *Background Information* »

Sources of renewable energy:

1. Solar energy
2. Wind power
3. Hydroelectric power
4. Wave and tidal power
5. Biomass

Benefits of renewable energy:

- Lower CO_2 emissions, reducing global climate change.
- They are inexhaustible.
- They are a secure and stable energy supply.
- Ireland has many indigenous resources, mainly in rural areas. Their extraction would reduce out-migration in these often peripheral areas, and reduce our dependence on foreign fuel imports.

Case study: wind energy

1 high pressure to low pressure . . . .

2 wind is not a new source of energy . . . .

3 turbines with three long blades . . . .

Advantages of wind power

4 renewable/no pollution . . . .

5 operating costs are almost zero . . . .

6 production costs have declined . . . .

7 European Wind Energy Association . . . .

Disadvantages of wind power

8 not constant . . . .

9 many turbines will have to be constructed . . . .

10 blight on the landscape . . . .

Wind power in Ireland

11 increased in recent years . . . .

12 Irish Sea waters are shallow . . . .

13 Ireland's geography suits wind power . . . .

14 Sustainable Energy Ireland . . . .

15 USA is the largest user . . . .

16 Lansdowne Market Research . . . .

17 Arklow Bank wind farm . . . .

(b) Non-Renewable Resources

Sample Question 2

Define the term 'non-renewable resource'. In your answer refer to one type of non-renewable resource.

Insert the following terms ino the blanks below:

cleanest / the Kinsale gas field / finite resources / Europe / sixty-seven / Middle East / fossil fuel / 3 per cent /
water / Sustainable Energy Ireland / methane / permeable rock / 100m / mercapton / 60 per cent / carbon
dioxide / other gases / 1971 / Statoil / compounds / 3,000m / imports / 2020 / rate of flow / Corrib Gas Field /
fault / environmentally dangerous / seismic waves / 1976 / Marathon Petroleum / 35 per cent / three-
dimensional map / test hole / Soviet Union / anticline traps / 25 per cent / volume / 1,000m / Seven Heads /
Shell / process the gas offshore / 2003 / Environmental Protection Agency / odourless

- Non-renewable resources are .... Once used, they cannot be replaced. Fossil
fuels are finite resources. **(1 SRP)**

Case study: natural gas

- Natural gas is a .... composed primarily of .... which formed millions of
years ago from decomposed plant and animal life. The gas accumulated in layers of .... ,
like sand, becoming trapped between layers of impermeable rocks, such as shale, underneath the
surface of the earth. **(1 SRP)**

- It is perhaps the .... of all fossil fuels. It does not emit any particles such as soot or sulphur
dioxide into the atmosphere. It also releases less .... than oil. **(1 SRP)**

- Geologists explore gas fields by using their knowledge to detect likely locations of .... and/or
.... Preliminary exploration is done by detonating small explosions in shallow
wells and recording the .... Seismic waves react differently to various rock types and
a computer-generated .... of the rock layers can be constructed. **(1 SRP)**

- If there is a likelihood of a gas deposit an exploratory .... is drilled and if the ....
and .... are sufficient, the well will be commercially exploited. **(1 SRP)**

- There is enough gas globally to last .... years at current levels of output. Seventy-two
per cent of gas reserves are in the former .... and the ....
Only .... of reserves are in .... **(1 SRP)**

- On being brought ashore, ... and other gases and .... are removed. Natural gas is
.... so a strong odourant, ... , is added before distribution. **(1 SRP)**

- Natural gas accounts for .... of total energy demand in Ireland. By .... it will
account for .... of energy demand. **(1 SRP)**

Gas fields in Ireland

- The ...., located 50km off the coast of Cork, was discovered in ....
Production started in .... **(1 SRP)**

- The gas platform stands in .... of water. The gas is extracted from .... below the sea bed. **(1 SRP)**

- The field was operated by .... It no longer produces large amounts of gas,
but gas reserves have been replaced by the gas from the nearby Ballycotton and Seven Heads gas fields.
.... (SEI) and the ....

.... (EPA) plan to develop the Kinsale gas field as a mass storage container for CO_2 with a capacity of up to 330 million tonnes in order to reduce Ireland's carbon gas emissions. **(1 SRP)**

- ...., close to the Kinsale gas field, came into production in .... **(1 SRP)**

- The ...., 70km off the Mayo coast, is operated by ...., but owned by a group including Shell, Marathon and .... The gas lies over .... below the sea bed. **(1 SRP)**

- However, the project has been hindered due to protests by locals. They want Shell to .... The locals fear that onshore processing would be .... for the local area. **(1 SRP)**

- Once on-stream it will provide up to .... of Ireland's gas needs, reducing our dependence on .... **(1 SRP)**

(c) Acid Rain

Sample Question 3

What are the causes and consequences of acid rain and what can be done to remedy the problem?

1   first observed in Scandinavia . . . .

2   destruction of forests . . . .

Causes of acid rain

3   burning fossil fuels . . . .

Consequences of acid rain

4   damage to forests . . . .

5   damage to lakes . . . .

6   damage to buildings . . . .

7   aeroplanes . . . .

8   respiratory problems . . . .

9   Alzheimer's disease . . . .

Solutions

10   filters on chimneys . . . .

11   alternative sources of energy . . . .

12 car pool ....

13 public transport infrastructure ....

14 cleanest emission technology ....

15 liming ....

16 conserving energy ....

17 diagram of acid rain cycle

Sulphur dioxide and nitrogen oxides are released into the atmosphere from power plants, industries and vehicles

Carbon dioxide

The gases are transported by winds to eventually form clouds

Acid rain falls, damaging flora and fauna

(d) Conflict Between Local and National Interests

Sample Question 4

Examine, with reference to examples you have studied, how conflicts may develop between local and national interests.

Insert the following terms ino the blanks below:

dead organic / 130 / fracture / run-off / 3,000m / wells / anti-corrosion / pipeline / untreated / platform / habitats directive / Shell / whales and dolphins / clean burning / explosion / tax breaks / pressure / processing / twelve towns / Special Area of Conservation / local community / fossil fuels / unpolluted / adversely affected / landslides / odourless / GDP / economic activity / opposed / 60 per cent / 25 per cent / imports / unstable bog / reservoir / nine chimneys / declined

Case study: natural gas in Ireland

■ Natural gas accounts for .... of total primary energy demand in Ireland. It is ....
.... and emits lower levels of harmful by-products into the air, making it one of the lowest polluting .... available. **(1 SRP)**

■ The gas in the Corrib field, 70km off the Mayo coast, is 250 million years old. It was formed due to the decay of .... material. The gas lies over .... below the sea bed. It will be brought from the reservoir to the surface via .... drilled using high-technology drilling equipment. **(1 SRP)**

■ The gas will then be treated with an .... agent and anti-freeze before being sent to the shore. The gas will then travel by a .... constructed on the seabed to the shore, at Broadhaven Bay. It will then travel to a gas .... terminal at Bellanaboy. **(1 SRP)**

■ The gas is being processed on shore to reduce the dangers involved with working on and travelling to an offshore .... **(1 SRP)**

■ While the field is operated by .... , it is owned by a consortium which also includes Statoil and Marathon Petroleum. These companies are attracted by .... and low rates of corporation tax. **(1 SRP)**

Arguments in favour of the Corrib gas project

■ It will boost Ireland's .... by €3 billion over the lifespan of the project. Over 800 jobs will be created during the construction phase, with approximately .... high-quality permanent jobs, reducing emigration from this rural area. **(1 SRP)**

■ It will provide .... of Ireland's natural gas needs, reducing our dependence on .... , helping to improve our balance of payments. Successful completion of the Corrib project will encourage investment by other firms in energy exploration off the west coast. **(1 SRP)**

■ The project will increase the availability of natural gas to .... in Co. Mayo and Co. Galway, making the west more attractive for investment. The project will provide funds for .... projects. **(1 SRP)**

Arguments against the Corrib gas project

■ Over 80 per cent of the local population living in the affected parish of Kilcommon are ....
to the project for a number of reasons.

■ The area enjoys excellent air quality and .... rivers. Locals fear that the quality of the environment will be .... by the project. **(1 SRP)**

■ The construction of the gas pipeline is unprecedented. The proposed pipeline will send ....
gas across unstable bog land to a land-based gas refinery. The unstable bog land is subject to
.... This would have adverse effects on the pipeline, causing it to .... and inflicting terrible damage on the local environment. **(1 SRP)**

■ The gas travelling through the pipeline will be .... Locals are concerned that gas leaks would almost be impossible to detect. **(1 SRP)**

■ The gas will travel through the pipeline at very high .... The pressure is much higher than that allowed for the biggest Bord Gáis pipelines. This only serves to increase the likelihood of a gas .... **(1 SRP)**

■ Huge concerns exist over the safety of the refinery.

(a) The refinery will comprise .... which will emit harmful gases such as carbon dioxide and methane into the environment.

(b) The refinery will be constructed on .... Following heavy rainfall it may be subject to a landslide. The foundations of the refinery might be affected, with grave consequences for the local environment. **(1 SRP)**

■ Carrowmore Lake, which supplies the area with water, may be polluted by .... The ...., built to store the waste water from the refinery, is not equipped to deal with the levels of rainfall associated with the west of Ireland. **(1 SRP)**

■ Even though Carrowmore Lake is a protected area under the EU's .... it has already been damaged. Fish species have .... in numbers. Water quality has deteriorated. Algal blooms are developing. **(1 SRP)**

■ Broadhaven Bay is a .... (SAC). It is home to countless species of fish and the greatest variety of cetaceans in Ireland. Consequently, fishing is an important .... which could now be in danger. The future of the .... which inhabit the bay will also be in doubt when gas refining begins. **(1 SRP)**

(e) Sustainable Economic Development

« Background Information »

The **Environmental Protection Agency** was established in 1993 to protect the Irish environment. Its mission is to protect and improve the environment for both present and future generations in a sustainable manner.

The EPA is responsible for:

■ Licensing and control of large waste and industrial activities to ensure that they do not damage human health and the environment.

■ Regulating Ireland's greenhouse gas emissions.

■ Undertaking environmental research and development.

■ Monitoring of Ireland's water quality.

■ Prosecuting those who break environmental law and damage the environment.

An **Environmental Impact Assessment** (EIA) evaluates the environmental effects of a proposed development or project.

Sample Question 5

Examine, with reference to an example you have studied, the importance of ensuring that development is environmentally sustainable.

Introduction

1 sustainable economic development ....

2 Environmental Protection Agency ....

Case study: Tara Mines

3 Navan, Co. Meath ....

4 shallow tropical sea ....

5 deposits discovered in 1970 ....

6 lead and zinc concentrate ....

7 2.6 million tonnes of ore ....

8 under the surface ....

9 environmentally sensitive area ....

10 Brú na Bóinne ....

11 architectural compatibility ....

12 placement and orientation ....

13 recycling ....

14 stored in sand tanks ....

15 health and safety ....

(f) The Consequences of Ignoring Sustainable Development

Sample Question 6

Examine, with reference to one activity, the environmental, economic and social consequences of ignoring sustainable development.

Insert the following terms into the blanks below:

abandonment of spoil heaps / Euralille / Sambre-Meuse / social / water pollution / noise pollution / mine subsidence / conversion poles / GNP / water pollution / jobs / dependency ratio / underground / out-migration / valuable minerals / sustainable / deindustrialisation / the EU / Nord-Pas-de-Calais / technopoles / other geological materials / dust / economic / disturbance of the natural environment / surface / unemployment / economic depression / environment / secondary economic activities

Case study: mining

- Mining is the extraction of .... such as lead and zinc or .... from the earth. There are two types of mining – .... and .... (1 SRP)

- Mining, while it may boost .... and generate ...., does not always treat the .... in a .... manner. Mining can result in major environmental, ... and .... consequences. (1 SRP)

Environmental consequences

- .... Mining involves the temporary disturbance of large areas of land. When the Sambre-Meuse coalfields in Belgium finally closed, 150km² of coalfield was left idle with damaging consequences for the environment such as water and air pollution. (1 SRP)

- .... and .... Noise pollution results from machinery involved in drilling operations. Dust pollution is caused by mining trucks travelling over poor surfaces, coal being crushed, the use of high-powered drills, and strong winds which deposit dust over large areas. Mining dust can cause respiratory problems in humans. (1 SRP)

- .... Acid mine drainage (AMD) is metal-rich water formed as a result of chemical reactions between rocks containing sulphur-bearing minerals and water. The run-off enters nearby rivers and streams, polluting water supplies and damaging aquatic life. (1 SRP)

- .... As a consequence of the extraction of the minerals in an underground mine, the roof of the cave may collapse and the land above it subsides. Subsidence increases mining costs and exposes the miners to increased risks. (1 SRP)

- .... and run-down mine buildings. They are a blight on the landscape. Many old mining buildings and spoil heaps still dominate the landscapes of the Nord-Pas-de-Calais and the Sambre-Meuse. (1 SRP)

Economic and social consequences

- Economic and social consequences also occur when the mine closes as happened in the .... in the north-east of France. (1 SRP)

- On closure there is a rise in .... When the .... coalfield in Belgium closed in 1964 over 55,000 miners lost their jobs. This puts huge pressure on the government to find alternative employment. Social welfare payments also increase. (1 SRP)

- As a result, there is often the problem of .... Many of the younger unemployed miners who are unable to find jobs locally migrate to other cities or regions or emigrate further afield. This results in huge social problems for the mining areas concerned. Whole communities can be devastated. The migration of the younger miners also increases the .... in the worst affected areas. (1 SRP)

- As a consequence of unemployment and out-migration the entire region can fall into an .... Incomes are reduced and spending in the affected regions declines. Sectors dependent on coal-mining also suffer a drop in employment. Schools and other services often have to close in the affected areas. (1 SRP)

- .... often follows. The entire region becomes run down. Industries that were once dependent on the coal mines for their power source move to coastal areas to avail of alternative energy imports. As a consequence of unemployment and out-migration, income in the area falls and what was once an attractive market is now a poor market. (1 SRP)

- To solve the massive unemployment problem in these run-down areas, massive investment is required. The French government and .... invested large amounts in the regeneration of the Nord coalfield. They introduced .... whereby emphasis was placed on developing secondary and tertiary economic activities. If the mining industry had not fallen into decline, this money could have been invested elsewhere. **(1 SRP)**

- In the city of Lille the creation of '...........................' or technology parks for footloose high-tech industry on the city's ring motorway and the development of .... , a new international business centre, provide thousands of jobs in the secondary and tertiary sectors respectively. **(1 SRP)**

- The Nord has now transformed itself from an industrial region in decline to a well-developed modern economy focusing on .... and services industries. **(1 SRP)**

(g) Global Warming

Sample Question 7

Examine the causes and impact of one global environmental issue you have studied.

The Greenhouse Effect

1 natural phenomenon ....

The major greenhouse gases

2 carbon dioxide ....

3 manufactured gases ....

The consequences of global warming

4 world's temperature is increasing...

5 monoculture ....

6 increase in tropical storms...

7 increased rate of glacial melt ....

8 circulation system of the oceans..

Ireland and the Greenhouse Effect

9 Mediterranean climate ....

10 increased coastal erosion...

11 decreased rainfall in the summer ....

Solutions

12 reduction in the use of fossil fuels ....

13 stopping rainforest destruction..

14 carbon tax...

15 nuclear power ....

16 Kyoto Protocol ....

17 Copenhagen climate conference ....

(h) Tropical Rainforests

Sample Question 8

Why are tropical rainforests being damaged? What are the consequences of deforestation and what are the solutions?

Tropical rainforests

1 1975 ....

Reasons for deforestation

2 foreign debts ....

3 commercial logging...

4 cattle ranching...

5 collection of wood for fuel ....

6 increased demand in the First World...

Consequences of rainforest depletion

7 indigenous people ....

8 variety of species ....

9 source of medicinal plants ....

10 siltation of rivers ....

11 global and local climate patterns ....

Solutions to rainforest destruction

12 debt-for-nature swaps ....

13 fuel wood plantations..

14 greater recycling..

15 sustainable development ....

16 educational programmes ....

17 eco-tourism ....

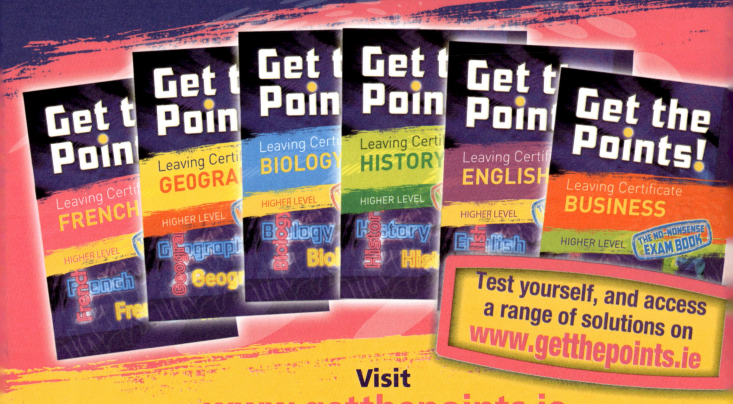